A CAMPER'S GUIDE TO OREGON & WASHINGTON

A GUIDE TO THE STATES' IMPROVED CAMPGROUNDS

A CAMPER'S GUIDE TO OREGON & WASHINGTON

By KiKi Canniff

Illustrations by Janora Bayot

Ki² Enterprises
P.O. Box 13322
Portland, Oregon 97213

Copyright © 1988
by
KiKi Canniff

Library of Congress Cataloging-in-Publication Data

Canniff, KiKi
   A camper's guide to Oregon & Washington.

   Includes index.
   1. Camp sites, facilities, etc. – Oregon – Directories. 2. Camp sites, facilities, etc. – Washington (State) – Directories. I. Title. II. Camper's guide to Oregon and Washington.
GV191.42.07C36   1988   647'.94795   88-8812
ISBN 0-941361-00-4   (pbk.)

ISBN #0-941361-00-4

Ki² Enterprises
P.O. Box 13322
Portland, Oregon 97213

TABLE OF CONTENTS

INTRODUCTION

Together, Oregon and Washington have more than 2,000 individual campgrounds. Those listed in this book are the "improved" campgrounds; those which have improved facilities and charge a fee for overnight use. You will find those which do not charge a fee detailed in **Free Campgrounds of Washington & Oregon**. Free campgrounds generally offer very minimal facilities.

Improved campgrounds in Oregon and Washington offer a variety of facilities. You might find complete utility hookups, swimming pools, hot tubs, game rooms, showers, laundry facilities, boat rental, charter fishing and more at some; while others provide little more than picnic tables, fire pits and toilet facilities. The price of an overnight stay ranges from less than $1.00 to more than $20.00. Each type of campground affords a different type of experience. This book was designed to help you locate the type of camping experience you desire.

In order to provide the best information, Ki² books do not accept advertising. All campgrounds receive the same treatment; no matter what their advertising budget. I have attempted to include all of the improved campgrounds located in Oregon and Washington but if you come across any I've missed, please let me know. I will try to add them to future editions. I have made every effort to insure that the information provided is accurate. However, time brings changes so if you visit a listed campground and find the facilities differ please let me know. Updated information may be sent to me at Ki² Enterprises, P.O. Box 13322, Portland, Oregon 97213.

Happy camping!

KiKi Canniff

KiKi Canniff
Author

HOW TO USE THIS BOOK

Start by reading the opening chapter. It will give you facts about the variety of elevations, terrains, scenery and climates campers can encounter in Oregon and Washington. Plus tips on avoiding rain. It also explains who the major campground operators are and what facilities you can expect to find at their campsites.

Each state's campground listings opens with a small locator map. This is followed by a grouping of cities arranged by area. This will help you to locate the cities referenced in the area you plan to visit. Towns where only a few campgrounds exist are referenced from the nearest city with a high concentration of campgrounds. These locator maps were not intended for navigation since travelers can get a full-size highway map free from either state's tourism office.

Campgrounds are then listed alphabetically by city. Each individual listing begins with the campground name followed by that of its operating agency. Next, you'll find a brief, but complete, listing of facilities. The type of toilet is listed only when it differs from the normal facilities offered by that agency. At the end of the facilities line you will find one, two or three dollar signs; $ tells you it is less than $5, $$ means $5 to $10, and $$$ more than $10. The final information consists of simply stated directions. FSR has been subsituted for Forest Service Road and CR for County Road.

CAMPING IN OREGON & WASHINGTON

Camping in Oregon and Washington offers an opportunity to enjoy the real Northwest experience, getting in touch with nature. This enchanting corner has it all. Picturesque ocean beaches, rugged mountain ranges, lush old growth forests, world renowned fishing, crystal clear high mountain lakes, sun drenched desert landscapes, snow capped peaks, an array of geological wonders, restful small towns and bustling big cities.

This is a land where getting close to nature is always within reach. The Northwest's outstanding physical features and wildlife are what attracted the first settlers; and although civilization has brought many changes to the area, much of the landscape remains uncluttered. Large parcels of land have been protected as public lands and wilderness areas so that you, and future generations, might enjoy the same experience that enticed those early pioneers and explorers. Much of the area's early history was preserved with it.

There are many similarities in these two states. The Cascade Mountain Range divides them both from north to south. The western portion has summers where beautiful sunny weather comes mixed with rain. It's this same rainfall however, that gives this part of the states the lush green beauty that brings visitors from all over the world. The drier, eastern half of the two states is hot and dry all summer long. Summer temperatures on both sides of the mountains are often over 90°, while higher elevations can see nighttime temperatures below 40°.

Archeological digs have unearthed proof that people have lived in this area for more than 9,000 years. Other discoveries have documented prehistoric plant and animal life as well as flooding by a great inland sea. Volcanos and ice age glaciers have sculpted much of this land's present terrain. Settled in the 1800's, Indians roamed this land freely until about 100 years ago. Their culture is still very visible. They knew how to hide from the rain and bad weather, and many of the most popular campgrounds and recreational areas exist in areas where they once had their winter camps.

Camping in Oregon

In Oregon, practically all of the Pacific Ocean's beaches are public land. The variety of these coastal playgrounds includes spots where the mountains reach the shore, beaches that range from sparkling white sands, to agate strewn or black sand beaches, plus tidal pools and secluded coves. The southern portion harbors the state's "banana belt", the wild Rogue River and one of the world's largest coastal dune areas. The northern half has historic lighthouses, wildlife refuges, estuaries, Indian shell mounds, spouting horns, whale watching and a number of interesting seaside towns.

When fog blankets the Oregon coast you can often escape its clutches with a short drive eastward, into the mountains. There you will encounter rushing streams, forested lands, wildlife and quiet towns. Campgrounds are plentiful both near the beach and in the mountains.

The I-5 corridor, in Oregon, is the most often used route for travelers in a hurry. Yet just off its asphalt expanse a myriad of experiences beckon. Along that corridor you'll encounter heavily forested mountain passes, scenic valleys, historic towns, thriving cities, spectacular views and access routes to a half dozen National Forests. Most of the state's 50 covered bridges are within a short drive as well. Wildlife is abundant and history, if you know where to look, is easy to view.

The southern portion of this corridor harbors Crater Lake National Park, Oregon Caves National Monument, the mind boggling Oregon Vortex, historic Jacksonville, and many great fishing streams. In the northern half you'll discover pristine wilderness areas, 11,235' Mt. Hood, the scenic Columbia River Gorge, the first incorporated city west of the Rocky Mountains, the state's capitol city and its largest city. Even the biggest of towns has rugged campgrounds within an hours drive and RV parks are everywhere.

The eastern side of the Cascade Mountain Range and central Oregon offer plenty of sunshine. The sheer height of these mountains snags most rain clouds causing them to dump their rain before they can ascend. This creates a desert environment where campers can retreat when the western side is too wet for their plans.

The largest collection of volcanic remains in the continental United States can be found in the southern half of this section. Ice caves, lava cast forests, obsidian flows, fissures and cracks; plus beautiful Newberry Crater are all fun to visit. The John Day Fossil Beds, Smith Rock's mountain climbers, sun bleached ghost towns, plus the Deschutes, Metolius, Crooked and Columbia Rivers entice you north.

Cross Oregon to it's very eastern edge and you'll find yet another experience waiting. It is here, in the very northeast corner, that you'll encounter what residents refer to as the Little Switzerland of America. Hell's Canyon, the world's deepest canyon, guards its eastern border. Two National Forests occupy much of this land and a number of recreation areas and wilderness lands protect its use. The southeast corner shelters a 30 mile long, 4 mile wide, lava flow filled with obsidian, agate and petrified wood plus Leslie Gulch Canyon, Lake Owyhee and lots of great rockhounding areas.

Camping in Washington

A camping outing in Washington has plenty of rewards too. The northern portion of its Pacific Ocean coastline hides America's last unspoiled wilderness beach. Together, Olympic National Park and Olympic National Forest protect most of the area's best natural features. This section's rain forests, old growth trees, wildlife refuges, whale watching viewpoints, hiking trails, pristine lakes and unique plants are all worth investigating. Along the southern coast you'll encounter the world's longest driveable beach, historic Forts Columbia and Canby, sheltered bays, aging lighthouses, colorful cranberry bogs, charter fishing boats, and lots of great beachcombing areas.

A trip along Washington's I-5 corridor will give you access to many of the state's better known attractions. These include Mt. St. Helens, where you can view and visit an active volcano; Mt. Rainier National Park, which protects the 14,410' Mt. Rainier; Hood Canal; Puget Sound; the spectacular San Juan Islands; and the western beginnings for the famed Cascade Loop. History is easy to enjoy at Port Townsend, Coupeville, Snohomish, and Fort Lewis to name just a few sites. This corridor and its surrounding land also harbors both Washington's capitol city Olympia, and Seattle the state's largest. At 55-65 mph it all goes by in a quick blur but anyone taking the time to leave the freeway will find lots to see and plenty of great camping areas.

Heading east over the Cascade Mountain Range, toward central Washington, you'll find a slightly drier climate. Less rain falls east of the mountains since clouds heavy with moisture must empty before making the ascent. These mountains do not run due north and south, so you'll find some of the cities included with this section actually sit on the western slopes.

The full glory of northern Washington's Cascade Loop unfolds here. Most of the land it passes by is protected by National Forests and Park lands. Along the way you'll have the chance to visit pristine wilderness areas, a bald eagle sanctuary, recreational lakes, a multitude of hiking trails, and two unique villages. A visit to Winthrop is like a trip to the old west; Leavenworth is situated high in the Cascades and resembles a Bavarian village.

As you leave the Cascade Mountains, heading east, you will find a dry, desert climate. Recreation here generally centers around lakes and rivers. Moses Lake, Lake Conconully, Roosevelt Lake and the Columbia River are four good examples. Geological wonders like Dry Falls and Ginkgo Petrified Forest provide a look at prehistoric Washington. More recent historical attractions include Indian rock paintings, ghost towns, small town museums and displays.

Washington's most eastern portion holds the state's largest limestone cave, the reconstructed 1880 Fort Spokane, Indian caves and writings, and the tragic remains of Whitman Mission. Water oriented camping is popular here too and much activity is centered along the Snake, Columbia and Pend Oreille Rivers. Spokane is this region's largest city and offers a wide range of recreational opportunities.

Campground operators

The **National Park Service** provides campground facilities at Washington's Mount Rainier, Olympic and North Cascades National Parks as well as Oregon's Crater Lake National Park. National Parks were established at these locations to regulate land use toward the conservation of wildlife, scenery, natural and historic objects for the enjoyment of future generations. Fees are charged for entrance to some National Park areas. Although camping permits are not required for the campgrounds listed in this book, anyone who wants to backpack and/or camp in the less traveled portions of these lands must obtain a Backcountry Use Permit. These permits help to regulate visitor use and are cost free. For further information on area National Parks contact the regional headquarters at 83 South King Street, Seattle, WA 98104, (206)442-0170. Handicapped visitors and those over the age of 62 should inquire about Golden Eagle and Golden Age Passports.

Mount Rainier National Park protects a 14,410' mountain that harbors more glaciers than any other single mountain in the continental U.S. Sunrise, the highest point in the park open to automobiles is at 6,400'. To get higher, you'll need to hike some of the park's 305 miles of trails. These range from short family hikes to one 95 mile route that completely circles the mountain. This land is inhabited by bears, mountain goats, deer, elk, mountain lions, beavers, marmots, rabbits and raccoons. Waterfalls, ice caves, wildflowers, undisturbed wilderness and crisp mountain lakes add to its beauty. Lower elevation campgrounds are open from late May thru October, higher elevation camps do not open until late June and close in late September. Improved camps offer piped water, flush toilets, picnic tables, fireplaces, garbage pickup and have a 14 day limit. Nighttime temperatures drop to 40° throughout the summer and many trails are not completely free of snow until mid-July. Call (206)569-2211 or write Mt. Rainier National Park, Star Route - Tahoma Woods, Ashford, WA 98304 for more information.

The **Olympic National Park** protects two distinct areas on Washington's Olympic Peninsula. The first, a 57 mile stretch of wild Pacific Ocean coastline, contains a unique coastal rain forest. Hiking in this area will reveal foaming sea stacks, undisturbed tidepools, and perhaps a glimpse of harbor seals, river otters or migrating gray whales. The second area is nearly surrounded by the Olympic National Forest and covers a magnificent region of glacier-clad peaks, alpine meadows, cascading streams and virgin forests. An average annual rainfall of 140″ creates lush vegetation and enormous trees. No firearms are allowed in the park and no pets or motorized vehicles are allowed on the trails. Most trails are open to pack and saddle horses. Visitor centers can be found at Port Angeles, Lake Crescent and the Hoh Rain Forest; park headquarters are located at 600 East Park Avenue, Port Angeles, WA 98362 or call (206)452-9235. Park campgrounds offer picnic tables, fireplaces, piped water and toilet facilities. A 25 mile drive around scenic Lake Quinault, three temperate rain forests, abundant wildlife and the view from atop Hurricane Ridge provide visitors with plenty of things to see. An entry fee is charged at some sites during the summer.

North Cascades National Park encompasses 1,053 square miles of alpine scenery. You can explore deep glaciated canyons, frozen glaciers, stark jagged peaks, ice cold mountain lakes and streams, or perhaps see a mountain goat, deer, wolverine, cougar or moose. Four district units; North, South, Ross Lake and Lake Chelan National Recreation Areas are included within the park. Year round ranger stations are operated at Marblemount, Stehekin, Chelan, and during the summer at Concrete too. The only road into this area is the Cascade River Road which extends from Marblemount to below Cascade Pass. The best weather occurs between mid-June and late-September, although summer storms are not uncommon. Snow is off all but the higher trails by July, and you'll generally find less rain on the eastern side of the mountains. For further information write North Cascades National Park, Marblemount, WA 98267 or call (206)873-4590.

Oregon's **Crater Lake National Park** is situated on the crest of the Cascade Mountain Range, 80 miles northeast of Medford. This park was once the site of a 12,000 foot volcano, Mount Mazama, which was destroyed nearly 7,000 years ago by successive flows of molten rock. Centuries of rain water and melting snows have filled its caldera with water creating the United States' deepest lake. Additional volcanic activity caused Wizard Island to appear in its crystal clear pool. At its greatest depth this lake reaches nearly 2,000′ making it the seventh deepest lake in the world. Eagles, deer, bears, coyote, porcupine, bobcat, elk, fox and cougar frequent the area. Trails access the land and panoramic vistas, wildflower filled meadows and crisp mountain air unfold to the hardy hiker.

The **Coulee Dam National Recreation Area** consists of Roosevelt Lake and a 660 mile long narrow strip of land adjacent to the lakeshore. Roosevelt Lake was created by the construction of Grand Coulee Dam, the largest and most important dam on the Columbia River. The lake's western shores offer very little shade and are generally warm and sunny; the north arm tends to be forested and cooler. The lake is at its maximum level by early July and remains that way thru Labor Day. Water skiing is popular, sailing is excellent and fish abundant. Summertime temperatures range from a daytime high of 75-100° to a nighttime low of 50-60°. Deer, coyotes, marmots, porcupine and an occasional bear are spotted. Recent archeological excavations have unearthed evidence that people have lived in this area for more than 9,000 years. Fort Spokane, a reconstructed 1880's army post, relates the more recent past belonging to America's colorful frontier period. Additional information may be obtained by visiting park headquarters in Coulee Dam or by writing to P.O. Box 37, Coulee Dam, WA 99116.

There are nineteen **National Forests** in Oregon and Washington. No matter where you go, you're always within a few hours drive of at least one National Forest, sometimes two or three. This public land provides recreational land for camping, hiking, picnics, boating, fishing, swimming, mountain climbing, skiing and more. A quick visit to any National Forest ranger station will provide you with current information on area trails, weather, special attractions and avoiding crowds. Although there are no entrance fees for National Forests most improved campgrounds charge a fee. Lower elevation campgrounds are open year round and high country camps from about mid-June thru August, depending upon weather. Improved campgrounds generally offer designated spaces, drinking water, road access, toilet facilities, and firepits. Many campgrounds are accessible to the physically challenged. Group campsites are available in some areas. Boat ramps, picnic areas and visitor centers are free. Maps of each National Forest showing roads, trails, camps and natural areas are available for a small cost. For further information contact the Pacific Northwest Regional Headquarters, 319 SW Pine Street (P.O. Box 3623), Portland, OR 97208, (503)221-2877. They can also supply details on their participation in the National Park Golden Eagle/Age Passport and how to obtain camp stamps.

Oregon's National Forests include Deschutes, Fremont, Malheur, Mt. Hood, Ochoco, Rogue River, Siskiyou, Siuslaw, Umatilla, Ump- qua, Wallowa-Whitman, Willamette and Winema. Washington's are Colville, Gifford Pinchot, Mt. Baker-Snoqualmie, Okanogan, Olym- pic and Wenatchee. These lands encompass some of the region's best recreational areas. Many also protect and regulate roadless wilderness lands where backpackers can enjoy a pristine wilderness adventure. Visitors to wilderness areas must obtain a permit for overnight trips; some overused areas also require per- mits for all day journeys. A stop at the local ranger station will get you full details on these free permits and information that will allow you to avoid crowded areas and travel as a minimum impact visitor.

The **Bureau of Land Management (BLM)** manages 15.7 million acres in Oregon. Recreational lands are scattered throughout the state with district offices located in Salem, Eugene, Roseburg, Coos Bay, Medford, Lakeview, Prineville, Burns, Baker and Vale. Several white water rivers flow through this land; Deschutes, John Day, Grande Ronde, Owyhee and Rogue Rivers are some. Areas for off-road vehicles are also provided. The gathering for personal use of rocks, minerals, gemstones, berries, nuts and flowers is okay. Permits are required for large collections. Historic and related artifacts must be left undisturbed. Unless posted otherwise, the maximum stay in BLM campgrounds is 14 days. Facilities generally include drinking water, picnic tables, toilets, firepits, and recrea- tional opportunities. National Park Golden Eagle/Age Passport holders receive a discount on fees. The main office is located at 825 NE Multnomah Street (P.O. Box 2965), Portland, OR 97208, (503)231-6274.

Nearly 100 **Washington State Parks** offer camping. Most provide flush toilets, hot showers, picnic tables, firepits, garbage service, running water, utility hookups, and have a 10 day maximum stay. Parks featuring picnic areas offer tables, piped water, fireplaces or stoves, and shelters; some also have kitchens. Sites with inter- pretive displays focus on historical or geological events. Many of these campgrounds are open year round; others from April 1 thru September 30. Most parks offer facilities which meet barrier-free guidelines for accessibility. The fee for standard campsites if $7.00, an additional $2.50 is charged for utility hookups. Campers from states where an out of state surcharge is levied are required to pay the same surcharge. Summer boat camping at one of the many moorage areas will cost you $3.50-$5.50 per night depending on the length of your craft. Horses are permitted only in designated areas and pets must be leashed at all times. For further information write the Washington State Parks & Recreation Commission, 7150 Cleanwater Lane, KY-11, Olympia, WA 98504-5711, or call (206)753-2027. If you're in Washington you can call their summer-time toll free number; (800)562-0990.

The **Washington State Department of Natural Resources** manages 5 million acres. Capitol Forest, Tahuya, Sultan-Pilchuck, Okanogan, Yacolt, Hoh-Clearwater and Ahtanum Multiple Use Areas all have campgrounds. Multiple Use Areas balance forest production with recreational opportunities. Capitol Forest, southwest of Olympia, is the most heavily used. It offers 76,000 acres accessed by a good trail system for hikers, horses and trailbikes. Tahuya, inside the Hood Canal Loop, has 33,000 acres, numerous lakes and streams and is another heavily used area. Sultan-Pilchuck is a scenic 62,000 acre area east of Everett; Okanogan 176,600 acres of mountainous pine forests, lakes and streams. Yacolt is a former burn area and has 73,000 acres with hard-surfaced roads and trails for hikers, horses and trailbikes. Hoh-Clearwater has a rain forest and Ahtanum 39,400 acres which range from desert to alpine. For additional information on these areas write to Washington State Department of Natural Resources, Division of Recreation, 120 E. Union, Room 106 -EK-12, Olympia, WA 98504 or call (206)753-5338.

Oregon State Parks manage most of the state's Pacific Ocean beaches; some as day-use areas and others as campgrounds. Other state park campgrounds are situated along rivers and lakes, or near natural attractions. A few are open year round; others from mid-April to late October. Most have flush toilets, showers, picnic tables and firepits; many offer full utility hookups. During the summer, a campsite with full utilities is $10.00, tent sites $8.00, primitive sites $7.00, overnight moorage $3.00, and hiker/biker campgrounds $2.00. Group campsites are $30.00 with advance reservation required. Reservations are also taken by mail for 13 high use camps in Brookings, Coos Bay, Detroit, Florence, Joseph, Lincoln City, Madras, Newport, Prineville, Tillamook and Waldport. For further information, and reservation applications, write Oregon State Parks, 525 Trade Street SE, Salem, OR 97310 or call (503)238-7488. The summertime toll free number within Oregon is (800)452-5687.

Private Campgrounds, and a couple operated by agencies like the **Corp of Engineers** and **Pacific Power** provide the balance of improved campgrounds. Private campgrounds sometimes offer the most deluxe facilities. Swimming pools, hot tubs, saunas, game rooms, full utility hookups and laundry facilities are among the amenities offered. Most provide accommodations for RV's and some do not permit tents. Rates for individual sites range from $5.00 to more than $20.00 depending upon location and facilities. These campgrounds are operated by individuals, families and businesses. Most take reservations and phone numbers have been provided within the listings.

Getting the most out of your camping experience

Planning ahead is the best way to avoid hassles. Those new to the area will want to start by contacting each state's tourism office. Besides general and camping information, ask about receiving a calendar of annual events, map and specific information on attractions geared toward your interests (fishing, hiking, history, etc.). In Washington you can call (206)586-2088. For information on Oregon call (800)233-3306 from within the state or (800)547-7842 from outside the state.

Next, check with your local bookstore or library for some good regional guidebooks; those which pertain only to the northwest corner. Something published within the area, or written by someone who lives here, will often show you more. These can be especially helpful when you're looking for information on a specific type of attraction or worthwhile sites that most visitors overlook. Upon comparison, you will generally find that a book which tries to cover more than a couple of states in one volume includes far less specific information than something devoted strictly to the area. Books that do not carry advertising or charge businesses for their listings are also more likely to give you an unbiased look at available attractions.

With all of this information in hand, you're ready to plan your trip. Keep your schedule flexible, this will allow you to escape an extended bout of wet weather by fleeing to the drier side of the mountains. You'll find plenty of campgrounds on either side. Start by listing your "must see" spots. Hitting these sights first will help you to remain flexible. Then, if the weather changes, you can check your list and head elsewhere.

Campers who live here year round always pack for a variety of weather conditions and so should you. Having warm clothes along will make gray skies seem sunny because it won't slow you down. You may actually find that the cooler weather makes hiking and other strenuous activities less so. Wet weather is great for visiting museums and other inside attractions.

WHERE TO FIND OREGON'S IMPROVED CAMPGROUNDS

All campgrounds in this section are arranged alphabetically by city. The following map and area listings will help you to locate cities in your destination area. The page number is shown in parenthesis. This book should be used together with your state highway map. See page 13 for complete information on how to use this guide.

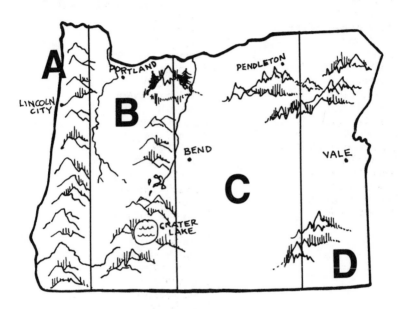

SECTION A – COASTAL TOWNS

North
Astoria (35)
Beaver (36)
Cannon Beach (43)
Depoe Bay (52)
Eddyville (54)
Garibaldi (61)
Hebo (68)
Lincoln City (78)
Newport (82)
Pacific City (85)
Tidewater (100)
Tillamook (100)
Waldport (104)
Yachats (109)

South
Bandon (36)
Brookings (39)
Cave Junction (45)
Charleston (46)
Coos Bay (47)
Coquille (48)
Florence (57)
Gardiner (61)
Gold Beach (62)
Lakeside (74)
Langlois (75)
Mapleton (80)
North Bend (83)
Port Orford (88)
Powers (89)
Reedsport (92)
Remote (93)

SECTION B – I-5 & NEIGHBORING AREAS

North
Albany (33)
Aurora (35)
Camp Sherman (41)
Cascade Locks (44)
Corbett (48)
Dee (52)
Detroit (53)
Elsie (54)
Estacada (55)
Government Camp (63)
Gresham (67)
Idanha (69)
McMinnville (82)
Mehama (82)
Newberg (82)
Parkdale (86)
Philomath (88)
Portland (89)
Rhododendron (93)
Salem (95)
Sweet Home (98)
Tollgate (101)
Vernonia (104)
Welches (106)

South
Ashland (33)
Azalea (35)
Blue River (38)
Butte Falls (41)
Canyonville (44)
Cascade Summit (45)
Cottage Grove (48)
Crater Lake National Park (49)
Crescent (49)
Crescent Lake (50)
Creswell (51)
Diamond Lake (53)
Drain (54)
Eugene (57)
Fort Klamath (60)
Glide (61)
Gold Hill (63)
Grants Pass (65)
Idleyld Park (70)
Jacksonville (71)
Keno (72)
Klamath Falls (72)
Lowell (79)
McKenzie Bridge (81)
Oakridge (83)
Prospect (91)
Rogue River (94)
Roseburg (94)
Selma (95)
Springfield (97)
Sutherlin (97)
Talent (99)
Westfir (107)
White City (109)

SECTION C – CASCADES EAST/CENTRAL OREGON

North
Arlington (33)
Condon (47)
Culver (51)
Fossil (60)
Fox (60)
Heppner (68)
Hermiston (68)
Hood River (69)
John Day (71)
Madras (79)
Maupin (80)
Pendleton (87)
Prairie City (90)
Spray (97)
The Dalles (99)
Tygh Valley (102)
Ukiah (102)
Wamic (106)
Warm Springs (106)
Weston (107)

South
Bend (37)
Bly (39)
Burns (40)
Chemult (46)
Chiloquin (46)
Frenchglen (61)
Lakeview (74)
LaPine (75)
Paulina (87)
Prineville (90)
Redmond (92)
Sisters (96)

SECTION D – EASTERN OREGON

North
Baker (35)
Dale (51)
Elgin (54)
Enterprise (54)
Haines (67)
Halfway (68)
Huntington (69)
Joseph (71)
La Grande (74)
Oxbow (85)
Richland (94)
Troy (102)
Union (103)
Unity (103)

South
Juntura (72)
Vale (103)

OREGON CAMPGROUNDS

ALBANY

ALBANY TRAILER PARK (Private)
12 trailer sites w/hookups for water/electricity/sewer, trailers to 35', no tents, reservations - (503)928-8532, showers, laundry, groceries, $$$.
East of Albany. Take I-5 south to Viewcrest exit #237, east to Century Drive, follow this 3.0 miles to trailer park.

"BABE THE BLUE OX" RV PARK (Private)
100 trailer sites w/hookups for water/electricity/sewer, reservations -(503)926-2886, showers, laundry, groceries, $$$.
In Albany. Leave I-5 on exit #233 and head east to Price Road. Campground is located at 4000 Blue Ox Drive.

ARLINGTON

TERRACE HEIGHTS MOTOR HOME PARK (Private)
10 trailer sites w/hookups for water/electricity/sewer, reservations - (503)454-2757, showers, laundry, $$$.
In Arlington. Leave I-84 at Arlington exit #137, take Main Street .5 mile south to motor home park.

ASHLAND

CAMPERS COVE (Private)
25 trailer units w/hookups for water/electricity/sewer, reservations - (503)482-1201, showers, ice, lake, swimming, fishing, boat launch, hiking, elev. 5000', $$$.
Southeast of Ashland. I-5 to State 66, east 18.0 miles to Hyatt Lake Road, northeast 3.0 miles to Hyatt Prairie Road, north 1.5 miles.

EMIGRANT CAMPGROUND (Jackson County)
40 campsites, reservation information - (503)776-7001, showers, laundry, trailer waste disposal, lake, fishing, boat launch, boat rental, swimming, playground, hiking, $$.
Southeast of Ashland. I-5 to State 66, east 5.0 miles to campground.

GLENYAN KOA (Private)
68 campsites, 11 w/hookups for water/electricity/sewer, 35 w/hookups for water & electricity, plus 22 w/hookups for water only, reservations - (503)482-4138, showers, laundry, groceries, trailer waste disposal, swimming pool, pond, fishing, playground, $$$.
Southeast of Ashland. I-5 to State 66, east 3.5 miles to campground.

GRIZZLY CAMPGROUND (Jackson County)
36 campsites, trailers to 25', lake, fishing, boat launch, hiking, elev. 4500', $.
East of Ashland. Take I-5 south to State 66, after 1.0 mile follow Dead Indian Road 20.0 miles east, Hyatt Prairie Road 2.0 miles south to campground.

HOWARD PRAIRIE LAKE RESORT (Private)
300 campsites, 60 w/hookups for water/electricity/sewer, 90 w/hookups for water & electricity, plus 150 tent units, reservation information - (503)482-1979, showers, laundry, groceries, trailer waste disposal, lake, swimming, fishing, boat launch, boat rental, hiking, wheelchair access, elev. 4500', $$.
East of Ashland. Take I-5 south to State 66, after 1.0 mile follow Dead Indian Road 20.0 miles east, Hyatt Prairie Road 3.5 miles south to campground.

HYATT LAKE (BLM)
25 units, trailers okay, picnic area w/shelter, drinking water, boat launch, boating, hiking, fishing, swimming, nature study, elev. 5000', $$.
Southeast of Ashland. State 66 16.0 miles east, then take East Hyatt Lake Road 4.0 miles north to campground.

HYATT LAKE RESORT (Private)
65 campsites, 35 w/hookups for water/electricity/sewer, 23 w/hookups for water & electricity, plus 7 tent units, reservations - (503)482-0525, showers, ice, trailer waste disposal, lake, swimming, fishing, boat launch & rental, playground, hiking, $$.
Southeast of Ashland. I-5 to State 66, east 18.0 miles to Hyatt Lake Road, northeast 3.0 miles to Hyatt Prairie Road, north 1.0 mile.

JACKSON HOT SPRINGS (Private)
52 campsites, 14 w/hookups for water/electricity/sewer, 13 w/hookups for water & electricity, plus 25 tent units, reservations - (503)482-3776, showers, laundry, ice, mineral water swimming pool & baths, $$-$$$.
North of Ashland. I-5 to exit #19, South Valley View Road .5 mile southwest to campground.

SUGAR PINE (Jackson County)
11 group campsites, reservations - (503)776-7001, lake, swimming, fishing, boat launch, hiking, elev. 4500', $$$.
East of Ashland. Take I-5 south to State 66, after 1.0 mile follow Dead Indian Road 20.0 miles east, Hyatt Prairie Road 2.0 miles south to campground.

LILY GLEN CAMPGROUND (Jackson County)
15 campsites, some group sites, reservation information - (503)776-7001, lake, fishing, hiking, $.
East of Ashland. Take I-5 south to State 66, after 1.0 mile follow Dead Indian Road 21.0 miles east.

WILLOW POINT CAMPGROUND (Jackson County)
30 campsites, reservation information - (503)776-7001, lake, swimming, fishing, boat launch, hiking, elev. 5000', $$.
East of Ashland. Take I-5 south to State 66, after 1.0 mile follow Dead Indian Road 20.0 miles east, Hyatt Prairie Road 5.0 miles south to campground.

ASTORIA

FORT STEVENS (Oregon State Park)
605 campsites, 213 w/hookups for water/electricity/sewer, 130 w/hookups for electricity, plus 262 tent units, mail reservations available, trailers to 56', group campsites, wheelchair access, picnic area, historical museum, self-guided walking tour, remains of Civil War era fort visible, showers, trailer waste disposal, boat launch, swimming, fishing, ocean beach access, beachcombing, bicycle trail, hiking trails, $-$$$.
West of Astoria. Campground is located 10.0 miles west of Astoria, off US 101, near Warrenton.

KAMPERS WEST KAMPGROUND RV PARK (Private)
200 campsites, 100 w/hookups for water & electricity, plus 100 tent units, reservation information - (503)861-1814, showers, laundry, ice, trailer waste disposal, river, fishing, $$.
West of Astoria. Campground is located 10.0 miles west of Astoria, off US 101, following the Warrenton/Fort Stevens signs. Campground is located at 1140 NW Warrenton Drive.

NEACOXIE LAKE TRAILER PARK (Private)
40 trailer sites, 10 w/hookups for water/electricity/sewer, plus 30 w/hookups for water & electricity, no tents, no pets, reservation information - (503)861-3921, showers, laundry, lake, swimming, fishing, nearby boat launch, $$-$$$.
Southwest of Astoria. Leave Astoria heading toward Warrenton, take US 101 4.0 miles south of Warrenton to Sunset Beach Road, campground is .5 mile.

AURORA

ISEBERG PARK RV (Private)
84 campsites w/hookups for water/electricity/sewer, tents okay, reservations -(503)678-2646, showers, laundry, groceries, trailer waste disposal, rec room, miniature golf course, hiking, $$$.
West of Aurora. Leave I-5 at exit #278 and look for signs.

AZALEA

MEADOW WOOD RV RESORT & CAMPGROUND (Private)
63 trailer sites w/hookups for water & electricity, reservation information -(503)832-2959, showers, laundry, groceries, trailer waste disposal, swimming pool, playground, $$$.
Southwest of Azalea. I-5 9.0 miles south to exit #86, Frontage Road 4.0 miles south. Located at 862 Autumn Lane in Glendale.

BAKER

ALPENDORF RV PARK (Private)
30 campsites, 26 w/hookups for water/electricity/sewer, plus 4 w/hookups for water & electricity, reservation information - (503)523-7171, showers, groceries, $$-$$$.
Northeast of Baker. Leave I-84 at exit #302 and drive west .1 mile to park.

MOUNTAIN VIEW CAMPGROUND/HOLIDAY TRAV-L-PARK (Private)
60 campsites, 52 w/hookups for water/electricity/sewer, plus 8 tent units, reservations - (503)523-4824, showers, laundry, trailer waste disposal, swimming pool, playground, $$-$$$.
In Baker. Leave I-84 on exit #304 and travel west .5 mile on Campbell, 1.0 mile north on Cedar, 1.0 mile west on Hughes Lane to campground.

UNION CREEK (Wallowa-Whitman National Forest)
58 campsites, 24 w/hookups for water & electricity, trailers to 22', group sites, picnic area, piped water, flush toilets, trailer waste disposal, wheelchair access, gasoline, ice, boat launch, boating, swimming, fishing, water skiing, hiking, adjacent to Phillips Reservoir, bicycling, elev. 4100', $$.
Southwest of Baker. State 7 20.0 miles south.

BANDON

BLUE JAY CAMPGROUND (Private)
40 campsites, 2 w/hookups for water/electricity/sewer, 2 w/hookups for water & electricity, 16 w/hookups for electricity, plus 20 tent units, reservation information - (503)347-3258, showers, $$-$$$.
South of Bandon. US 101 4.0 miles south, Scenic Beach Loop Drive .5 mile west to campground.

BULLARDS BEACH (Oregon State Park)
192 campsites, 92 w/hookups for water/electricity/sewer, plus 100 w/hookups for electricity, trailers to 55', picnic area, wheelchair access, showers, trailer waste disposal, boat launch, fishing, horse trails & camp facilities, ocean access, beachcombing, 1896 Coquille Lighthouse, $$-$$$.
North of Bandon. US 101 1.0 mile north to campground.

DRIFTWOOD SHORES RV PARK (Private)
40 trailer sites w/hookups for water/electricity/sewer, reservation information - (503)347-4122, showers, laundry, groceries, trailer waste disposal, $$-$$$.
In Bandon. West of US 101 junction with State 42 1 block at 935 E. 2nd Street.

BEAVER

BEAVER CREEK (Siuslaw National Forest)
5 tent units, picnic area, well, fishing, hiking, sand dunes, elev. 400', $.
Northeast of Beaver. US 101 north approximately 3 miles to Hemlock, FSR 375 5.0 miles along East Beaver Creek Road to campground.

CAMPER COVE (Private)
19 campsites, 12 w/hookups for water/electricity/sewer, plus 7 tent units, trailers to 35', reservation information - (503)398-5334, showers, laundry, trailer waste disposal, river, fishing, hiking, $$-$$$.
North of Beaver. US 101 2.5 miles north.

BEND

BEACH (Deschutes National Forest)
10 units, some trailers, piped water, river, lake - speed limits, boating, fishing, swimming, elev. 4900', $$.
Southwest of Bend. CR 46 approximately 36 miles. Campground is located at south end of Elk Lake.

BEND KOA (Private)
73 campsites, 42 w/hookups for water/electricity/sewer, 29 w/hookups for water & electricity, plus 2 tent units, reservations - (503)382-7728, showers, laundry, groceries, trailer waste disposal, swimming pool, pond, fishing, playground, $$$.
At Bend. US 97 2.0 miles north.

BENHAM FALLS (Deschutes National Forest)
5 tent units, no trailers, on Deschutes River, boat launch, boating, fishing, elev. 4100', $$.
South of Bend. US 97 8.0 miles south to Lava Butte, FSR 1831 west 4 miles to campground.

CROWN VILLA RV PARK (Private)
106 trailer sites w/hookups for water/electricity/sewer, no tents, reservations - (503)388-1131, showers, laundry, ice, trailer waste disposal, pond, bicycle rentals, playground, wheelchair access, nearby golf, $$$.
Southeast of Bend. US 97 south just past city limits, 2.0 miles southeast on Brosterhaus Road.

ELK LAKE (Deschutes National Forest)
22 units, trailers to 22', picnic area, piped water, lake - speed limits, boating, swimming, fishing, elev. 4900', $$.
West of Bend. CR 46 31.5 miles west to campground.

LITTLE FAWN (Deschutes National Forest)
28 units, 5 group sites, reservations required (503)388-5664, trailers to 22', on Elk Lake - speed limits, boat launch, boating, swimming, fishing, elev. 4900', $$.
West of Bend. CR 46 31.3 miles west, FSR 1822 2.1 miles southeast, FSR 18228 .2 mile southwest.

LOWES RV PARK (Private)
45 campsites, 35 w/hookups for water/electricity/sewer, plus 10 tent units, reservation information - (503)382-6206, showers, laundry, $$-$$$.
At Bend. US 97 south, located near city limits 2.5 miles south of junction with US 20.

MEADOW (Deschutes National Forest)
13 tent units, on Deschutes River, fishing, elev. 4000', $$.
Southwest of Bend. CR 46 5 miles southwest of Bend.

POINT (Deschutes National Forest)
9 units, trailers to 22', piped water, on Elk Lake - speed limits, boating, swimming, fishing, elev. 4900', $$.
West of Bend. CR 46 33.0 miles west to campground.

QUINN MEADOW HORSE CAMP (Deschutes National Forest)
22 units, reservations required (503)388-5664, trailers to 18', well, stream, fishing, hiking & horse trails, elev. 5100', $.
West of Bend. CR 46 30.0 miles west, FSR 450 .3 mile southeast.

SATAN CREEK (Deschutes National Forest)
2 tent units, on Sparks Lake, fishing, hiking, elev. 5400', $$.
West of Bend 28 miles. CR 46 west to Sparks Lake and campground.

TUMALO (Oregon State Park)
88 campsites, 20 w/hookups for water/electricity/sewer, plus 68 tent units, trailers to 35', group campsites, showers, fishing, hiking trails, $$-$$$.
Northwest of Bend. US 20 5.0 miles northwest to campground.

BLUE RIVER

DELTA (Willamette National Forest)
39 units, trailers to 22', picnic area, well, river, wheelchair access, fishing, old growth nature trail, elev. 1200', $$-$$$.
East of Blue River. State 126 3.5 miles east, FSR 19 .3 mile south, FSR 194 .7 mile west.

FRENCH PETE (Willamette National Forest)
17 units, trailers to 18', well, river, wheelchair access, boating, swimming, fishing, water skiing, hiking, elev. 2000', $$-$$$.
Southeast of Blue River. State 126 3.5 miles east, FSR 19 11.0 miles south.

FRISSELL CROSSING (Willamette National Forest)
12 units, trailers to 18', well, river, fishing, hiking, elev. 2600', $-$$.
Southeast of Blue River. State 126 3.5 miles east, FSR 19 23.0 miles south.

HORSE CREEK (Willamette National Forest)
42 units, trailers to 22', group sites - reservations required (503)854-3366, well, fishing, elev. 1400', $$-$$$.
Southeast of Blue River. State 126 .2 mile east, CR 161 5.1 miles southeast.

LAZY DAZE MOTOR HOME PARK (Private)
18 trailer sites w/hookups for water/electricity/sewer, reservations - (503)822-3889, showers laundry, ice, river, fishing, $$.
East of Blue River. State 126 1.5 miles east.

MAPLE LEAF RV PARK & CAMPGROUND (Private)
30 campsites, 25 w/hookups for water/electricity/sewer, plus 5 tent units, reservation information - (503)822-3912, showers, laundry, river, fishing, playfield, $$$.
East of Blue River. State 126 2.5 miles east.

McKENZIE RIVER TRAILER COURT (Private)
12 trailer sites, 6 w/hookups for water/electricity/sewer, plus 6 w/out hookups, reservation information - (503)822-6067, showers, laundry, river, fishing, $$$.
East of Blue River. State 126 1.5 miles east.

MONA (Willamette National Forest)
23 units, trailers to 22', piped water, river, flush toilets, wheelchair access, boat launch, boating, swimming, fishing, water skiing, elev. 1400', $$-$$$.
Northeast of Blue River. State 126 2.0 miles east, FSR 15 3.9 miles northeast, FSR 15120 .3 mile south.

PATIO RV PARK (Private)
66 trailer sites, 44 w/hookups for water/electricity/sewer, plus 22 w/hookups for water & electricity, no tents, reservations - (503)822-3596, showers, laundry, trailer waste disposal, river, fishing, playfield, hiking, $$$.
East of Blue River. State 126 6.0 miles east, McKenzie River Drive east 2.5 miles to park.

SLIDE CREEK (Willamette National Forest)
16 units, trailers okay, picnic area, lake, boating, swimming, fishing, water skiing, elev. 1700', $$-$$$.
Southeast of Blue River. State 126 3.5 miles east, FSR 19 11.6 miles south, FSR 195 1.5 miles north.

BLY

GERBER RESERVOIR (BLM)
50 units, trailers okay, picnic area, drinking water, fishing, hiking, swimming, boat launch, boating, $.
Southwest of Bly. Take Gerber Road approximately 19.0 miles southwest to west side of reservoir and campground.

BROOKINGS

CHETCO RV PARK (Private)
121 trailer sites w/hookups for water/electricity/sewer, reservation information - (503)469-3863, showers, laundry, ice, trailer waste disposal, $$$.
South of Brookings. US 101 south 1.0 mile past the Chetco River Bridge.

DRIFTWOOD RV PARK (Private)
108 campsites, 100 w/hookups for water/electricity/sewer, plus 8 w/hookups for water & electricity, reservations - (503)469-3213, showers, laundry, ocean access, fishing, boat launch, $$-$$$.
South of Brookings. US 101 south over Chetco River Bridge, Lower Harbor Road west .7 mile.

HARRIS BEACH (Oregon State Park)
151 campsites, 34 w/hookups for water/electricity/sewer, 51 w/hookups for electricity, plus 66 tent units, group campsites, mail reservations available, trailers to 50', picnic area, wheelchair access, showers, trailer waste disposal, fishing, ocean access, beachcombing, hiking trails, $$-$$$.
North of Brookings. US 101 2.0 miles north to campground.

LITTLE REDWOOD (Siskiyou National Forest)
12 units, trailers to 18', picnic area, piped water, river, boating, swimming, fishing, elev. 100', $.
Northeast of Brookings. US 101 .5 mile south, CR 784 7.5 miles northeast, FSR 376 6.0 miles northeast.

LOEB (Oregon State Park)
53 campsites w/hookups for electricity, trailers to 50', picnic area, fishing, swimming, $$.
Northeast of Brookings. Leave US 101 at Brookings on Chetco River Road, follow this 10.0 miles northeast.

LUDLUM PLACE (Siskiyou National Forest)
1 group site, reservations advised - (503)469-2196, trailers to 32', river, swimming, fishing, elev. 200', $$.
East of Brookings, US 101 5.7 miles southeast, CR 896 6.3 miles northeast, FSR 3907 1.0 miles east, FSR 4029 1.5 miles north.

PORT OF BROOKINGS SPORTHAVEN TRAILER PARK (Port)
173 campsites, 42 w/hookups for water/electricity/sewer, 56 w/hookups for water & electricity, plus 75 w/out hookups, reservation information - (503)469-5867, showers, laundry, trailer waste disposal, ocean access, river, swimming, fishing, boat launch, boat rental, wheelchair access, $$-$$$.
In Brookings. US 101 south to Lower Harbor Road, located at Benham Lane and Lower Harbor Road.

RIVER BEND PARK (Private)
120 trailer sites w/hookups for water/electricity/sewer, reservations -(503)469-3356, showers, laundry, trailer waste disposal, river, swimming, fishing, boat ramp, $$-$$$.
Southeast of Brookings. US 101 south over Chetco River Bridge, Southbank Chetco River Road 1.5 miles east.

SEA BIRD RV PARK (Private)
60 trailer sites w/hookups for water/electricity/sewer, no tents, reservation information - (503)469-3512, showers, laundry, trailer waste disposal, $$.
In Brookings. US 101 south over Chetco River Bridge, proceed 1 block to park.

WINCHUCK (Siskiyou National Forest)
13 units, trailers to 18', picnic area, piped water, river, swimming, fishing, elev. 100', $.
East of Brookings, US 101 5.7 miles southeast, CR 896 6.3 miles northeast, FSR 3907 1.1 miles east.

BURNS

DELINTMENT LAKE (Ochoco National Forest)
24 units, trailers to 22', picnic area, well, boat launch, boating, swimming, fishing, elev. 5600', $.
Northwest of Burns. FSR 47 15 miles northwest, FSR 41 25 miles northwest, FSR 4365 3 miles west, FSR 41 5 miles west.

EMIGRANT (Ochoco National Forest)
6 units, trailers to 22', piped water, stream, fishing, $.
Northwest of Burns. FSR 47 15 miles northwest, FSR 41 20 miles northwest.

FALLS (Ochoco National Forest)
5 units, trailers to 22', piped water, stream, fishing, $.
Northwest of Burns. FSR 47 15 miles northwest, FSR 41 18 miles north-west.

SANDS TRAILER PARK (Private)
16 campsites, 10 w/hookups for water/electricity/sewer, plus 6 tent units, reservation information - (503)573-7010, showers, nearby golf, elev. 4200', $$.
South of Burns. US 395/20 south 1.0 mile.

VILLAGE TRAILER PARK (Private)
41 campsites, 32 w/hookups for water/electricity/sewer, plus 9 tent units, reservation information - (503)573-7640, showers, laundry, river, playground, $$.
At Burns. US 395/20 northeast to Seneca Drive, located at 1273 Seneca Drive.

BUTTE FALLS

FOURBIT FORD (Rogue River National Forest)
6 tent units, well, stream, fishing, elev. 3200', $.
East of Butte Falls. CR 30 9.3 miles southeast, FSR 3065 1.2 miles northeast.

PARKER MEADOWS (Rogue River National Forest)
6 tent units, piped water, picnic area, fishing, elev. 5000', $.
Northeast of Butte Falls. CR 30 10.0 miles southeast, FSR 37 11.0 miles northeast.

WHISKEY SPRINGS (Rogue River National Forest)
36 units, trailers to 18', picnic area, piped water, hiking, elev. 3200', $.
Southeast of Butte Falls. CR 30 9.3 miles southeast, FSR 3065 .3 mile east.

WILLOW LAKE RESORT (Private)
75 campsites, 25 w/hookups for water/electricity/sewer, 20 w/ hookups for water & electricity, plus 30 tent units, reservations - (503)865-3229, showers, groceries, trailer waste disposal, lake, swimming, fishing, boat launch, boat rental, hiking, elev. 3000', $$.
Southeast of Butte Falls. Fish Lake Road 8.0 miles southeast, Willow Lake Road 2.0 miles southwest.

WILLOW PRAIRIE (Rogue River National Forest)
6 tent units, well, elev. 4400', $.
Southeast of Butte Falls. Leave Butte Falls heading southeast toward State 140, take FSR 3738 west 1.5 miles to campground.

CAMP SHERMAN

ALLEN SPRINGS (Deschutes National Forest)
16 units, 1 group site, trailers to 22', piped water, river, fishing, hiking, elev. 2800', $$-$$$.
North of Camp Sherman. FSR 900 5.0 miles north to campground.

ALLINGHAM (Deschutes National Forest)
6 units, 4 group sites, trailers to 22', piped water, river, fishing, hiking, elev. 2900', $$.
North of Camp Sherman. FSR 900 1.0 mile north to campground.

BLACK BUTTE MOTEL & RV PARK (Private)
28 campsites, 18 w/hookups for water/electricity/sewer, plus 10 w/hookups for water & electricity, reservation information - (503)595-6514, showers, laundry, trailer waste disposal, river, fishing, playfield, playground, hiking, $$$.
At Camp Sherman. Located on Camp Sherman Road.

CAMP SHERMAN (Deschutes National Forest)
13 units, 2 group sites, trailers to 22', piped water, river, fishing, hiking, elev. 3000', $$.
North of Camp Sherman. FSR 900 .2 mile north to campground.

FOSTER'S COLD SPRINGS RESORT (Private)
35 trailer sites w/hookups for water/electricity/sewer, no tents, reservation information - (503)595-6271, river, fishing, hiking, elev. 3000', $$$.
North of Camp Sherman. Located on Camp Sherman Road, just north of town.

GORGE (Deschutes National Forest)
12 units, 6 group sites, trailers to 22', piped water, river, fishing, hiking, elev. 2900', $$.
North of Camp Sherman. FSR 900 2.0 miles north to campground.

LOWER BRIDGE (Deschutes National Forest)
11 units, 1 group site, trailers to 22', piped water, river, fishing, hiking, elev. 2800', $$-$$$.
North of Camp Sherman. FSR 14 9.0 miles north to campground.

METOLIUS RIVER RESORT (Private)
35 trailer sites w/hookups for water/electricity/sewer, no tents, reservation information - (503)595-6281, showers, ice, river, fishing, hiking, elev. 2900', $$$.
At Camp Sherman. Located on Camp Sherman Road.

PINE REST (Deschutes National Forest)
8 tent sites, piped water, river, fishing, hiking, elev. 2900', $$.
North of Camp Sherman. FSR 900 1.5 miles north to campground.

PIONEER FORD (Deschutes National Forest)
16 units, 4 group sites, trailers to 22', piped water, river, wheelchair access, fishing, hiking, elev. 2800', $$-$$$.
North of Camp Sherman. FSR 14 7.0 miles north to campground.

SHEEP SPRINGS HORSE CAMP (Deschutes National Forest)
11 units, 9 group sites, trailers to 18', well, horse facilities, elev. 3200', $$-$$$.
Northwest of Camp Sherman. FSR 1420 4.0 miles west, FSR 12 1.0 miles north, campground road .5 mile.

SMILING RIVER (Deschutes National Forest)
27 units, 10 group sites, trailers to 22', piped water, river, fishing, hiking, elev. 2900', $$.
North of Camp Sherman. FSR 900 1.0 mile north to campground.

CANNON BEACH

BUD'S CAMPGROUND & RV PARK (Private)
25 trailer sites w/hookups for water/electricity/sewer, trailers to 35', no tents, reservation information - (503)738-6855, showers, laundry, groceries, $$$.
North of Cannon Beach. US 101 11.0 miles north, just past Gearhart.

NEHALEM BAY (Oregon State Park)
291 campsites w/hookups for electricity, trailers to 60', wheelchair access, picnic area, showers, trailer waste disposal, boat launch, fishing, ocean access, beachcombing, bicycle trail, horse trails, $-$$.
South of Cannon Beach. US 101 south approximately 17.0 miles, campground is located 3.0 miles south of Manzanita junction.

NEHALEM BAY TRAILER PARK (Private)
12 trailer sites w/hookups for water/electricity/sewer, no tents, reservation information - (503)368-5180, showers, laundry, groceries, $$.
South of Cannon Beach. US 101 south 14.0 miles.

NEHALEM SHORES RV PARK (Private)
25 trailer sites w/hookups for water/electricity/sewer, reservation information - (503)368-6670, showers, laundry, ice, river, fishing, $$.
South of Cannon Beach. US 101 15.0 miles south to Nehalem, 7th Street .2 mile north, North Fork Road .6 mile east.

OSWALD WEST (Oregon State Park)
36 primitive campsites, hike-in only, picnic area, hiking, fishing, situated in rain forest w/massive spruce & cedar trees, $$.
South of Cannon Beach. US 101 10.0 miles south, take trail to campground.

RIVERSIDE LAKE RESORT (Private)
69 campsites, 20 w/hookups for water/electricity/sewer, 19 w/hookups for water & electricity, plus 30 tent units, reservation information - (503)738-6779, showers, laundry, river, swimming, fishing, $$-$$$.
North of Cannon Beach. US 101 7.0 miles north.

RV RESORT AT CANNON BEACH (Private)
100 trailer sites w/hookups for water/electricity/sewer, no tents, reservations - (503)436-2231, showers, laundry, groceries, propane & gasoline, swimming pool, therapy pool, river, fishing, boat rental, game room, playfield, playground, hiking, wheelchair access, $$$.
At Cannon Beach. Located just off the Cannon Beach exit ramp; about .6 mile past milepost 29.

SADDLE MOUNTAIN (Oregon State Park)
9 primitive campsites, picnic area, hiking, $$.
Southeast of Cannon Beach. US 26 southeast, campground is 8.0 miles northeast of Necanicum junction.

SEA RANCH RESORT (Private)
71 campsites, 25 w/hookups for water/electricity/sewer, 13 w/hookups for electricity, plus 33 tent units, reservation information - (503)436-2815, showers, ice, trailer waste disposal, ocean access, swimming, fishing, hiking, $$-$$$.
North of Cannon Beach. Resort is located 6 blocks north of city center on old US 101.

VENICE RV PARK (Private)
30 trailer sites w/hookups for water/electricity/sewer, no tents, reservation information - (503)738-8851, showers, laundry, trailer waste disposal, river, fishing, $$$.
North of Cannon Beach. US 101 north approximately 10.0 miles, located at south end of Newana River Bridge in Seaside.

CANYONVILLE

CHARLES V. STANTON PARK (Douglas County)
37 campsites, 20 w/hookups for water/electricity/sewer, plus 17 tent units, showers, river, fishing, playground, hiking, wheelchair access, $$.
North of Canyonville. I-5 northbound take exit #99; southbound exit #101. Campground is located 1.0 mile north of Canyonville.

SURPRISE VALLEY MOBIL VILLAGE (Private)
25 campsites, 15 w/hookups for water/electricity/sewer, 8 w/hookups for water & electricity, plus 2 tent sites, reservation information - (503)839-8181.
Northeast of Canyonville. I-5 to exit #102, Gazley Road 1.0 mile east.

CASCADE LOCKS

CASCADE LOCKS KOA CAMPGROUND (Private)
81 campsites, 32 w/hookups for water/electricity/sewer, 40 w/hookups for water & electricity, plus 9 tent units, reservation information - (503)374-8668, showers, laundry, groceries, swimming pool, playground, trailer waste disposal, hiking, $$$.
East of Cascade Locks. At east end of town take Forest Lane 1.0 mile southeast to park.

CASCADE LOCKS MARINE PARK (Port of Cascade Locks)
38 campsites, reservation information - (503)374-8619, showers, trailer waste disposal, river, fishing, boat launch, playground, wheelchair access, wind surfing area, historic site, $$.
In Cascade Locks. Located 3 blocks north of Cascade Locks exit off I-84.

EAGLE CREEK (Mt. Hood National Forest)
19 units, trailers to 22', piped water, flush toilets, wheelchair access, swimming, fishing, hiking, bicycling, elev. 200', $$.
West of Cascade Locks. I-84 4.5 miles west, I-84 2.0 miles east, FSR 240 .1 mile southeast.

HERMAN CREEK (Mt. Hood National Forest)
4 tent units, spring, fishing, geology, hiking, elev. 1000', $.
West of Cascade Locks. US 30 to Herman Creek Road N22, 2 miles southeast of Columbia Gorge Work Station, follow this to campground.

OVERLOOK (Mt. Hood National Forest)
Group campsites, trailers to 22', reservations required - (503)695-2276, picnic area w/community kitchen, piped water, river, flush toilets, boating, swimming, fishing, bicycling, elev. 200', $$$.
West of Cascade Locks. I-84 4.5 miles west, I-84 2.0 miles east, FSR 243 .3 mile north.

WYETH (Mt. Hood National Forest)
3 units, trailers to 32', piped water, stream, flush toilets, wheelchair access, swimming, fishing, hiking, elev. 200', $$.
East of Cascade Locks. I-84 7.0 miles east.

CASCADE SUMMIT

PEBBLE BAY (Deschutes National Forest)
Campsites, on Odell Lake, boat-in only, swimming, fishing, water skiing, elev. 4800', $.
Southeast of Cascade Summit. On southwest end of Odell Lake.

CAVE JUNCTION

CAVE CREEK (Siskiyou National Forest)
18 tent units, piped water, fishing, hiking, elev. 2900', $.
East of Cave Junction. State 46 16.0 miles east, FSR 4032 1.0 mile south. Located 4 miles northwest of Oregon Caves National Monument.

CAVES HIGHWAY (Private)
24 campsites, 20 w/hookups for water/electricity/sewer, 2 w/hookups for water & electricity, plus 2 tent units, reservation information - (503)592-3338, showers, trailer waste disposal, $$-$$$.
Southeast of Cave Junction. Leave US 199 at southern end of town and head east on State 46 1.0 mile.

GRAYBACK (Siskiyou National Forest)
35 units, trailers to 22', picnic area, piped water, stream, flush toilets, swimming, fishing, elev. 1800', $.
East of Cave Junction. State 46 12.0 miles east. Located 8 miles northwest of Oregon Caves National Monument.

KERBY TRAILER PARK (Private)
14 campsites, 5 w/hookups for water/electricity/sewer, plus 9 w/hookups for water & electricity, reservation information - (503)592-2897, showers, laundry, trailer waste disposal, $$.
North of Cave Junction. US 199 2.8 miles north.

SHADY ACRES RV PARK (Private)
20 campsites, 12 w/hookups for water/electricity/sewer, 4 w/hookups for water & electricity, plus 4 tent units, reservation information - (503)592-3702, showers, trailer waste disposal, $$.
South of Cave Junction. US 199 1.0 mile south.

TRAILS END CAMPGROUND (Private)
50 campsites, 11 w/hookups for water/electricity/sewer, 7 w/hookups for water & electricity, plus 32 tent units, reservation information - (503)592-3354, showers, trailer waste disposal, river, swimming, playground, $$-$$$.
South of Cave Junction. US 199 2.5 miles south, Burch Drive .1 mile southwest.

CHARLESTON

BASTENDORFF BEACH PARK (Coos County)
80 campsites, 55 w/hookups for water & electricity, plus 25 tent units, showers, trailer waste disposal, ocean access, fishing, playground, hiking, $$.
South of Charleston. Take Cape Arago Highway 2.0 miles south.

CHARLESTON MARINA & TRAVEL PARK (Port of Coos Bay))
100 campsites, 60 w/hookups for water/electricity/sewer, 32 w/hookups for water & electricity, plus 12 tent units, reservation information - (503)888-9512, showers, laundry, ice, trailer waste disposal, ocean access, river, fishing, boat launch, playground, $-$$.
In Charleston. At west end of Charleston Bridge turn north on Boat Basin Drive, after 2 blocks turn east on Kingfisher Drive, park is 1 block.

HUCKLEBERRY HILL MOBILE HOME PARK (Private)
20 trailer sites w/hookups for water/electricity/sewer, reservation information - (503)888-3611, showers, laundry, ice, trailer waste disposal, hiking, $$.
In Charleston. Located .2 mile west of Charleston Bridge, on Cape Arago Highway.

THREE TREES RV PARK (Private)
26 trailer sites w/hookups for water/electricity/sewer, trailers to 35', reservation information - (503)888-4325, showers, groceries, ocean access, fishing, boat launch, $$.
In Charleston. At west end of Charleston bridge, turn north on Boat Basin Drive and follow to park.

CHEMULT

DIGIT POINT (Winema National Forest)
64 units, trailers to 32', piped water, lake - speed limits, flush toilets, trailer waste disposal, boat launch, boating, swimming, fishing, hiking, mosquitoes, elev. 5600', $$.
West of Chemult. US 97 1.0 mile north, FSR 9772 12.0 west.

CHILOQUIN

COLLIER (Oregon State Park)
68 campsites, 50 w/hookups for water/electricity/sewer, plus 18 tent units, trailers to 40', picnic area, wheelchair access, showers, trailer waste disposal, fishing, horse facilities, hiking trails, historic logging museum & pioneer cabins, $$-$$$.
North of Chiloquin. US 97 north to Collier State Park.

JACKSON F. KIMBALL (Oregon State Park)
6 primitive campsites, trailers to 15', no drinking water, fishing, $.
North of Chiloquin. US 97 to State 232; campground is located 3.0 miles north of Fort Klamath.

NEPTUNE PARK RESORT (Private)
25 campsites, 8 w/hookups for water/electricity/sewer, 12 w/hookups for water & electricity, plus 5 tent units, reservation information - (503)783-2489, showers, groceries, lake, swimming, fishing, boat launch, boat rental, elev. 4200', $$-$$$.
West of Chiloquin. West 6.0 miles, Lakeside Road 3.0 miles south.

SPRING CREEK (Winema National Forest)
26 units, trailers to 32', fishing, elev. 4200', $.
North of Chiloquin. US 97 6.0 miles north, FSR 9732 2.0 miles west. Campground is located 6.5 miles from Collier Memorial State Park.

WALT'S COZY CAMP (Private)
34 campsites, 12 w/hookups for water/electricity/sewer, 2 w/hookups for water & electricity, plus 20 tent units, reservation information - (503)783-2537, showers, elev. 4200', $$.
Southwest of Chiloquin. Near milepost #248 on US 97.

WATER WHEEL CAMPGROUND (Private)
44 campsites, 10 w/hookups for water/electricity/sewer, 14 w/hookups for water & electricity, plus 20 tent units, reservation information - (503)783-2738, showers, laundry, groceries, trailer waste disposal, river, swimming, fishing, boat launch, playground, elev. 4200', $$-$$$.
Southwest of Chiloquin. Campground is located on US 97 .1 mile north of US 97/State 62 junction.

WILLIAMSON RIVER (Winema National Forest)
10 units, trailers to 32', piped water, fishing, elev. 4200', $.
North of Chiloquin. US 97 5.0 miles north, FSR 9730 1.0 mile northeast. Campground is 1 mile from Collier State Park.

WILLIAMSON RIVER TRAILER PARK (Private)
18 trailer sites w/hookups for water/electricity/sewer, reservation information - (503)783-2834, showers, laundry, river, swimming, fishing, boat launch, elev. 4100', $$.
Southwest of Chiloquin. US 97 9.0 miles south to Modoc Point Road, northwest 5.0 miles to park.

CONDON

CONDON MOBILE HOME & RV PARK (Private)
17 trailer sites w/hookups for water/electricity/sewer, reservation information - (503)384-6611, laundry, playground, $$.
In Condon. At west city limits on State 206.

COOS BAY

DRIFTWOOD RV PARK (Private)
15 trailer sites w/hookups for water/electricity/sewer, reservation information - (503)888-6103, showers, laundry, ocean access, fishing, $$.
West of Coos Bay. US 101 to Cape Arago Highway, west 7.0 miles to park.

KELLEY'S RV PARK (Private)
38 trailer sites w/hookups for water/electricity/sewer, no tents, reservation information - (503)888-6531, showers, laundry, trailer waste disposal, river, $$.
West of Coos Bay. US 101 to Cape Arago Highway, west 4.5 miles to park.

PLAINVIEW TRAILER PARK (Private)
34 trailer sites, 32 w/hookups for water/electricity/sewer, plus 2 w/hookups for water & electricity, reservation information - (503)888-5166, showers, laundry, ocean access, lake, fishing, $$.
West of Coos Bay. US 101 to Cape Arago Highway, west 7.5 miles to park.

SUNSET BAY (Oregon State Park)
137 campsites, 29 w/hookups for water/electricity/sewer, plus 108 tent units, group campsites, mail reservations available, picnic area, wheelchair access, showers, swimming, fishing, beach access, beach-combing, hiking access to Oregon Coast Trail, $$-$$$.
Southwest of Coos Bay. Leave US 101 at Coos Bay heading west past Charleston to Sunset Bay.

COQUILLE

LAVERNE PARK (Coos County)
85 campsites, community kitchen, flush toilets, showers, fish ladder, playfield, playground, swimming, hiking, rockhounding, $$.
East of Coquille. Take Coquille/Fairview Road 15.0 miles.

CORBETT

CROWN POINT RV PARK (Private)
15 trailer sites w/hookups for water/electricity/sewer, reservation information - (503)695-5207, showers, laundry, trailer waste disposal, $$$.
East of Corbett. Take Scenic Loop Highway to milepost #9, .2 mile east of town.

COTTAGE GROVE

BAKER BAY (Lane County)
34 campsites, trailers to 25', showers, groceries, trailer waste disposal, lake, swimming, fishing, boat launch, boat rental, wheelchair access, $$.
East of Cottage Grove. Take Dorena Reservoir Road 7.0 miles east to campground.

COTTAGE GROVE LAKE PRIMITIVE AREA (Corps)
34 campsites, lake, fishing, $.
South of Cottage Grove. London Road 3.5 miles south, Reservoir Road .5 mile east to campground.

PASS CREEK (Douglas County)
30 trailer sites w/hookups for water/electricity/sewer, information - (503)942-3281, showers, stream, playground, wheelchair access, $$.
South of Cottage Grove. Leave I-5 at exit #163, campground is 10.0 miles south of Cottage Grove, in Curtin.

PINE MEADOWS (Corps)
93 campsites, showers, trailer waste disposal, lake, swimming, fishing, playground, $$.
South of Cottage Grove. London Road 3.5 miles south, Reservoir Road .5 mile east to campground.

SCHWARZ PARK/DORENA LAKE (Corps)
50 campsites, showers, trailer waste disposal, river, fishing, wheelchair access, $$.
East of Cottage Grove. Take Dorena Lake exit #174 off I-5, Row River Road 5.0 miles east.

THE VILLAGE GREEN (Private)
42 trailer sites w/hookups for water/electricity/sewer, reservation information - (503)942-2491, swimming pool, spa, $$$.
East of Cottage Grove. Take Dorena Lake exit #174 off I-5, Row River Road .1 mile east to 725 Row River Road.

CRATER LAKE NATIONAL PARK

LOST CREEK (Crater Lake National Park)
12 campsites, information - (503)594-2211, elev. 6000', $$.
In Crater Lake National Park. Follow signs on Pinnacles Road.

MAZAMA (Crater Lake National Park)
200 campsites, information - (503)594-2211, groceries, trailer waste disposal, lake, fishing, hiking, wheelchair access, elev. 6000', $$.
In Crater Lake National Park. Located east of Annie Spring entrance .5 mile.

CRESCENT

BOUNDARY SPRING (Deschutes National Forest)
Campsites, trailers to 22', primitive, at base of Walker Rim, elev. 4400', $.
Southeast of Crescent. US 97 2.2 miles southwest, FSR 257 5.6 miles southeast.

CRESCENT CREEK (Deschutes National Forest)
10 units, trailers to 22', stream, fishing, elev. 4500', $.
West of Crescent. CR 61 8.2 miles west. Campground is located on Crescent Creek at County Road crossing.

EAST DAVIS LAKE (Deschutes National Forest)
33 units, trailers to 22', well, on Davis Lake - speed limits, boating, fishing, hiking, elev. 4400', $.
Northwest of Crescent. CR 61 9.0 miles west, FSR 46 6.5 miles north, FSR 46855 1.5 miles west. Located on south end of Davis Lake at mouth of Odell Creek.

SIMAX BAY (Deschutes National Forest)
6 units, some trailers, piped water, on Crescent Lake, boating, fishing, swimming, water skiing, elev. 4850', $.
West of Crescent 30 miles. Take State 58 west of Crescent to Crescent Lake. Campground is on east end of lake.

SIMAX BEACH (Deschutes National Forest)
6 units, some trailers, lake, river, boating, fishing, swimming, water skiing, elev. 4850', $.
West of Crescent 30 miles. Take State 58 west of Crescent to Crescent Lake Area. Campground is located on east side of lake.

TANDY BAY (Deschutes National Forest)
4 units, some trailers, river, fishing, swimming, water skiing, hiking, elev. 4850', $.
West of Crescent 30 miles. Take State 58 west of Crescent to Crescent Lake. Campground is at west end of Crescent Lake.

WEST DAVIS LAKE (Deschutes National Forest)
25 units, trailers to 22', well, on Davis Lake - speed limits, boating, fishing, elev. 4400', $.
Northwest of Crescent. CR 61 9.0 miles west, FSR 46 3.3 miles north, FSR 4660 3.8 miles northwest, FSR 46604 2.0 miles east. Located on south end of Davis Lake at mouth of Odell Creek.

CRESCENT LAKE

CRESCENT LAKE (Deschutes National Forest)
44 units, trailers to 22', picnic area, piped water, on Crescent Lake, boat launch, boating, swimming, fishing, elev. 4800', $$.
Southwest of Crescent Lake. FSR 60 2.7 miles southwest to campground. Located at north end of Crescent Lake, across creek from resort.

ODELL CREEK (Deschutes National Forest)
22 units, trailers to 22', well, on Odell Lake, boating, swimming, fishing, elev. 4800', $.
Northwest of Crescent Lake. State 58 1.6 miles northwest, FSR 5811 .4 mile southwest. Located on east end of Odell Lake, at head of Odell Creek.

ODELL TRAILER PARK (Private)
33 trailer sites w/hookups for water/electricity/sewer, no tents, reservation information - (503)433-2411, showers, laundry, groceries, trailer waste disposal, elev. 4800', $$$.
At Crescent Lake. State 58 at Crescent Lake.

PRINCESS CREEK (Deschutes National Forest)
46 units, trailers to 22', picnic area, piped water, on Odell Lake, boating, swimming, fishing, water skiing, elev. 4800', $$.
Northwest of Crescent Lake. State 58 5.4 miles northwest to campground. Located on north shore of Odell Lake.

SPRING (Deschutes National Forest)
68 units, trailers to 22', picnic area, well, on Crescent Lake, boating, swimming, fishing, water skiing, elev. 4800', $$.
Southwest of Crescent Lake. State 209 3.0 miles southwest, FSR 244-1 5.6 miles southwest, FSR 244F .1 mile northeast to campground. Located on south side of Crescent Lake.

SUNSET COVE (Deschutes National Forest)
27 units, trailers to 22', picnic area, well, on Odell Lake, boat launch, boating, swimming, fishing, water skiing, elev. 4800', $$.
Northwest of Crescent Lake. State 58 2.6 miles northwest to campground. Located at northeast end of Odell Lake.

TRAPPER CREEK (Deschutes National Forest)
32 units, trailers to 22', piped water, on Odell Lake, boat launch, boating, swimming, fishing, water skiing, hiking, near Diamond Peak Wilderness, elev. 4800', $$.
Northwest of Crescent Lake. State 58 6.9 miles northwest, FSR 5810 1.8 miles southwest to campground. Located at west end of Odell Lake.

WHITEFISH HORSE CAMP (Deschutes National Forest)
19 units, trailers okay, stream, hiking, elev. 4800', $.
Southwest of Crescent Lake. FSR 60 6.7 miles west to campground. Located at west end of Crescent Lake.

CRESWELL

SHERWOOD FOREST KOA (Private)
150 campsites, 100 w/hookups for water/electricity/sewer, 25 w/hookups for water, plus 25 tent units, reservations - (503)895-4410, showers, laundry, groceries, trailer waste disposal, swimming pool, therapy pool, playground, $$-$$$.
At Creswell. Located .1 mile off I-5 on Creswell exit #182.

TAYLOR'S TRAVEL PARK (Private)
24 campsites, 17 w/hookups for water/electricity/sewer, plus 7 w/hookups for water & electricity, reservation information - (503)895-4715, showers, trailer waste disposal, playfield, playground, $$.
West of Creswell. Leave I-5 at exit #182 and head west to Hwy. 99S, go south 1.3 miles to Davisson Road then .4 mile south to campground.

CULVER

PERRY SOUTH (Deschutes National Forest)
63 units, trailers to 22', well, on Metolius Arm of Lake Billy Chinook, flush toilets, wheelchair access, boat launch, boating, swimming, fishing, elev. 2000', $.
Northwest of Culver. CR 1 20.0 miles west, FSR 64 5.0 miles northwest to campground. Near Cove State Park.

DALE

GOLD DREDGE (Umatilla National Forest)
3 units, trailers okay, fishing, hiking, trail bikes, elev. 3400', $.
Northeast of Dale. US 395 1.0 miles northeast, FSR 55 5.0 miles northwest, FSR 5506 1.9 miles southeast.

MEADOWBROOK RV PARK (Private)
16 campsites, 2 w/hookups for water/electricity/sewer, plus 14 w/hookups for electricity, reservation information - (503)421-3104, groceries, trailer waste disposal, stream, fishing, hiking, elev. 4000', $-$$$.
At Dale. Located at milepost #71 on US 395.

ORIENTAL CREEK (Umatilla National Forest)
5 tent units, fishing, hiking, motor bikes, elev. 3500', $.
Northeast of Dale. US 395 1.0 miles northeast, FSR 55 5.0 miles northwest, FSR 5506 8.0 miles southeast.

TOLLBRIDGE (Umatilla National Forest)
6 units, trailers to 32', piped water, stream, fishing, at mouth of Desolation Creek, elev. 2800', $.
Northeast of Dale. US 395 1.0 mile northeast, FSR 55 .6 mile southeast, FSR 10 .1 mile southeast.

WELCH CREEK (Umatilla National Forest)
1 unit, trailer to 22', picnic area, fishing, elev. 4500', $.
Southeast of Dale. US 395 1.0 mile northeast, FSR 55 .6 mile southeast, FSR 10 13.9 miles southeast.

DEE

LADD CREEK (Mt. Hood National Forest)
2 tent units, stream, fishing, elev. 2000', $.
Southwest of Dee 15 miles. Reached via US 26 or State 35 to Lolo Pass Road, follow this to campground.

DEPOE BAY

FOGARTY CREEK RV PARK (Private)
53 trailer sites w/hookups for water/electricity/sewer, no tents, reservation information - (503)764-2228, showers, laundry, trailer waste disposal, $$$.
North of Depoe Bay. US 101 2.0 miles north.

HOLIDAY HILLS MOTOR HOME PARK (Private)
22 trailer sites w/hookups for water/electricity/sewer, no tents, reservation information - (503)764-2430, showers, laundry, ocean access, swimming, fishing, playground, $$$.
North of Depoe Bay. US 101 3.5 miles north.

HOLIDAY RV PARK (Private)
110 trailer sites w/hookups for water/electricity/sewer, no tents, reservation information - (503)765-2302, showers, laundry, groceries, indoor swimming pool, therapy pool, ocean access, fishing, $$$.
In Depoe Bay. Located 1.0 mile north of Depoe Bay city center on US 101.

MARTIN'S TRAILER HARBOR (Private)
16 trailer sites w/hookups for water/electricity/sewer, no tents, reservation information - (503)765-2601, showers, laundry, $$$.
In Depoe Bay. Leave US 101 2 blocks north of bridge on Collins Street, campground is 2 blocks.

SEA & SAND RV PARK (Private)
95 campsites, 51 w/hookups for water/electricity/sewer, 35 w/hookups for water & electricity, plus 9 tent units, trailers to 35', reservation information -(503)764-2313, showers, laundry, trailer waste disposal, ocean access, swimming, fishing, $$-$$$.
North of Depoe Bay. US 101 3.5 miles north.

DETROIT

BREITENBUSH (Willamette National Forest)
30 units, group sites, trailers to 18', piped water, wheelchair access, river, groceries, gasoline, fishing, elev. 2200', $$-$$$.
Northeast of Detroit. FSR RS46 9.8 miles northeast. Campground is located 1 mile from Breitenbush Hot Springs Resort and 3 miles north of Breitenbush Gorge National Recreation Trail.

CLEATOR BEND (Willamette National Forest)
9 units, trailers to 18', river, fishing, elev. 2200',$.
Northeast of Detroit. FSR RS46 9.6 miles northeast. Campground is located 1.0 mile from Breitenbush Hot Springs Resort and 3.0 miles north of Breitenbush Gorge National Recreation Trail.

DETROIT LAKE (Oregon State Park)
320 campsites, 106 w/hookups for water/electricity/sewer, 70 w/hookups for electricity, plus 144 tent units, trailers to 67', group sites, mail reservations available, picnic area, showers, boat launch, fishing, swimming, $$-$$$.
West of Detroit. State 22 2.0 miles west to campground.

HOOVER (Willamette National Forest)
37 units, trailers to 22', piped water, on Detroit Lake, flush toilets, wheelchair access, boat launch, interpretive services, boating, swimming, fishing, water skiing, elev. 1600', $$-$$$.
Southeast of Detroit. State 22 2.9 miles southeast, FSR 10 .8 mile northwest.

HOOVER GROUP CAMP (Willamette National Forest)
5 units, 1 group site, trailers to 18', reservations required - (503)854-3366, piped water, picnic shelter, playfield, boating, swimming, fishing, water skiing, elev. 1600', $$-$$$.
Southwest of Detroit. State 22 2.9 miles southwest, FSR 10 .8 mile northwest.

HUMBUG (Willamette National Forest)
22 units, trailers to 22', piped water, river, fishing, hiking, elev. 1800', $$.
Northeast of Detroit. FSR RS46 4.8 miles northeast. Located 5 miles from Detroit Reservoir on Breitenbush River.

SOUTHSHORE (Willamette National Forest)
30 units, trailers to 22', picnic area, well, on Detroit Lake, wheelchair access, boat launch, boating, swimming, fishing, water skiing, elev. 1600', $$.
Southwest of Detroit. State 22 2.9 miles southeast, FSR 10 4.1 miles west.

DIAMOND LAKE

DIAMOND LAKE RV PARK (Private)
160 campsites, 140 w/hookups for water/electricity/sewer, plus 20 w/hookups for water & electricity, reservation information - (503)793-3318, showers, laundry, groceries, trailer waste disposal, lake, swimming, fishing, boat launch, hiking, wheelchair access, elev. 5300', $$$.
Southwest of Diamond Lake. South to Diamond Lake South Shore Road, north 1.0 mile to park.

LEMOLO LAKE RESORT (Private)
34 campsites, 24 w/hookups for water/electricity/sewer, plus 10 w/hookups for water & electricity, showers, laundry, groceries, trailer waste disposal, lake, swimming, fishing, boat launch, boat rental, hiking, elev. 4200', $$.
Northwest of Diamond Lake. State 138 8.0 miles northwest, Lemolo Lake Road #2610 north 5.0 miles.

DRAIN

ELKTON RV PARK (Private)
46 campsites, 11 w/hookups for water/electricity/sewer, 25 w/hookups for water & electricity, plus 10 tent units, reservation information - (503)849-2298, groceries, river, swimming, fishing, $-$$.
West of Drain. State 38 14.0 miles west to Elkton, 2 blocks west of bridge turn on 2nd Street, park is 1 block.

EDDYVILLE

BIG ELK (Siuslaw National Forest)
9 units, 1 group site, trailers to 18', piped water, stream, swimming, fishing, elev. 200', $.
Southeast of Eddyville. US 20 10.0 miles east, CR 547 7.5 miles south, CR 538 1.1 miles west.

ELGIN

JUBILEE LAKE (Umatilla National Forest)
51 units, trailers to 22', picnic area, piped water, flush toilets, lake - no motors, hiking, elev. 4700', $$.
North of Elgin. State 204 23.5 miles northwest, FSR 64 11.2 miles northeast, FSR 250 .7 mile southeast.

MINAM (Oregon State Park)
12 primitive campsites, trailers to 60', picnic area, fishing, $.
Northeast of Elgin. State 82 15.0 miles northeast to campground.

ELSIE

SPRUCE RUN (Clatsop County)
40 campsites, trailers to 25', stream, swimming, fishing, hiking, $$.
At Elsie. Located north of US 26 at Elsie.

ENTERPRISE

OUTPOST RV PARK (Private)
40 trailer sites w/hookups for water/electricity/sewer, reservation information - (503)426-4745, showers, elev. 3500', $$.
North of Enterprise. State 3 .5 mile north to park.

ESTACADA

ARMSTRONG (Mt. Hood National Forest)
18 units, trailers to 32', well, on Clackamas River, wheelchair access, fishing, elev. 900', $$.
Southeast of Estacada. State 224 15.4 miles southeast.

BARTON PARK (Clackamas County)
97 campsites w/hookups for water & electricity, reservation information -(503)637-3015, trailer waste disposal, river, swimming, fishing, boat launch, playground, $$.
Northwest of Estacada. State 224 northwest 9.0 miles, County Road .5 mile south to park.

BIG SLIDE LAKE (Mt. Hood National Forest)
2 tent sites, swimming, fishing, hike-in only, elev. 4300', $.
Southeast of Estacada. State 224 26.7 miles southeast, FSR S46 3.7 miles south, FSR S63 5.4 miles south, FSR S708 2.9 miles southwest, FSR S708A 2.0 miles to Dickey Creek Trailhead, Trail #533 4.0 miles to campground. Also accessible via Trails #550 and 555.

CARTER BRIDGE (Mt. Hood National Forest)
11 units, trailers to 32', piped water, on Clackamas River, wheelchair access, trailer waste disposal, fishing, elev. 800', $$.
Southeast of Estacada. State 224 15.0 miles southeast.

FISH CREEK (Mt. Hood National Forest)
21 units, trailers to 18', well, on Clackamas River, fishing, elev. 900', $$.
Southeast of Estacada. State 224 15.6 miles southeast.

HARRIET LAKE (Mt. Hood National Forest)
13 units, trailers to 32', well, wheelchair access, boat launch, boating, fishing, elev. 2100', $$.
Southeast of Estacada. State 224 southeast 27 miles, FSR 57 6.5 miles east, FSR 4630 1.2 miles west.

HIDEAWAY LAKE (Mt. Hood National Forest)
9 units, trailers to 18', piped water, lake - no motors, boating, swimming, fishing, hiking, elev. 4500', $.
Southeast of Estacada. State 224 27.0 miles southeast, FSR 57 7.5 miles east, FSR 58 3.0 miles north, FSR 5830 5.3 miles northwest.

INDIAN HENRY (Mt. Hood National Forest)
88 units, trailers to 22', piped water, on Clackamas River, flush toilets, wheelchair access, reservations advised for wheelchair accessible campsites -(503)630-6861, trailer waste disposal, interpretive services, fishing, hiking, elev. 1200', $$.
Southeast of Estacada. State 224 23.0 miles southeast, FSR 53 .5 mile southeast.

KINGFISHER (Mt. Hood National Forest)
25 units, trailers to 18', well, on Hot Springs Fork of Collawash River, fishing, elev. 1600', $$.
Southeast of Estacada. State 224 26.5 miles southeast, FSR 46 3.5 miles south, FSR 63 3.0 miles south, FSR 70 2.0 miles southwest. Bagby Hot Springs Trailhead 4.3 miles southwest of campground.

LAZY BEND (Mt. Hood National Forest)
19 units, trailers to 22', piped water, on Clackamas River, flush toilets, swimming, fishing, elev. 800', $$.
Southeast of Estacada. State 224 10.7 miles southeast.

LOCKABY (Mt. Hood National Forest)
14 units, trailers to 32', well, on Clackamas River, fishing, elev. 900', $$.
Southeast of Estacada. State 224 15.3 miles southeast.

MILO McIVER (Oregon State Park)
44 campsites w/hookups for electricity, trailers to 60', group campsites, group picnic area, wheelchair access, showers, trailer waste disposal, boat launch, fishing, horse & hiking trails, $$.
West of Estacada. Leave State 211 at Estacada; campground is 5.0 miles west.

PAUL DENNIS (Mt. Hood National Forest)
19 units, trailers to 18', lake - no motors, groceries, gasoline, ice, boat launch, boat rental, boating, swimming, fishing, hiking trails, elev. 5000', $.
Southeast of Estacada. State 224 27.0 miles southeast, FSR 46 21.8 miles south, FSR 4690 8.2 miles southeast, FSR 4200 6.3 miles south.

PENINSULA (Mt. Hood National Forest)
38 units, trailers to 22', well, lake - no motors, wheelchair access includes trails and fishing, boat launch, boating, swimming, fishing, elev. 4900', $.
Southeast of Estacada. State 224 27.0 miles southeast, FSR 46 21.8 miles south, FSR 4690 8.2 miles southeast, FSR 4220 6.6 miles south.

PROMONTORY (Clackamas County)
58 campsites, trailers to 20', reservation information - (503)630-5153, showers, groceries, lake, fishing, boat launch, boat rental, playground, hiking, $$.
Southeast of Estacada. State 224 7.0 miles southeast.

RAINBOW (Mt. Hood National Forest)
15 units, trailers to 18', piped water, river, wheelchair access, swimming, fishing, hiking, elev. 1400', $$.
Southeast of Estacada. State 224 27.0 miles southeast, FSR 46 .1 mile south.

RIPPLEBROOK (Mt. Hood National Forest)
14 units, trailers to 18', piped water, stream, wheelchair access, fishing, elev. 1500', $$.
Southeast of Estacada. State 224 26.5 miles southeast.

RIVERSIDE (Mt. Hood National Forest)
16 units, trailers to 22', well, river, wheelchair access, fishing, hiking, elev. 1400', $$.
Southeast of Estacada. State 224 27.0 miles southeast, FSR 46 2.7 miles south.

ROARING RIVER (Mt. Hood National Forest)
11 units, trailers to 18', well, at junction of Roaring River & Clackamas River, fishing, hiking, elev. 1000', $$.
Southeast of Estacada. State 224 18.2 miles southeast.

SKOOKUM LAKE (Mt. Hood National Forest)
2 tent units, fishing, elev. 4500', $.
Southeast of Estacada 32 miles. State 224 15.6 miles southeast to Fish Creek, FSR S54 to FSR S505 to campground.

SUNSTRIP (Mt. Hood National Forest)
8 units, trailers to 18', well, on Clackamas River, trailer waste disposal, fishing, elev. 1000', $$.
Southeast of Estacada. State 224 18.6 miles southeast.

EUGENE

EUGENE KOA (Private)
104 campsites, 41 w/hookups for water/electricity/sewer, plus 63 w/hookups for water & electricity, reservation information - (503)343-4832, showers, laundry, groceries, trailer waste disposal, mini-golf, playground, $$-$$$.
North of Eugene. I-5 north 6.0 miles to exit #199, campground is .3 mile west.

EUGENE MOBILE VILLAGE (Private)
20 trailer sites w/hookups for water/electricity/sewer, no tents, reservation information - (503)747-2257, showers, laundry, groceries, trailer waste disposal, playground, $$.
South of Eugene. I-5 south to exit #189, east over I-5, Frontage Road 1.0 mile north toward Springfield and park.

SHAMROCK MOBILE HOME VILLAGE (Private)
81 trailer sites, 73 w/hookups for water/electricity/sewer, plus 8 w/hookups for water & electricity, no tents, adults only, reservation information -(503)747-7473, showers, laundry, trailer waste disposal, river, fishing, $$$.
South of Eugene. I-5 to exit #191, Glenwood Blvd. north .7 mile, Franklin Blvd 1.0 mile east/southeast to campground.

FLORENCE

ALDER LAKE (Siuslaw National Forest)
22 units, trailers to 32', piped water, flush toilets, lake - no motors, swimming, fishing, elev. 100', $$.
North of Florence. US 101 7.0 miles north, FSR 792 .2 mile west.

CARL G. WASHBURNE (Oregon State Park)
58 campsites w/hookups for water/electricity/sewer, trailers to 45', picnic area, showers, ocean access, beachcombing, hiking, fishing, swimming, wildlife, $$$.
North of Florence. US 101 14.0 miles north to campground.

CARTER LAKE EAST (Siuslaw National Forest)
11 units, trailers to 18', piped water, lake - speed limits, boat launch, boating, swimming, fishing, sand dunes, elev. 100', $$.
South of Florence. US 101 8.6 miles south, FSR 1086 .2 mile west.

CARTER LAKE WEST (Siuslaw National Forest)
22 units, trailers to 22', piped water, lake - speed limits, flush toilets, boat launch, boating, swimming, fishing, hiking, sand dunes, elev. 100', $$.
South of Florence. US 101 8.5 miles south, FSR 1084 .1 mile west.

DRIFTWOOD II (Siuslaw National Forest)
100 units, trailers to 22', piped water, flush toilets, wheelchair access, swimming, fishing, hiking, ORV, elev. 100', $.
South of Florence. US 101 7.0 miles south, FSR 1078 1.4 miles west.

DUNE LAKE (Siuslaw National Forest)
17 units, trailers to 22', picnic area, piped water, lake - no motors, flush toilets, swimming, fishing, hiking, elev. 100', $$.
North of Florence. US 101 7.0 miles north, FSR 791 .2 mile west.

FLORENCE DUNES KOA (Private)
126 campsites, 94 w/hookups for water/electricity/sewer, plus 32 tent units, reservation information (503)997-6431, showers, laundry, groceries, trailer waste disposal, playground, hiking, $$-$$$.
In Florence. US 101 2.0 miles north, 35th Street 1.2 miles west, Rhododendron Drive .1 mile north.

JESSIE M HONEYMAN (Oregon State Park)
382 campsites, 66 w/hookups for water/electricity/sewer, 75 w/hookups for electricity, plus 241 tent units, mail reservations available, trailers to 55', group campsites, picnic area, wheelchair access, showers, trailer waste disposal, boat launch, fishing, swimming, hiking trails, sand dunes, lakes, wild rhododendrons, $$-$$$.
South of Florence. US 101 3.0 miles south to campground.

LAGOON (SILTCOOS) (Siuslaw National Forest)
51 units, trailers to 22', piped water, river, flush toilets, swimming, fishing, hiking, ocean beach access, elev. 100', $$.
South of Florence. US 101 7.0 miles south, FSR 1076 1.3 miles west.

LAKE VIEW PARK (Private)
6 trailer sites w/hookups for water/electricity/sewer, trailers to 40', no tents, reservation information - (503)997-6688, showers, laundry, lake, swimming, fishing, $$.
North of Florence. US 101 5.5 miles north, Mercer Lake Road 1.0 mile east.

LAKE'S EDGE RV PARK (Private)
13 trailer sites w/hookups for water/electricity/sewer, no tents, trailers to 35', reservation information - (503)997-6056, showers, laundry, groceries, lake, fishing, boat launch, boat rental, hiking, $$$.
South of Florence. US 101 6.0 miles south, Pacific Avenue .5 mile east, Laurel Street east .01 mile.

LAKESHORE TRAVEL PARK (Private)
12 trailer sites w/hookups for water/electricity/sewer, no tents, reservation information - (503)997-2741, showers, laundry, lake, swimming, fishing, $$.
South of Florence. US 101 4.5 miles south, located near milepost #195.

LANE COUNTY HARBOR VISTA (Lane County)

26 campsites, showers, trailer waste disposal, ocean access, river, fishing, hiking, $$.
West of Florence. US 101 2.0 miles north, 35th Street 1.2 miles west, Rhododendron Drive 5.0 miles southwest.

MID-WAY MARINA & RV PARK (Private)

40 trailer sites w/hookups for water/electricity/sewer, reservation information - (503)997-3031, showers, laundry, trailer waste disposal, river, fishing, boat launch, boat rental, hiking, $$.
East of Florence. State 126 6.0 miles east.

PORT OF SIUSLAW RV PARK & MARINA (Port)

78 campsites, 33 w/hookups for water/electricity/sewer, plus 45 w/hookups for water & electricity, reservation information - (503)997-3040, showers, laundry, trailer waste disposal, ocean access, river, fishing, boat launch, $$-$$$.
In Florence. At north end of bridge proceed north on US 101 3 blocks to Maple, go 2 blocks southeast to 1st Street, park is 3 blocks east.

RHODODENDRON TRAILER PARK (Private)

18 trailer sites w/hookups for water/electricity/sewer, reservation information - (503)997-2206, showers, laundry, groceries, $$.
North of Florence. US 101 3.0 miles north, located at Heceta Beach Junction.

SILTCOOS LAKE RESORT (Private)

12 campsites, 9 w/hookups for water/electricity/sewer, plus 3 w/hookups for water & electricity, trailers to 32', reservation information - (503)997-3741, showers, lake, swimming, fishing, boat launch, boat rental, playground, hiking, $$-$$$.
South of Florence. US 101 6.0 miles south, Pacific Avenue .03 mile, located at corner of Pacific and Fir Street.

SUTTON CREEK (Siuslaw National Forest)

91 units, 1 group site, trailers to 22', piped water, flush toilets, swimming, fishing, hiking trail to ocean, elev. 100', $$.
North of Florence. US 101 6.0 miles north, FSR 794 1.6 miles northwest. Bicycles can take access route from US 101.

SUTTON CREEK GROUP CAMP (Siuslaw National Forest)

6 group sites, trailers to 22', reservations advised - (503)268-4473, piped water, flush toilets, swimming, fishing, hiking, elev. 100', $$.
North of Florence. US 101 6.0 miles north, FSR 794 1.6 miles northwest, FSR 793 .3 mile northeast. Pacific Ocean is 1 mile west.

TYEE (Siuslaw National Forest)

15 units, trailers to 22', piped water, boat launch, boating, swimming, fishing, elev. 100', $.
South of Florence. US 101 6.0 miles south, FSR 1068 .1 mile southeast. Campground is 1 mile from Siltcoos Lake.

WAXMYRTLE (SILTCOOS) (Siuslaw National Forest)

53 units, trailers to 22', piped water, river, flush toilets, access to Pacific Ocean & sand dunes, swimming, fishing, hiking, elev. 100', $$.
South of Florence. US 101 7.0 miles south, FSR 1078 1.4 miles west.

WAYSIDE RV & MOBILE PARK (Private)
22 trailer sites w/hookups for water/electricity/sewer, no tents, reservation information - (503)997-6451, showers, laundry, trailer waste disposal, lounge, tennis, $$$.
North of Florence. US 101 1.7 miles north.

WOAHINK LAKE RESORT (Private)
Campsites, adults only - no pets, reservation information - (503)997-6454, laundry, lake, $$$.
South of Florence. US 101 4.5 miles south.

FORT KLAMATH

CRATER LAKE RV PARK (Private)
75 campsites, 5 w/hookups for water/electricity/sewer, 20 w/hookups for water & electricity, plus w/out hookups, trailers to 35', reservation information -(503)381-2275, showers, laundry, groceries, lake, stream, swimming, fishing, playfield, playground, elev. 4300', $$-$$$.
Northwest of Fort Klamath. State 62 5.0 miles northwest, located about 1.0 mile south of Crater Lake National Park.

FORT CREEK RESORT (Private)
50 campsites, 13 w/hookups for water/electricity/sewer, 8 w/hookups for water & electricity, plus 29 tent units, reservation information - (503)381-2349, showers, laundry, swimming pool, playfield, playground, stream, fishing, elev. 4100', $$$.
South of Fort Klamath. State 62 1.5 miles south.

FORT KLAMATH LODGE & RV PARK (Private)
16 campsites, 11 w/hookups for water/electricity/sewer, plus 5 tent units, reservation information - (503)381-2234, showers, laundry, groceries, river, fishing, elev. 4100', $$-$$$.
In Fort Klamath. State 62 near city center.

FOSSIL

FOSSIL MOTEL & TRAILER PARK (Private)
12 trailer sites w/hookups for water/electricity/sewer, reservation information - (503)763-4075, laundry, stream, fishing, elev. 3000', $-$$.
At Fossil. Located on State 19 at Fossil Junction.

SHELTON (Oregon State Park)
43 primitive campsites, trailers to 30', picnic area, $.
Southeast of Fossil. State 19 10.0 miles southeast to campground.

FOX

THE HITCHING POST (Private)
16 trailer sites w/hookups for water/electricity/sewer, reservation information - (503)421-3344, showers, laundry, elev. 4000', $$.
Northeast of Fox. US 395 8.0 miles north to Long Creek.

FRENCHGLEN

AMERICAN ADVENTURE STEENS MOUNTAIN RESORT (Private)
97 campsites, 55 w/hookups for water/electricity/sewer, plus 42 w/hookups for water & electricity, reservation information - (503)493-2415, showers, laundry, groceries, trailer waste disposal, river, swimming, fishing, hiking, elev. 4100', $$.
Southeast of Frenchglen. Located 3.0 miles southeast on Fishlake Road.

GARDINER

LOST LAKE (Siuslaw National Forest)
4 units, trailers to 22', boat launch, fishing, within Oregon Dunes National Recreation Area, elev. 100', $.
Northwest of Gardiner. US 101 9.0 miles northwest.

GARIBALDI

BAR VIEW JETTY COUNTY PARK (Tillamook County)
257 campsites, 40 w/hookups for water/electricity/sewer, 20 w/hookups for electricity, plus 197 tent units, reservation information - (503)322-3522, showers, trailer waste disposal, ocean access, swimming, fishing, playground, hiking, $$.
North of Garibaldi. US 101 2.0 miles north.

BIAK BY THE SEA MOTOR HOME PARK (Private)
41 campsites, 35 w/hookups for water/electricity/sewer, plus 6 tent units, trailers to 35', reservation information - (503)322-3206, laundry, ocean access, swimming, fishing, boat launch, boat rental, $-$$.
In Garibaldi. West of city center 1 block on 7th Street.

GLIDE

CAVITT CREEK (BLM)
8 units, trailers okay, picnic area, drinking water, swimming, fishing, nature study, elev. 1100', $.
South of Glide. Campground is located 8.0 miles south of Glide on Cavitt Creek County Road.

LAKE IN THE WOODS (Umpqua National Forest)
4 units, shelter, trailers to 18', picnic area, well, lake - no motors, flush toilets, boating, fishing, hiking trails to Hemlock & Yakso Falls plus Hemlock Lake, elev. 3200', $.
East of Glide. CR 17 16.5 miles east, FSR 27 10.5 miles north.

WOLF CREEK (Umpqua National Forest)
8 units, trailers to 22', piped water, flush toilets, swimming, fishing, hiking, elev. 1100', $.
Southeast of Glide. CR 17 12.4 miles southeast. Campground is located 1 mile east of Job Corp Center on Little River Road.

GOLD BEACH

ANGLERS TRAILER VILLAGE (Private)
40 trailer sites w/hookups for water/electricity/sewer, no tents, reservation information - (503)247-7922, showers, laundry, $$.
East of Gold Beach. Located 3.5 miles east of US 101 on the south bank of Rogue River via Jerrys Flat Road.

ARIZONA BEACH (Private)
127 campsites, 11 w/hookups for water/electricity/sewer, 85 w/hookups for water & electricity, plus 31 tent units, reservations - (503)332-6491, showers, laundry, groceries, trailer waste disposal, ocean access, stream, swimming, fishing, playfield, playground, $$-$$$.
North of Gold Beach. US 101 14.0 miles north.

COUGAR LANE RV PARK & CAMPGROUND (Private)
84 campsites, 53 w/hookups for water & electricity, plus 31 w/hookups for water/electricity/sewer, reservations - (503)247-2813, showers, laundry, groceries, trailer waste disposal, river, swimming, fishing, boat launch, hiking, $$$.
Northeast of Gold Beach. Just before the bridge take Jerrys Flat Road and go 28.0 miles east to Agness and campground.

FOUR SEASONS RV RESORT (Private)
45 campsites, 36 w/hookups for water/electricity/sewer, 9 w/hookups for water & electricity, reservation information - (503)247-7959, showers, laundry, groceries, trailer waste disposal, river, swimming, fishing, boat launch, playfield, hiking, $$-$$$.
East of Gold Beach. US 101 to north end of Rogue River bridge, Rogue River Road east 3.5 miles, North Bank Rogue southeast 3.0 miles.

HONEY BEAR CAMPGROUND (Private)
150 campsites, 18 w/hookups for water/electricity/sewer, 46 w/hookups for water & electricity, plus 86 tent units, reservation information - (503)247-2765, showers, laundry, groceries, trailer waste disposal, ocean access, stream, swimming, fishing, playfield, playground, hiking, nearby golf, $$-$$$.
North of Gold Beach. US 101 7.0 miles north, Ophir Road 2.0 miles north.

INDIAN CREEK RECREATION PARK (Private)
125 campsites, 100 w/hookups for water/electricity/sewer, plus 25 tent units, reservation information - (503)247-7704, showers, laundry, groceries, river, fishing, playfield, playground, wheelchair access, $$-$$$.
East of Gold Beach. Leave US 101 at south end of Rogue River bridge, east .5 mile on Jerry's Flat Road.

KIMBALL CREEK BEND RV RESORT (Private)
66 campsites, 56 w/hookups for water/electricity/sewer, plus 10 tent units, reservation information - (503)247-7580, showers, laundry, groceries, trailer waste disposal, river, swimming, fishing, boat launch, playfield, hiking, $$-$$$.
East of Gold Beach. US 101 to north end of Rogue River bridge, Rogue River Road east 3.5 miles, North Bank Rogue southeast 4.5 miles.

LUCKY LODGE RV PARK (Private)
42 campsites, 32 w/hookups for water/electricity/sewer, 4 w/hookups for water & electricity, plus 6 tent units, trailers to 35', reservation information -(503)247-7618, showers, laundry, trailer waste disposal, river, swimming, fishing, boat launch, $$.
East of Gold Beach. US 101 to north end of Rogue River bridge, Rogue River Road east 3.5 miles, North Bank Rogue southeast 4.5 miles.

NESIKA BEACH RV PARK CAMPGROUND (Private)
37 campsites, 15 w/hookups for water/electricity/sewer, 12 w/hookups for water & electricity, plus 10 tent units, trailers to 35', reservation information -(503)247-6077, showers, laundry, groceries, ocean access, fishing, $$.
North of Gold Beach. US 101 7.0 miles north, Nisika Road .7 mile southwest.

QUOSATANA (Siskiyou National Forest)
42 units, trailers to 32', piped water, river, flush toilets, wheelchair access, trailer waste disposal, boat launch, boating, swimming, fishing, on recreational section of Wild & Scenic Rogue River, elev. 100', $$.
Northeast of Gold Beach. CR 595 4.2 miles northeast, FSR 33 10.0 miles northeast.

SANDY CAMP/RV PARK (Private)
86 campsites, 36 w/hookups for water/electricity/sewer, plus 50 tent units, reservation information - (503)247-2301, showers, ocean access, river, fishing, boat launch, $$.
At Gold Beach. Take Port of Gold Beach exit off US 101 and head west .5 mile to the South Jetty.

GOLD HILL

GOLD'N ROGUE KOA (Private)
90 campsites, 20 w/hookups for water/electricity/sewer, 30 w/hookups for water & electricity, 24 w/hookups for water, plus 16 tent units, reservations -(503)855-7710, showers, laundry, groceries, trailer waste disposal, swimming pool, stream, playground, $$$.
At Gold Hill. Leave I-5 at Gold Hill exit #40, north .3 mile to Blackwell Road, travel east .2 mile.

LAZY ACRES MOTEL & RV PARK (Private)
24 campsites, 18 w/hookups for water/electricity/sewer, plus 6 w/hookups for water & electricity, reservation information - (503)855-7000, ice, river, swimming, fishing, playfield, playground, $$-$$$.
West of Gold Hill. Leave I-5 at Gold Hill exit #40, north .3 mile, State 99 west 1.5 miles.

GOVERNMENT CAMP

ALPINE (Mt. Hood National Forest)
7 units, trailers to 18', piped water, elev. 5400', $.
Northeast of Government Camp. US 26 .8 mile east, State 173 4.6 miles northeast. Located 1 mile below Timberline Lodge National Historic Site.

CLACKAMAS LAKE (Mt. Hood National Forest)
47 units, trailers to 18', well, lake - speed limits, elev. 3400', $.
Southeast of Government Camp. US 26 15.0 miles southeast, FSR 42 8.0 miles south, FSR 4270 .5 mile east.

CLEAR LAKE (Mt. Hood National Forest)
28 units, trailers to 22', well, lake, boating, swimming, fishing, water skiing, elev. 3600', $$.
Southeast of Government Camp. US 26 9.0 miles southeast, FSR 2630 1.0 mile south, FSR 220 1.0 mile south.

FROG LAKE (Mt. Hood National Forest)
33 units, trailers to 18', well, lake - no motors, boating, swimming, fishing, elev. 3800', $$.
Southeast of Government Camp. US 26 7.0 miles southeast, FSR 2610 1.0 mile southeast FSR 230 .5 mile south.

GONE CREEK (Mt. Hood National Forest)
50 units, trailers to 32', piped water, lake - speed limits, boating, swimming, fishing, elev. 3200'. $$.
South of Government Camp. US 26 15.0 miles southeast, FSR 42 8.0 miles south, FSR 57 3.5 miles west.

JOE GRAHAM HORSE CAMP (Mt. Hood National Forest)
14 units, trailers to 32', reservations advisable - (503)328-6211, elev. 3400', $$.
South of Government Camp. US 26 15.0 miles southeast, FSR 42 8.0 miles south.

HOOD VIEW (Mt. Hood National Forest)
43 units, trailers to 32', piped water, lake - speed limits, boating, swimming, fishing, elev. 3200', $$.
South of Government Camp. US 26 15.0 miles southeast, FSR 42 8.0 miles south, FSR 57 4.0 miles west.

LITTLE CRATER (Mt. Hood National Forest)
16 units, trailers to 18', picnic area, well, stream, elev. 3200', $.
South of Government Camp. US 26 15.0 miles southeast, FSR 42 6.0 miles south, FSR 58 2.7 miles west, FSR 230 .3 mile west.

LOWER TWIN (Mt. Hood National Forest)
5 tent units, fishing, hike-in, elev. 4200', $.
Southeast of Government Camp. US 26 2 miles east, State 35 north to Frog Lake Turnoff, take trail to this camp on Lower Twin Lake.

OAK FORK (Mt. Hood National Forest)
47 units, trailers to 22', well, lake - speed limits, boating, swimming, fishing, elev. 3200', $$.
South of Government Camp. US 26 15.0 miles southeast, FSR 42 8.0 miles south, FSR 57 3.0 miles west, FSR 170 .5 mile north.

PINE POINT (Mt. Hood National Forest)
20 units, trailers to 32', piped water, lake - speed limits, boat launch, boating, fishing, swimming, hiking trail, elev. 3200', $-$$.
South of Government Camp. US 26 15 miles southeast, FSR 42 8 miles south, FSR 57 5.0 miles west to campground.

STILL CREEK (Mt. Hood National Forest)
27 units, trailers to 18', piped water, fishing, elev. 3700', $.
Southeast of Government Camp. US 26 1.2 miles southeast, FSR 2650 .5 mile south.

TRILLIUM LAKE (Mt. Hood National Forest)
39 units, trailers to 32', piped water, lake - no motors, wheelchair access, boat launch, boating, swimming, fishing, bicycling, elev. 3600', $$.
Southeast of Government Camp. US 26 2.2 miles southeast, FSR 2656 1.3 miles south.

GRANTS PASS

BEND O' THE RIVER CAMPGROUND (Private)
21 campsites, 10 w/hookups for water/electricity/sewer, 11 w/hookups for water & electricity, plus 4 tent units, reservation information - (503)479-2547, showers, laundry, groceries, trailer waste disposal, river, swimming, fishing, boat launch, playground, $$.
West of Grants Pass. Take G Street 7.5 miles west (becomes Upper & Lower River Roads), campground is located just past milepost #7.

BIG PINE (Siskiyou National Forest)
14 units, trailers to 22', picnic area, piped water, fishing, outstanding ponderosa pine stand, elev. 2400', $.
West of Grants Pass. I-5 3.4 miles north, CR 2-6 12.4 miles northwest, FSR 355 12.8 miles southwest.

GRANTS PASS OVER-NITERS (Private)
40 trailer sites, 29 w/hookups for water/electricity/sewer, plus 11 w/hookups for water & electricity, reservation information - (503)479-7289, showers, laundry, ice, swimming pool, $$-$$$.
Northwest of Grants Pass. I-5 north 3.0 miles to Merlin exit #61, east to Frontage Road, north .5 mile.

GRIFFIN PARK (Josephine County)
20 campsites, 15 w/hookups for water/electricity/sewer, plus 5 tent units, reservations - (503)474-5285, showers, trailer waste disposal, river, swimming, fishing, boat launch, playfield, playground, hiking, $$.
Southwest of Grants Pass. US 199 approximately 4.0 miles west, Riverbanks Road 2.5 miles to campground.

HAVE-A-NICE DAY CAMPGROUND (Private)
39 campsites, 15 w/hookups for water/electricity/sewer, 19 w/hookups for water & electricity, plus 5 w/hookups for water, reservation information - (503)582-1421, showers, laundry, ice, playground, trailer waste disposal, river, swimming, fishing, boat launch, hiking, $$-$$$.
Southeast of Grants Pass. I-5 8.0 miles southeast to Rogue River exit #48, southwest .1 mile to Rogue River Highway (Old Highway 99), west 1.5 miles.

INDIAN MARY PARK (Josephine County)
89 campsites, 42 w/hookups for water/electricity/sewer, plus 47 tent units, trailers to 32', showers, ice, river, swimming, fishing, boat launch, playfield, playground, hiking, $$.
Northwest of Grants Pass. I-5 north to Merlin exit #61, Merlin-Galice Road 7.6 miles west.

JOE CREEK WATERFALLS RV RESORT (Private)
66 campsites, 46 w/hookups for water/electricity/sewer, plus 20 tent units, reservation information - (503)474-0250, showers, laundry, groceries, trailer waste disposal, stream, swimming, fishing, mini-golf, playfield, hiking, $$-$$$.
North of Grants Pass. I-5 north 10.0 miles to Hugo exit #66, Jumpoff Joe Creek Road .7 mile east.

LES CLARE RV PARK & CAMPGROUND (Private)
47 campsites, 26 w/hookups for water/electricity/sewer, 12 w/hookups for water & electricity, plus 9 tent units, reservations - (503)479-0046, showers, laundry, ice, trailer waste disposal, river, fishing, $$-$$$.
Southeast of Grants Pass. I-5 south to exit #58, State 99 3.0 miles south, Rogue River Highway (Old Highway 99) 2.5 miles east, located at 2956 Rogue River Highway.

RIVERFRONT RV TRAILER PARK (Private)
22 campsites, 16 w/hookups for water/electricity/sewer, 4 w/hookups for water & electricity, plus 2 tent units, reservation information - (503)582-0985, showers, laundry, ice, trailer waste disposal, river, swimming, fishing, boat launch, $$-$$$.
Southeast of Grants Pass. I-5 8.0 miles southeast to Rogue River exit #48, southwest .1 mile to Rogue River Highway/State 99, west 2.0 miles.

ROGUE VALLEY OVERNIGHTERS (Private)
80 trailer sites w/hookups for water/electricity/sewer, reservation information - (503)479-2208, showers, laundry, playground, trailer waste disposal, $$$.
In Grants Pass. I-5 south to exit #58, south 1 block to NW 6th Street, located at 1806 NW 6th Street.

SCHROEDER (Josephine County)
30 trailer sites w/hookups for water/electricity/sewer, trailers to 35', showers, tennis, playfield, playground, river, fishing, boat launch, $$.
West of Grants Pass. Located 4.0 miles west on Schroeder Lane.

SELMAC LAKE (Josephine County)
81 campsites, trailers to 32', reservation information - (503)474-5285, showers, trailer waste disposal, lake, swimming, fishing, boat launch, playfield, playground, hiking, $$.
Southwest of Grants Pass. US 199 23.0 miles southwest of Grants Pass on Lakeshore Drive.

SUNNY VALLEY KOA (Private)
72 campsites, 11 w/hookups for water/electricity/sewer, plus 61 w/hookups for water & electricity, reservation information - (503)479-0209, showers, laundry, groceries, trailer waste disposal, swimming pool, playfield, playground, $$$.
North of Grants Pass. I-5 17.0 miles north to Sunny Valley exit #71.

VALLEY OF THE ROGUE (Oregon State Park)
174 campsites, 97 w/hookups for water/electricity/sewer, 55 w/hookups for electricity, plus 22 tent units, group campsites, trailers to 40', group picnic area, wheelchair access, showers, trailer waste disposal, boat launch, fishing, $$-$$$.
East of Grants Pass. I-5 south/east 12.0 miles to campground.

WHITE HORSE (Josephine County)
39 campsites, 8 w/hookups for water/electricity/sewer, 2 w/hookups for electricity, plus 29 tent units, trailers to 35', reservation information -(503)474-5285, showers, river, fishing, boat launch, playground, hiking, $$.
In Grants Pass. At city center take G Street west to Upper River Road, head north 6.0 miles to campground.

GRESHAM

BELLACRES MOBILE ESTATE (Private)
12 trailer sites w/hookups for water/electricity/sewer, trailers to 35', no tents, adults only, reservation information - (503)665-4774, showers, laundry, game room, lounge, $$$.
In Gresham. From I-84 take Wood Village exit, NE 238th Drive south 2.6 miles (road becomes 242nd then Hogan Drive), NE Division Street .6 mile east.

OXBOW (Multnomah County)
45 campsites, trailers to 30', no pets, river, fishing, boat launch, playfield, playground, hiking, wheelchair access, golden age passports honored, $$.
East of Gresham. Take Division Street 8.0 miles east of Gresham to campground.

ROLLING HILLS MOBILE TERRACE (Private)
101 trailer sites w/hookups for water/electricity/sewer, no tents, reservation information - (503)666-7282, showers, laundry, groceries, trailer waste disposal, swimming pool, game room, lounge, wheelchair access, $$$.
West of Gresham. Leave I-84 westbound at Sandy Blvd. exit #15, campground is west .7 mile at 20145 NE Sandy Blvd.

HAINES

ANTHONY LAKE (Wallowa-Whitman National Forest)
47 campsites, trailers to 22', piped water, 20 acre lake - no motors, wheelchair access includes trails & fishing, boat launch, boat rental, ice, cafe/snack bar, boating, swimming, good fishing, hiking, cool in summer, elev. 7100', $$.
Northwest of Haines. State 411 17.0 miles northwest, FSR 73 7.0 miles west.

GRANDE RONDE LAKE (Wallowa-Whitman National Forest)
8 units, 2 group sites, trailers to 18', picnic area, piped water, 10 acre lake - no motors, boat launch, boating, swimming, fishing, cool in summer, elev. 7200', $.
Northwest of Haines. State 411 17.0 miles northwest, FSR 73 8.5 miles west, FSR 43 .5 mile northwest.

MUD LAKE (Wallowa-Whitman National Forest)
14 units, trailers to 18', piped water, small lake, boating, swimming, fishing, elev. 7100', cool in summer with periodic mosquito problems, $.
Northwest of Haines. State 411 17.0 miles northwest, FSR 73 7.3 miles west.

HALFWAY

LAKE FORK (Hells Canyon National Recreation Area)
11 units, trailers to 22', well, stream, fishing, hiking, elev. 3200', $.
Northeast of Halfway. State 86 9.2 miles east, FSR 39 8.3 miles north.

HEBO

HEBO LAKE (Siuslaw National Forest)
16 units, trailers to 18', picnic area w/shelter, piped water, lake - no motors, boating, swimming, fishing, hiking, elev. 1600', $.
East of Hebo. US 101 .1 mile north, State 22 .3 mile southeast, FSR 14 5.0 miles east.

HEPPNER

ANSON WRIGHT COUNTY PARK (Morrow County)
12 campsites, 6 w/hookups for water/electricity/sewer, plus 6 tent units, trailers to 30', showers, stream, swimming, fishing, playground, hiking, wheelchair access, elev. 4000', $$.
South of Heppner. State 207 27.0 miles south.

CUTSFORTH COUNTY PARK (Morrow County)
18 campsites, 10 w/hookups for water/electricity/sewer, plus 8 tent units, trailer to 30', showers, lake, swimming, fishing, hiking, elev. 4000', $$.
Southeast of Heppner. Willow Creek Highway 20.0 miles southeast.

HERMISTON

BUTTERCREEK RECREATIONAL COMPLEX (Private)
24 trailer sites w/hookups for water/electricity/sewer, reservation information - (503)567-5469, showers, laundry, groceries, trailer waste disposal, lounge, $$.
Southwest of Hermiston. Leave I-84 at exit #182, located at junction with State 207.

HAT ROCK CAMPGROUND (Private)
60 campsites, 27 w/hookups for water/electricity/sewer, 22 w/hookups for water & electricity, plus 11 w/hookups for water, reservation information - (503)567-4188, showers, laundry, groceries, swimming pool, playfield, trailer waste disposal, river, swimming, fishing, boat launch, $$-$$$.
Northeast of Hermiston. US 395 5.0 miles north, US 730 8.0 miles east, Hat Rock State Park Road 1.0 mile north.

SHADY REST RV PARK (Private)
24 trailer sites, 18 w/hookups for water/electricity/sewer, plus 6 w/hookups for water & electricity, reservation information - (503)922-5041, showers, laundry, swimming pool, $$.
North of Hermiston. US 395 5.0 miles north, US 730 .5 mile west.

HOOD RIVER

KINGSLEY (Mt. Hood National Forest)
11 tent units, piped water, lake, fishing, elev. 2800', $.
South of Hood River. FSR N20 12 miles to campground.

TOLL BRIDGE PARK (Hood River County)
20 trailer sites w/hookups for water/electricity/sewer, reservation information - (503)352-6300, showers, trailer waste disposal, river, swimming, fishing, playfield, playground, hiking, wheelchair access, $$.
South of Hood River. US 35 18.0 miles south.

VIENTO (Oregon State Park)
63 campsites, 58 w/hookups for electricity, plus 5 tent units, trailers to 30', picnic area, showers, stream, hiking, $$.
West of Hood River. I-84 8.0 miles west to campground.

HUNTINGTON

FAREWELL BEND (Oregon State Park)
93 campsites, 53 w/hookups for electricity, plus 40 primitive campsites, group sites, trailers to 45', picnic area, showers, trailer waste disposal, boat launch, fishing, swimming, Oregon Trail display, $-$$.
Southeast of Huntington. I-84 5.0 miles southeast to campground.

SPRING (BLM)
Campsites, water, boating, swimming, picnic sites, elev. 2000', $.
Northeast of Huntington. CR 1 7.0 miles to Brownlee Reservoir, on Snake River.

IDANHA

MARION FORKS (Willamette National Forest)
8 units, trailers to 22', piped water, stream, swimming, fishing, hiking, salmon hatchery adjacent to campground, elev. 2500', $$.
Southeast of Idanha. State 22 12.0 miles southeast, FSR 502 .1 mile southeast.

MOUNTAIN VIEW MOBILE PARK (Private)
15 trailer sites w/hookups for water/electricity/sewer, reservation information - (503)854-3774, lake, river, water sports, $$.
In Idanha. From city center head east 1 block on State 22, Church Street 2 blocks south, Willow Street 2 blocks east, Mountain Avenue 1 block to park.

RIVERSIDE (Willamette National Forest)
37 units, trailers to 22', piped water, on North Santiam River, fishing, hiking, elev. 2400', $$.
Southeast of Idanha. State 22 9.6 miles southeast.

WHISPERING FALLS (Willamette National Forest)
12 units, trailers to 22', piped water, flush toilets, on North Santiam River, waterfalls across river, fishing, elev. 1900', $$.
East of Idanha. State 22 4.1 miles east.

IDLEYLD PARK

BOGUS CREEK (Umpqua National Forest)
6 units, trailers to 32', piped water, flush toilets, boating, fishing, elev. 1100', $.
East of Idleyld Park. State 138 14.0 miles east.

BROKEN ARROW (Umpqua National Forest)
142 units, 6 group sites, trailers to 32', piped water, flush toilets, wheelchair access, elev. 5200', $-$$.
East of Idleyld Park. State 138 54.3 miles east, FSR 4795 4.0 miles south. Located at Diamond Lake, 15 miles north of Crater Lake.

CANTON CREEK (Umpqua National Forest)
12 units, trailers to 18', picnic area w/shelter, piped water, flush toilets, swimming, on Steamboat Creek - no fishing, elev. 1200', $.
East of Idleyld Park. State 138 18.0 miles east, FSR 38 .4 mile northeast.

DIAMOND LAKE (Umpqua National Forest)
160 units, 23 group sites, trailers to 22', piped water, flush toilets, interpretive services, trailer waste disposal, on Diamond Lake - speed limits, boat launch, boating, swimming, fishing, bicycling, elev. 5200', $$.
East of Idleyld Park. State 138 54.3 miles east, FSR 4795 2.0 miles south. Located 15 miles north of Crater Lake.

EAGLE ROCK (Umpqua National Forest)
2 units, trailers to 22', well, on North Umpqua River, boating, swimming, fishing, elev. 1600', $.
East of Idleyld Park. State 138 30.0 miles east.

HORSESHOE BEND (Umpqua National Forest)
33 units, 1 group site - reservation required (503)496-3532, trailers to 22', piped water, on North Umpqua River, flush toilets, wheelchair access, boat launch, boating, fishing, hiking, bicycling, elev. 1300', $$-$$$.
East of Idleyld Park. State 138 25.6 miles east, FSR 4750 .1 mile south, FSR 2615C .7 mile southwest.

MILLPOND (BLM)
12 units, trailers okay, group picnic area w/shelters, drinking water, swimming, hiking, fishing, nature study, elev. 1100', $$.
Northeast of Idelyld Park. Take Rock Creek Road 5.0 miles northeast to campground.

POOLE CREEK (Umpqua National Forest)
42 units, trailers to 22', piped water, at Lemolo Lake, boat launch, boating, swimming, fishing, water skiing, elev. 4200', $$.
East of Idleyld Park. State 138 49.4 miles east, FSR 2610 4.2 miles north.

ROCK CREEK (BLM)
17 units, trailers okay, picnic area, drinking water, swimming, fishing, nature study, elev. 1200', $.
Northeast of Idelyld Park. Take Rock Creek Road 8.0 miles northeast to campground.

SUSAN CREEK (BLM)
33 units, trailers okay, drinking water, swimming, hiking, $$.
East of Idleyld Park. State 138 2.0 miles east.

THIELSEN VIEW (Umpqua National Forest)
60 units, trailers to 32', piped water, on Diamond Lake - speed limits, boat launch, boating, swimming, fishing, elev. 5200', $$.
East of Idleyld Park. State 138 54.3 miles east, FSR 4795 3.1 miles west. Located 15 miles north of Crater Lake.

JACKSONVILLE

CANTRALL-BUCKLEY PARK (Jackson County)
42 campsites, trailers to 25', reservation information - (503)776-7001, showers, stream, swimming, fishing, playground, hiking, $$.
Southwest of Jacksonville. State 238 13.0 miles southwest.

FLUMET FLAT (Rogue River National Forest)
23 units, trailers to 22', piped water, flush toilets, wheelchair access, river, groceries, gasoline, ice, showers, laundry, interpretive trail, cafe/snack bar, swimming, fishing, hiking, elev. 1600', $$.
Southwest of Jacksonville. State 238 8.0 miles southwest, CR 859 9.9 miles south, FSR 1090 1.2 miles to campground.

FRENCH GULCH CAMP & TRAILHEAD (Rogue River National Forest)
9 units, trailers to 18', well, lake, wheelchair access, hiking, elev. 2100', $.
Southwest of Jacksonville. State 238 8.0 miles southwest, CR 10 14.0 miles southwest, FSR 1075 1.5 miles east.

JACKSON (Rogue River National Forest)
11 units, some trailers, piped water, picnic area, stream, fishing, swimming, historic area, elev. 1700', $.
Southwest of Jacksonville 19 miles. State 238 to Big Applegate Road #FH14, follow this to campground.

SQUAW LAKES (Rogue River National Forest)
11 tent units, picnic area, well, lake - no motors, boating, swimming, fishing, hiking, remote, elev. 3000', $-$$.
Southwest of Jacksonville. State 238 8.0 miles southwest, CR 10 14.0 miles southwest, FSR 1075 8.0 miles southeast to campground.

JOHN DAY

CLYDE HOLLIDAY (Oregon State Park)
30 campsites w/hookups for electricity, trailers to 60', picnic area, wheelchair access, showers, trailer waste disposal, fishing, $$.
West of John Day. US 26 7.0 miles west to campground.

JOSEPH

BLACKHORSE (Hells Canyon National Recreation Area)
17 units, trailers to 32', piped water, river, fishing, elev. 4000', $.
Southeast of Joseph. State 350 7.7 miles east, FSR 39 28.7 miles southeast.

COVERDALE (Hells Canyon National Recreation Area)
10 units, trailers to 32', piped water, river, fishing, elev. 4300', $.
Southeast of Joseph. State 350 7.7 miles east, FSR 39 28.8 miles southeast, FSR 3960 4.1 miles southwest.

HIDDEN (Hells Canyon National Recreation Area)
10 units, trailers to 32', piped water, river, fishing, hiking, elev. 4400', $.
Southeast of Joseph. State 350 7.7 miles east, FSR 39 28.8 miles southeast, FSR 3960 7.0 miles southwest.

INDIAN CROSSING (Hells Canyon National Recreation Area)
15 units, trailers to 32', well, river, fishing, trailhead into Eagle Cap Wilderness Area, elev. 4500', $.
Southeast of Joseph. State 350 7.7 miles east, FSR 39 28.8 miles south, FSR 3960 8.8 miles southwest.

LICK CREEK (Hells Canyon National Recreation Area)
12 units, trailers to 32', piped water, fishing, hiking, elev. 5400', $.
Southeast of Joseph. State 350 7.7 miles east, FSR 39 14.9 miles south.

OLLOKOT (Hells Canyon National Recreation Area)
12 units, trailers to 32', well, river, fishing, elev. 4000', $.
Southeast of Joseph. State 350 7.7 miles east, FSR 39 28.8 miles southeast.

WALLOWA LAKE (Oregon State Park)
210 campsites, 121 w/hookups for water/electricity/sewer, plus 89 tent units, group sites, trailers to 65', mail reservations available, picnic area, wheelchair access, showers, trailer waste disposal, lake, boating, fishing, swimming, hiking into Eagle Cap Wilderness, $$-$$$.
South of Joseph. Follow road south around Wallow Lake 6.0 miles.

JUNTURA

CHUKAR PARK (BLM)
16 units, water, swimming, hiking trails, elev. 3100', $.
North of Juntura. West of Juntura on US 20, take the road to Beulah Reservoir 6.0 miles to campground.

OASIS CAFE/MOTEL/RV PARK (Private)
22 trailer sites w/hookups for water/electricity/sewer, reservation information - (503)277-3605, river, fishing, lounge, elev. 2900', $$.
In Juntura. Located on US 20 in Juntura.

KENO

KENO CAMP (Pacific Power)
26 campsites, picnic area, showers, trailer waste disposal, on Klamath River, boat launch, fishing, swimming, $.
Northwest of Keno. State 66 approximately 2.0 miles northwest.

KLAMATH FALLS

ASPEN POINT (Winema National Forest)
61 units, trailers to 22', piped water, flush toilets, trailer waste disposal, at Lake of the Woods Recreation Area, boat launch, boating, swimming, fishing, trail to Mountain Lakes Wilderness, elev. 5000', $$.
Northwest of Klamath Falls. State 140 32.6 miles northwest, FSR 3704 .6 mile south.

HARRIMAN SPRINGS RESORT & MARINA (Private)
23 campsites, 17 w/hookups for water/electricity/sewer, plus 5 tent units, reservation information - (503)356-2323, showers, laundry, trailer waste disposal, lake, swimming, fishing, boat launch, boat rental, lounge, hiking, elev. 4100', $$.
Northwest of Klamath Falls. State 140 28.0 miles northwest, Rocky Point Road 1.5 miles north.

KLAMATH FALLS KOA (Private)
73 campsites, 36 w/hookups for water/electricity/sewer, 30 w/hookups for water & electricity, plus 7 tent units, reservations - (503)884-4644, showers, laundry, groceries, trailer waste disposal, swimming pool, stream, playground, elev. 4100', $$$.
In Klamath Falls. State 140 to Klamath Falls Lakeview exit, 5th Street to Washburn, left to Shasta Way, located at 3435 Shasta Way.

LAKE OF THE WOODS (Winema National Forest)
Campsites, picnic area, boat launch, hiking, $.
Northwest of Klamath Falls. State 140 35.0 miles northwest.

LAKE OF THE WOODS RESORT (Private)
45 campsites, 30 w/hookups for water/electricity/sewer, plus 15 tent units, trailers to 35', reservation information - (503)949-8300, showers, laundry, groceries, trailer waste disposal, lake, swimming, fishing, boat launch, boat rental, hiking, elev. 5000', $$.
Northwest of Klamath Falls. State 140 west 33.0 miles to milepost #36, south 1.0 mile on Lake of the Woods Road, west .5 mile.

MALLARD CAMPGROUND (Private)
55 campsites, 25 w/hookups for water/electricity/sewer, 18 w/hookups for water & electricity, plus 12 tent units, reservation information - (503)882-0482, showers, laundry, swimming pool, therapy pool, game room, elev. 4200', $$$.
North of Klamath Falls. US 97 3.0 miles north, on east side of road.

ROCKY POINT RESORT & MARINA (Private)
30 campsites, 18 w/hookups for water/electricity/sewer, 10 w/hookups for water & electricity, plus 2 tent units, reservation information - (503)356-2287, showers, laundry, trailer waste disposal, river, lake, swimming, fishing, boat launch, boat rental, lounge, hiking, elev. 4200', $$-$$$.
Northwest of Klamath Falls. State 140 28.0 miles northwest, Rocky Point Road 3.0 miles north.

SUNSET (Winema National Forest)
67 units, trailers to 22', piped water, lake, flush toilets, boat launch, boating, swimming, fishing, water skiing, adjacent to Mountain Lakes Wilderness, at Lake of the Woods Recreation Area, elev. 5000', $$.
Northwest of Klamath Falls. State 140 32.6 miles northwest, FSR 3704 1.0 mile south.

TINGLEY LAKE ESTATES (Private)
14 campsites, 4 w/hookups for water/electricity/sewer, 6 w/hookups for water & electricity, plus 4 tent units, reservation information - (503)882-8386, showers, laundry, trailer waste disposal, pond, swimming, fishing, boat rental, playground, elev. 4100', $$.
South of Klamath Falls. US 97 7.0 miles south to Midland, Old Midland Road 2.0 miles east, Tingley Lane .5 mile south.

WISEMAN'S MOBILE COURT (Private)
20 trailer sites w/hookups for water/electricity/sewer, reservation information - (503)883-8621, showers, laundry, trailer waste disposal, elev. 4200',
$$.
In Klamath Falls. US 97 5.0 miles east to 6th Street and park.

LA GRANDE

HILGARD JUNCTION (Oregon State Park)
18 primitive campsites, trailers to 20', picnic area, wheelchair access,
trailer waste disposal, fishing, Oregon Trail display, $.
Northwest of La Grande. I-84 8.0 miles northwest to campground.

SUNDOWNER MOBILE HOME PARK (Private)
24 trailer sites w/hookups for water/electricity/sewer, no tents, reservation
information - (503)963-2648, showers, laundry, trailer waste disposal, elev.
2800', $$$.
In La Grande. State 82 .3 mile east, Holmes Street .2 mile south.

LAKESIDE

NORTH LAKE RESORT & MARINA (Private)
100 campsites, 5 w/hookups for water/electricity/sewer, 31 w/hookups for
water & electricity, plus 64 tent units, reservation information -
(503)759-3515, showers, groceries, lake, swimming, fishing, boat launch,
boat rental, playground, $$.
In Lakeside. US 101 to Lakeside exit, .5 mile east to N. Lake Avenue, .5
mile east to 2090 North Lake Avenue.

SEADRIFT MOTEL & CAMPGROUND (Private)
45 trailer sites, 35 w/hookups for water & electricity, plus 10 w/out hookups,
no tents, reservation information - (503)759-3102, showers, trailer waste
disposal, playground, $$.
Northwest of Lakeside. US 101 .3 mile north of Lakeside exit.

LAKEVIEW

GOOSE LAKE (Oregon State Park)
48 campsites w/hookups for electricity, trailers to 30', boat launch, fishing,
$$.
South of Lakeview. US 396 15.0 miles south to campground.

HUNTER'S RV (Private)
23 trailer sites w/hookups for water & electricity, reservation information
-(503)947-4968, showers, groceries, trailer waste disposal, therapy pool,
ponds, lounge, playground, elev. 5000', $$-$$$.
North of Lakeview. US 395 2.0 miles north.

JUNIPERS RESERVOIR RV RESORT (Private)
20 campsites, 16 w/hookups for water/electricity/sewer, plus 4 w/hookups
for water & electricity, reservation information - (503)947-2050, showers,
laundry, trailer waste disposal, reservoir, stream, fishing, boat launch, hik-
ing, wheelchair access, $$$.
West of Lakeview. State 140 10.0 miles west.

PARKWAY MOTEL & RV PARK (Private)
19 campsites, 13 w/hookups for water/electricity/sewer, 1 w/hookups for electricity, plus 5 tent units, reservation information - (503)947-2707, showers, elev. 4800', $$-$$$.
In Lakeview. West of US 395/State 140 junction, on State 140, 2 blocks.

VALLEY FALLS STORE & CAMPGROUND (Private)
16 campsites, 6 w/hookups for water/electricity/sewer, 1 w/hookups for water & electricity, 1 w/hookups for water, plus 8 tent units, reservation information -(503)947-2052, groceries, playground, hiking, elev. 4200', $$.
North of Lakeview. US 395 23.0 miles north, located at junction with State 31.

LANGLOIS

LANGLOIS TRAVEL PARK (Private)
20 campsites, 10 w/hookups for water/electricity/sewer, plus 10 tent units, reservation information - (503)348-2256, showers, laundry, $$.
In Langlois. Located at south end of town on US 101.

PINE SPRINGS KOA (Private)
72 campsites, 11 w/hookups for water/electricity/sewer, 13 w/hookups for water & electricity, plus 48 tent units, reservations - (503)348-2358, showers, laundry, groceries, trailer waste disposal, pond, playground, hiking, $$-$$$.
South of Langlois. US 101 3.0 miles south.

LaPINE

ALLEN'S RIVERVIEW TRAILER PARK (Private)
25 campsites, 18 w/hookups for water/electricity/sewer, plus 7 tent units, reservation information - (503)536-2382, showers, laundry, river, swimming, fishing, elev. 4300', $$.
North of La Pine. US 97 2.6 miles north to Wickiup Junction, Burgess Road 1.0 mile west, Huntington Road 1.0 mile north.

CHIEF PAULINA HORSE CAMP (Deschutes National Forest)
14 units, trailers to 32', reservations required - (503)388-5674, in Newberry Crater, elev. 6300', $$.
East of LaPine. US 97 5.0 miles north, CR 21 15.0 miles east to campground.

CINDER HILL (Deschutes National Forest)
106 units, trailers to 32', piped water, flush toilets, boat launch, boating, fishing, in Newberry Crater, elev. 6300', $$.
East of LaPine. US 97 5.0 miles north, CR 21 18.0 miles east to campground. At east end of East Lake.

COVE (Deschutes National Forest)
1 tent unit, on Paulina Lake, hike-in or boat-in only, trails, fishing, elev. 6300', $.
East of LaPine. US 97 5 miles north, CR 21 15.8 miles north, located on northeast shore of Paulina Lake. Hikers can take trail behind Little Crater Campground approximately 3 miles to campground.

CULTUS LAKE (Deschutes National Forest)
16 units, trailers to 22', picnic area, well, lake, boating, swimming, fishing, water skiing, elev. 4700', $$.
Northwest of LaPine. US 97 2.4 miles northeast, FSR 204 20.0 miles west, State 46 6.4 miles north, FSR 2025 1.5 miles northwest.

CULTUS LAKE NORTH UNIT (Deschutes National Forest)
38 units, trailers to 22', picnic area, well, lake, boating, swimming, fishing, water skiing, elev. 4700', $$.
Northwest of LaPine. US 97 2.4 miles northeast, FSR 204 20.0 miles west, State 46 6.4 miles north.

DESCHUTES BRIDGE (Deschutes National Forest)
15 units, trailers to 22', picnic area, on Deschutes River, fishing, elev. 4600', $.
West of LaPine. US 97 2.4 miles northeast, CR 43 10.0 miles east, CR 42 10.0 miles west, CR 46 10.0 miles north.

EAST LAKE (Deschutes National Forest)
29 units, trailers to 32', piped water, on East Lake - speed limits, flush toilets, boat launch, boating, fishing, in Newberry Crater, elev. 6300', $$.
Northeast of LaPine. US 97 5.0 miles north, CR 21 17.0 miles east to campground. Located on southwest side of East Lake.

EAST LAKE RESORT & RV PARK (Private)
38 trailer sites w/hookups for water/electricity/sewer, trailers to 35', no tents, reservation information - (503)536-2230, showers, laundry, groceries, trailer waste disposal, lake, swimming, fishing, boat launch, boat rental, hiking, elev. 6300', $$$.
Northeast of LaPine. US 97 6.0 miles north, Paulina/East Lake Road 18.0 miles east.

FAR-E-NUF TRAILER PARK (Private)
18 trailer sites w/hookups for water/electricity/sewer, reservations - (503)536-2265, showers, laundry, ice, trailer waste disposal, elev. 4200', $$.
North of LaPine. US 97 2.6 miles north to Wickiup Junction, Burgess Road 2.5 miles west, Pine Forest Road .7 mile south, Wright Road 1 block.

GULL POINT (Deschutes National Forest)
5 units, 15 group sites, trailers to 32', picnic area, piped water, on Wickiup Reservoir, flush toilets, boating, swimming, fishing, water skiing, elev. 4300', $$.
West of LaPine. US 97 2.4 miles northeast, CR 43 10.0 miles west, CR 42 5.4 miles west, FSR 4260 3.5 miles south.

HOT SPRINGS (Deschutes National Forest)
43 units, trailers to 32', piped water, on East Lake - speed limits, fishing, in Newberry Crater, elev. 6300', $$.
East of LaPine. US 97 5.0 miles north, CR 21 17.6 miles east to campground. Located on south side of East Lake.

LAPINE (Oregon State Park)
145 campsites, 95 w/hookups for water,electricity/sewer, plus 50 w/hookups for electricity, trailers to 40', picnic area, wheelchair access, showers, trailer waste disposal, boating, fishing, $$-$$$.
North of LaPine. US 97 6.0 miles northeast, LaPine Recreation Area road 3.2 miles west.

LAVA LAKE (Deschutes National Forest)
38 units, trailers to 22', picnic area, well, lake - speed limits, trailer waste disposal, boat launch, boat rental, boating, fishing, hiking, elev. 4800', $$.
Northwest of LaPine. US 97 2.4 miles northeast, CR 43 10.0 miles west, CR 42 10.0 miles west, CR 46 13.5 miles north, FSR 1927 1.0 mile northeast.

LAVA LAKE RV CAMPGROUND (Private)
29 campsites, 24 w/hookups for water/electricity/sewer, plus 5 tent units, reservation information - (503)382-9443, groceries, trailer waste disposal, lake, swimming, fishing, boat launch, boat rental, hiking, elev. 4700', $$.
Northwest of La Pine. US 97 3.0 miles north, Pringle Falls Highway 9.0 miles northwest, Cascade Lakes Highway 26.0 miles west/north.

LITTLE CRATER (Deschutes National Forest)
53 units, trailers to 32', well, on Paulina Lake - speed limits, boat launch, boating, fishing, in Newberry Crater, elev. 6300', $$.
East of LaPine. US 97 5.0 miles north, CR 2129 15.0 miles east to campground. Located on east shore of Paulina Lake.

NORTH DAVIS CREEK (Deschutes National Forest)
17 units, trailers to 22', picnic area, well, on Wickiup Reservoir, boat launch, boating, fishing, water skiing, elev. 4400', $$.
West of LaPine. US 97 2.4 miles northeast, CR 43 10.0 miles west, CR 42 10.0 miles west, CR 46 4.0 miles south. Located between two springs at west end of Wickiup Reservoir.

OVERFLOW (Deschutes National Forest)
18 units, trailers to 32', reservations required - (503)382-6922, in Newberry Crater, elev. 6300', $$.
East of LaPine. US 97 5.0 miles north, CR 2129 15.1 miles east.

PAULINA LAKE (Deschutes National Forest)
69 units, trailers to 32', piped water, on Paulina Lake - speed limits, flush toilets, boat launch, boating, fishing, in Newberry Crater, elev. 6300', $$.
East of LaPine. US 97 5.0 miles north, CR 21 13.1 miles east to campground. Located on south shore of Paulina Lake.

PRAIRIE (Deschutes National Forest)
14 units, trailers to 32', well, stream, fishing, elev. 4400', $.
Northeast of LaPine. US 97 5.0 miles north, CR 21 3.0 miles southeast.

PRAIRIE GROUP AREA (Deschutes National Forest)
Group campsites, reservations required - (503)388-5674, stream, fishing, elev. 4300', $$.
Northeast of LaPine. US 97 5.0 miles north, CR 21 2.5 miles southeast.

QUINN RIVER (Deschutes National Forest)
41 units, trailers to 32', picnic area, well, river, boating, fishing, on Crane Prairie Reservoir - speed limits, historic site, elev. 4400', $$.
Northwest of LaPine. US 97 2.4 miles northeast, CR 43 10.0 miles west, CR 42 10.0 miles west, CR 46 4.0 miles north. Located at mouth of Quinn River, on Crane Prairie Reservoir, near Billy Quinn Historical Gravesite.

RIVER (Deschutes National Forest)
4 tent units, stream, fishing, elev. 4300', $.
West of LaPine 8 miles. Take US 97 west to Wickiup Road #216. This will lead you to the campground.

ROCK CREEK (Deschutes National Forest)
32 units, trailers to 22', well, on Crane Prairie Reservoir - speed limits, boating, fishing, elev. 4400', $$.
Northwest of LaPine. US 97 2.4 miles northeast, CR 43 10.0 miles west, CR 42 10.0 miles west, CR 46 2.4 miles north.

ROSLAND (Deschutes National Forest)
5 units, trailers to 22', no drinking water, on Little Deschutes River, swimming, fishing, elev. 4200', $.
North of LaPine. US 97 3.0 miles northeast, CR 1032 2.0 miles west to campground. Located 2.5 miles west of Wickiup junction.

ROUNDUP TRAVEL TRAILER PARK (Private)
27 campsites, 23 w/hookups for water/electricity/sewer, plus 4 w/hookups for water & electricity, adults only, reservation information - (503)536-2378, showers, laundry, trailer waste disposal, elev. 4300', $$$.
In La Pine. From city center take Huntington Road south 1 block, Finley Butte Road 1 block east.

SOUTH TWIN LAKE (Deschutes National Forest)
21 units, trailers to 22', piped water, lake - no motors, flush toilets, boating, swimming, fishing, elev. 4300', $$.
Southwest of LaPine. US 97 2.4 miles northeast, CR 43 10.0 miles west, CR 42 5.4 miles west, FSR 4260 1.6 miles south.

WEST SOUTH TWIN (Deschutes National Forest)
22 units, 2 group sites, trailers to 22', piped water, on Deschutes River channel - speed limits, flush toilets, boat launch, boat rental, cafe/snack bar, boating, swimming, fishing, elev. 4300', $$.
West of LaPine. US 97 2.4 miles northeast, CR 43 10.0 miles west, CR 42 5.4 miles west, FSR 4260 1.7 miles south.

LINCOLN CITY

COYOTE ROCK RV PARK (Private)
58 campsites, 38 w/hookups for water/electricity/sewer, plus 20 w/hookups for water & electricity, reservation information - (503)996-3436, showers, ice, river, fishing, boat launch, boat rental, $$-$$$.
Southeast of Lincoln City. US 101 1.5 miles south, State 229 1.0 mile east.

DEVIL'S LAKE (Oregon State Park)
100 campsites, 32 w/hookups for water/electricity/sewer, plus 68 tent units, group campsites, mail reservations available, trailers to 62', wheelchair access, showers, boat launch on East Devil's Lake, boating, fishing, swimming, $$-$$$.
At Lincoln City. Campground is at Lincoln City off US 101.

LINCOLN CITY KOA (Private)
80 campsites, 18 w/hookups for water/electricity/sewer, 20 w/hookups for water & electricity, plus 42 tent units, reservations - (503)994-2961, showers, laundry, groceries, trailer waste disposal, playground, $$$.
Northeast of Lincoln City. US 101 north 4.0 miles, East Devils Lake Road 1.0 miles southeast.

SALMON RIVER EVERGREEN PARK (Private)
77 campsites, 29 w/hookups for water/electricity/sewer, 23 w/hookups for water & electricity, plus 25 tent units, reservation information - (503)994-3116, showers, laundry, groceries, trailer waste disposal, river, fishing, hiking, $$-$$$.
Northeast of Lincoln City. US 101 5.0 miles north, State 18 6.0 miles east.

SPORTSMAN'S LANDING (Private)
30 trailer sites w/hookups for water/electricity/sewer, reservation information - (503)996-4225, laundry, river, fishing, boat launch & rental, $$.
South of Lincoln City. US 101 5.0 miles south, State 229 3.9 miles east.

TREE N' SEA TRAILER PARK (Private)
21 trailer sites w/hookups for water/electricity/sewer, no tents, reservation information - (503)996-3801, showers, trailer waste disposal, ocean access, river, swimming, fishing, $$$.
In Lincoln City. Located on SW 51st Street, 1 block west of US 101.

LOWELL

BEDROCK (Willamette National Forest)
20 units, trailers to 22', picnic area, well, stream, swimming, fishing, hiking, elev. 1100', $-$$.
Northeast of Lowell. CR 6220 1.8 miles north, CR 6240 9.9 miles east, FSR 181 4.8 miles east.

BIG POOL (Willamette National Forest)
5 tent units, piped water, stream, swimming, fishing, elev. 1000', $.
Northeast of Lowell. CR 6220 1.8 miles north, CR 6240 9.9 miles east, FSR 181 1.7 miles east.

CLARK CREEK (Willamette National Forest)
5 group sites w/shelters, reservations required (503)937-2129, no trailers, well, wheelchair access, interpretive services, hiking, $$$.
West of Lowell. CR 6220 2.0 miles north, CR 6240 8.0 miles east, FSR 18 3.0 miles east.

PUMA (Willamette National Forest)
11 units, trailers to 18', well, stream, swimming, fishing, hiking, elev. 1100', $.
Northeast of Lowell. CR 6220 1.8 miles north, CR 6240 9.9 miles east, FSR 181 6.5 miles east.

WINBERRY CREEK (Willamette National Forest)
6 units, 2 group sites, trailers to 18', well, fishing, swimming, hiking, elev. 1100', $-$$$.
East of Lowell. CR 6220 1.8 miles north, CR 6240 .4 mile east, CR 62450 5.8 miles southeast, FSR 191 3.5 miles southeast.

MADRAS

HAYSTACK RESERVOIR (Ochoco National Forest)
24 units, trailers to 22', piped water, flush toilets, lake, boat launch, boating, swimming, fishing, water skiing, elev. 2900', $$-$$$.
South of Madras. US 97 9.3 miles south, CR CR6 3.3 miles southeast, FSR 58 .6 mile north.

MADRAS/CULVER KOA (Private)
81 campsites, 16 w/hookups for water/electricity/sewer, 46 w/hookups for water & electricity, plus 19 tent units, reservations - (503)546-3073, showers, laundry, groceries, trailer waste disposal, swimming pool, playground, elev. 2800', $$-$$$.
Southwest of Madras. US 97 9.0 miles south, Jericho Lane .5 mile east.

THE COVE PALISADES (Oregon State Park)
272 campsites, 87 w/hookups for water/electricity/sewer, 91 w/hookups for electricity, plus 94 tent units, group campsites, trailers to 40', mail reservations available, picnic area, wheelchair access, showers, trailer waste disposal, boat launch, fishing, swimming, hiking trails, at confluence of Crooked/Deschutes/Metolius Rivers, $$-$$$.
Southwest of Madras. Just south of Madras leave US 97 and head east 5.0 miles, road will veer south, campground is 10.0 miles further.

MAPLETON

ARCHIE KNOWLES (Siuslaw National Forest)
9 units, trailers to 18', picnic area, piped water, stream, flush toilets, elev. 100', $.
East of Mapleton. State 126 3.0 miles east.

CLAY CREEK (BLM)
20 units, trailers okay, group picnic area w/shelters, drinking water, boating, swimming, fishing, nature study, elev. 500', $$.
Southeast of Mapleton. Highway 126 12.5 miles east of Mapleton to Siuslaw River Road, follow this road 16.0 miles south.

MAPLE-LANE TRAILER PARK & MARINA (Private)
46 campsites, 22 w/hookups for water/electricity/sewer, plus 24 w/hookups for water & electricity, reservation information - (503)268-4822, showers, river, fishing, boat launch, $$.
In Mapleton. Located on State 126 at milepost #14.

WHITTAKER CREEK (BLM)
31 units, trailers okay, picnic area, drinking water, boat launch, non-motorized boating only, swimming, fishing, nature study, elev. 300', $$.
East of Mapleton. State 126 14.0 miles southeast of Mapleton to Whittaker Creek Road and campground.

MAUPIN

BEAR SPRINGS (Mt. Hood National Forest)
21 units, trailers to 18', piped water, elev. 3200', $.
Northwest of Maupin. State 216 25.0 miles northwest.

MAUPIN CITY PARK (City)
27 trailer sites w/hookups for water/electricity/sewer, trailers to 24', laundry, groceries, trailer waste disposal, river, fishing, boat rental, $-$$.
In Maupin. Located in city of Maupin.

SOUTH JUNCTION (BLM)
8 units, hiking, $.
Southeast of Maupin. US 197 22.0 miles southeast, campground is just before its junction with US 97, on South Junction Road.

McKENZIE BRIDGE

BELKNAP WOODS RESORT (Private)
31 campsites, 23 w/hookups for water/electricity,sewer, plus 8 w/hookups for water & electricity, reservation information - (503)822-3535, showers, laundry, trailer waste disposal, swimming pool, therapy pool, river, fishing, hiking, $$.
East of McKenzie Bridge. State 126 5.0 miles east, Belknap Springs Road .3 mile north.

COLDWATER COVE (Willamette National Forest)
35 units, 2 group sites, trailers to 22', well, lake - no motors, wheelchair access includes trails, groceries, boat launch, boat rental, cafe-snack bar, boating, fishing, elev. 3100', $.
Northeast of McKenzie Bridge. State 126 14.2 miles northeast, FSR 1372 .1 mile southeast.

ICE CAP CREEK (Willamette National Forest)
22 units, trailers to 18', piped water, near Carmen Reservoir - no motors, Koosah & Sahalie Falls nearby, flush toilets, fishing, hiking, elev. 3000', $$.
Northeast of McKenzie Bridge. State 126 19.2 miles northeast, FSR 14071 .1 mile northeast.

McKENZIE BRIDGE (Willamette National Forest)
20 units, trailers to 22', well, on McKenzie River, boating, fishing, elev. 1400', $.
West of McKenzie Bridge. State 126 1.0 mile west.

OLALLIE (Willamette National Forest)
17 units, trailers to 22', at confluence of McKenzie River & Olallie Creek, boating, fishing, elev. 2000', $.
Northeast of McKenzie Bridge. State 126 11.1 miles northeast.

PARADISE (Willamette National Forest)
64 units, trailers to 22', piped water, group picnic area, flush toilets, on McKenzie River, fishing, hiking, elev. 1600', $$.
East of McKenzie Bridge. State 126 3.5 miles east.

THE HUB RV PARK (Private)
36 trailer sites w/hookups for water/electricity/sewer, reservation information - (503)822-3514, showers, laundry, trailer waste disposal, hiking, $$.
In McKenzie Bridge. On State 126, located between mileposts #50 and #51.

TRAIL BRIDGE (Willamette National Forest)
24 units, trailers to 32', picnic area, piped water, lake - speed limits, flush toilets, boating, fishing, elev. 2000', $.
Northeast of McKenzie Bridge. State 126 13.2 miles northeast, FSR 1477 .2 mile southwest.

McMINNVILLE

MULKEY RV PARK (Private)
18 campsites, 6 w/hookups for water/electricity/sewer, plus 12 w/hookups for water & electricity, reservation information - (503)472-2475, showers, river, swimming, fishing, $$.
Southwest of McMinnville. State 18 4.0 miles southwest.

MEHAMA

FISHERMEN'S BEND (BLM)
38 units, trailers okay, group campsites, group picnic area, drinking water, boat launch, non-motorized boating only, fishing, nature study, elev. 750', $$-$$$.
Southeast of Mehama. State 22 8.5 miles east, campground is west of Mill City.

JOHN NEAL MEMORIAL PARK (Linn County)
40 campsites, trailers to 22', river, fishing, boat launch, playfield, playground, hiking, $$.
Southeast of Mehama. South 1.0 mile to Lyons, east 1.5 miles to Memorial Park Road, north to park.

NEWBERG

CHAMPOEG (Oregon State Park)
48 campsites w/hookups for electricity, trailers to 30', group campsites, group picnic area, wheelchair access, showers, trailer waste disposal, boating, fishing, bicycle paths, hiking trails, historic area - site of Oregon's first government, interpretive center, $$.
Southeast of Newberg. Campground is located off US 99W, approximately 7.0 miles southeast of Newberg and is also accessible via I-5.

NEWPORT

AGATE BEACH TRAILER & RV PARK (Private)
35 campsites, 21 w/hookups for water/electricity/sewer, 9 w/hookups for water & electricity, plus 5 tent units, reservation information - (503)265-7670, showers, laundry, trailer waste disposal, therapy pool, lounge, $$-$$$.
North of Newport. US 101 3.0 miles north.

BEVERLY BEACH (Oregon State Park)
279 campsites, 52 w/hookups for water/electricity/sewer, 75 w/hookups for electricity, plus 152 tent units, group campsites, mail reservations available, trailers to 72', picnic area, wheelchair access, showers, trailer waste disposal, fishing, ocean access, beachcombing, hiking, $$-$$$.
North of Newport. US 101 7.0 miles north to campground.

CITY CENTER TRAILER PARK (Private)
10 trailer sites w/hookups for water/electricity/sewer, no tents, trailers to 35', reservation information - (503)265-5731, showers, laundry, $$-$$$.
In Newport. Located on US 101 at 8th Street.

HARBOR VILLAGE TRAILER PARK (Private)
140 trailer sites w/hookups for water/electricity/sewer, no tents, reservation information - (503)265-5088, showers, laundry, groceries, ocean access, fishing, boat rental, lounge, $$-$$$.
East of Newport. US 20 .5 mile east, SW Moore Drive .5 mile south, SE Bay Blvd. 1 block east.

SOUTH BEACH (Oregon State Park)
254 campsites w/hookups for electricity, group sites, mail reservations available, trailers to 53', wheelchair access, showers, trailer waste disposal, ocean access, beachcombing, fishing, hiking, $$-$$$.
South of Newport. US 101 2.0 miles south to campground.

SOUTH BEACH MARINA RV PARK (Port of Newport)
38 trailer sites w/hookups for water/electricity/sewer, no tents, reservation information - (503)867-3321, showers, laundry, groceries, trailer waste disposal, river, fishing, boat launch, lounge, playground, wheelchair access, $$-$$$.
In Newport. Leave US 101 at south end of Yaquina Bay bridge on Marine Science Center exit, park is .5 mile east.

SPORTSMAN'S TRAILER PARK (Private)
36 trailer sites, 33 w/hookups for water/electricity/sewer, plus 3 w/hookups for water & electricity, no tents, reservation information - (503)867-9588, ocean access, river, fishing, boat launch, boat rental, $$.
In Newport. Leave US 101 at south end of Yaquina Bay bridge on Marine Science Center exit, park is north 1 block.

NORTH BEND

BLUEBILL LAKE (Siuslaw National Forest)
18 units, 1 group site, trailers to 22', piped water, flush toilets, lake, fishing, hiking, ocean beach & dunes access, elev. 100', $$.
Northwest of North Bend. US 101 2.5 miles north, CR 609 .8 mile west, FSR 1099 2.3 miles northwest.

THE FIRS TRAILER PARK (Private)
25 trailer sites w/hookups for water/electricity/sewer, reservation information - (503)756-6274, showers, laundry, $-$$.
North of North Bend. US 101 7.0 miles north, Wildwood Drive 1.1 mile east.

OAKRIDGE

BLACK CANYON (Willamette National Forest)
71 units, trailers to 22', picnic area, piped water, river - speed limit, wheelchair access includes trails & fishing, boat launch, boating, fishing, swimming, hiking, at head of Lookout Point Reservoir, elev. 1000', $$-$$$.
Northwest of Oakridge. State 58 8.5 miles northwest.

BLUE POOL (Willamette National Forest)
22 units, trailers to 18', picnic area, piped water, river, flush toilets, fishing, swimming, near McCredie Hot Springs, elev. 1900', $$.
Southeast of Oakridge. State 58 8.8 miles southeast.

GOLD LAKE (Willamette National Forest)
25 units, trailers to 18', picnic area, well, lake - no motors, boat launch, boating, swimming, hiking, fly fishing only, elev. 4800', $$.
Southeast of Oakridge. State 58 25.6 miles southeast, FSR 500 2.2 miles northeast.

HAMPTON (Willamette National Forest)
5 units, trailers to 32', well, river, boat launch, boating, swimming, fishing, water skiing, elev. 1100', $.
Northwest of Oakridge. State 58 10.0 miles northwest.

ISLET (Willamette National Forest)
55 units, 3 group sites, trailers to 22', piped water, lake - speed limits, flush toilets, trailer waste disposal, boat launch, boating, swimming, fishing, hiking, elev. 5400', $$.
East of Oakridge. State 58 23.1 miles southeast, FSR 5897 10.5 miles northeast, FSR 5898 1.7 miles northwest, FSR 5898 1.7 miles southwest.

NORTH WALDO (Willamette National Forest)
58 units, trailers to 22', piped water, flush toilets, trailer waste disposal, lake - speed limits, boat launch, boating, swimming, fishing, hiking, elev. 5400', $$.
East of Oakridge. State 58 23.1 miles southeast, FSR 5897 10.5 miles northeast, FSR 5898 1.5 miles northwest, FSR 515 .6 mile northwest.

PACKARD CREEK (Willamette National Forest)
33 units, trailers to 32', picnic area, piped water, lake, wheelchair access includes trails, boat launch, boating, swimming, water skiing, fishing, hiking, elev. 1600', $$-$$$.
Southeast of Oakridge. State 58 2.2 miles southeast, CR 360 .5 mile southeast, FSR 21 5.2 miles south.

SALMON CREEK FALLS (Willamette National Forest)
15 units, trailers to 18', picnic area, well, fishing, swimming, elev. 1500', $$.
East of Oakridge. CR 149 3.0 miles east, FSR 24 3.7 miles northeast.

SAND PRAIRIE (Willamette National Forest)
20 units, trailers to 32', piped water, river, flush toilets, wheelchair access includes trails, near head of Hills Creek Reservoir, nearby boat launch, swimming, fishing, elev. 1600', $$-$$$.
South of Oakridge. State 58 2.2 miles southeast, CR 360 .5 mile southeast, FSR 21 11.6 miles south.

SHADOW BAY (Willamette National Forest)
92 units, 11 large group sites, trailers to 40', reservations advised -(503)782-2291, piped water, flush toilets, trailer waste disposal, lake - speed limits, boat launch, boating, swimming, fishing, elev. 5400', $$-$$$.
East of Oakridge. State 58 23.1 miles southeast, FSR 5897 6.5 miles northeast, FSR 5896 2.0 miles northwest.

SHADY DELL (Willamette National Forest)
9 units, trailers to 18', well, stream, fishing, elev. 1000', $.
Northwest of Oakridge. State 58 7.0 miles northwest.

OXBOW

DOVE CREEK (Wallowa-Whitman National Forest)
4 tent units, piped water, fishing, elev. 1700', $.
North of Oxbow. CR 210 8.0 miles north, FSR 1890 6.5 miles north.

KIRBY CREEK (Hells Canyon National Recreation Area)
4 tent units, piped water, boating, swimming, fishing, water skiing, hike-in, elev. 1700', $.
North of Oxbow. CR 210 8.0 miles north, Trail 1890 6.4 miles north.

LEEP CREEK (Hells Canyon National Recreation Area)
3 tent units, picnic area, lake, boating, swimming, fishing, water skiing, hike-in, elev. 1700', $.
North of Oxbow. CR 210 8.0 miles north, Trail 1890 4.7 miles north.

LYNCH CREEK (Hells Canyon National Recreation Area)
3 tent units, picnic area, lake, boating, swimming, fishing, water skiing, hike-in, elev. 1700', $.
North of Oxbow. CR 210 8.0 miles north, Trail 1890 7.3 miles northeast.

VERMILLION BAR (Hells Canyon National Recreation Area)
2 tent units, picnic area, lake, boating, swimming, fishing, water skiing, hike-in, elev. 1700', $.
North of Oxbow. CR 210 8.0 miles north, Trail 1890 6.9 miles north.

PACIFIC CITY

CAPE KIWANDA RV PARK (Private)
135 campsites, 95 w/hookups for water/electricity/sewer, plus 40 w/hookups for water & electricity, reservation information - (503)965-6230, showers, laundry, groceries, playground, trailer waste disposal, ocean access, swimming, fishing, boat launch, $$-$$$.
North of Pacific City. At city center take Brooten Road west .2 mile, then proceed north 1.0 mile to campground.

ISLAND PARK (Tillamook County)
40 campsites, trailer waste disposal, ocean access, pond, swimming, fishing, boat launch, $$.
North of Pacific City. US 101 5.0 miles north, at Sandlake.

PACIFIC CITY TRAILER PARK (Private)
15 trailer sites w/hookups for water/electricity/sewer, adults only, reservation information - (503)965-6820, showers, laundry, trailer waste disposal, river, fishing, $$.
In Pacific City. At city center take Pacific Avenue east 1 block.

RAINES RESORT (Private)
14 campsites, 12 w/hookups for water/electricity/sewer, plus 2 tent units, reservation information - (503)965-6371, laundry, river, fishing, boat launch, boat rental, $$.
In Pacific City. At city center take Brooten Road west .2 mile, then proceed north .8 mile, just past the bridge take Ferry Street west .1 mile.

RIVERVIEW LODGE CAMPGROUND (Private)

12 campsites w/hookups for water & electricity, reservation information -(503)965-6000, showers, river, swimming, fishing, boat rental, $-$$.
In Pacific City. Leave US 101 at northern Pacific City exit, campground is west 1.0 miles.

SAND BEACH (Siuslaw National Forest)

101 units, trailers to 32', piped water, flush toilets, trailer waste disposal, boating, swimming, fishing, Pacific Ocean & sand dunes access, ORV area, elev. 100', $$.
North of Pacific City. CR 536 .2 mile west, CR 535 8.4 miles north, CR 503 1.0 mile west, FSR S3001 .5 mile southwest.

SAND BEACH PARKING (Siuslaw National Forest)

100 units, trailers to 32', piped water, flush toilets, no tables, boating, swimming, fishing, Pacific Ocean & sand dunes access, ORV area, elev. 100', $.
North of Pacific City. CR 536 .2 mile west, CR 535 8.4 miles north, CR 503 1.8 miles southwest.

WEBB PARK (Tillamook County)

30 campsites, trailer waste disposal, ocean access, fishing, boat launch, $$.
North of Pacific City. At city center take Brooten Road west .2 mile then north 2.0 miles to park.

WOOD PARK (Tillamook County)

10 campsites, 5 w/hookups for water/electricity/sewer, 5 tent sites, river, fishing, $$.
North of Pacific City. Take Brooten Road west .2 mile then north 1.0 miles.

PARKDALE

LOST LAKE (Mt. Hood National Forest)

76 units, trailers to 22', piped water, lake - no motors, wheelchair access, groceries, ice, showers, boat launch, interpretive services, boat rental, cafe/snack bar, boating, swimming, fishing, hiking, bicycling, elev. 3200', $$.
Southwest of Parkdale. State 281 6.0 miles north, CR N22 10.0 miles southwest, FSR 13 4.0 miles southwest.

LOST LAKE GROUP CAMP (Mt. Hood National Forest)

12 group sites, trailers to 22', reservations required - (503)666-0701, piped water, lake - no motors, groceries, ice, showers, boat launch, interpretive services, boat rental, swimming, fishing, hiking, bicycling, elev. 3200', $$$.
Southwest of Parkdale. State 281 6.0 miles north, CR N22 10.0 miles southwest, FSR 13 4.0 miles southwest.

POLALLIE (Mt. Hood National Forest)

10 units, trailers to 18', well, river, swimming, fishing, elev. 3000', $$.
South of Parkdale. State 35 14.0 miles southeast.

ROBINHOOD (Mt. Hood National Forest)

24 units, trailers to 18', picnic area, wheelchair access, well, river, swimming, fishing, hiking, elev. 3600', $.
Southeast of Parkdale. State 35 12.0 miles south.

SHERWOOD (Mt. Hood National Forest)
18 units, trailers to 18', picnic area, well, river, wheelchair access, fishing, hiking, elev. 3000', $.
South of Parkdale. State 35 8.0 miles south.

WAHTUM LAKE (Mt. Hood National Forest)
8 tent units, fishing, lake, hike-in only, elev. 3700', $.
Northwest of Parkdale. State 281 6 miles north, CR 501 5 miles southwest, FSR N13/1300 5 miles west, FSR N18/1820 8 miles northwest, FSR N20/2820620 to Wahtum Lake, trail .3 mile to lakeside tent units.

PAULINA

SUGAR CREEK (Ochoco National Forest)
10 units, trailers to 22', picnic area, swimming, bicycling, elev. 4000', $.
Northeast of Paulina. CR 380 3.5 miles east, CR 113 6.5 miles north, FSR 158 1.8 miles east.

WOLF CREEK (Ochoco National Forest)
17 units, trailers to 22', piped water, bicycling, elev. 4100', $.
Northeast of Paulina. CR 380 3.5 miles east, CR 113 6.6 miles north, FSR 142 1.6 miles north, FSR 142 .2 mile north.

PENDLETON

ARROWHEAD RV PARK (Private)
100 trailer sites w/hookups for water/electricity/sewer, reservations -(503)276-8080, groceries, cafe, elev. 2600', $$.
East of Pendleton. I-84 4.0 miles east to exit #216, Market Road .1 mile northeast.

BROOKE TRAILER COURT (Private)
14 campsites, 8 w/hookups for water/electricity/sewer, plus 6 w/hookups for water & electricity, reservation information - (503)276-5353, showers, laundry, ice, river, fishing, $$-$$$.
In Pendleton. I-84 exit #210, State 11 .8 mile northeast, SE Court Avenue 2.5 miles west, SE 8th Street north 2 blocks.

EMIGRANT SPRINGS (Oregon State Park)
51 campsites, 18 w/hookups for water/electricity/sewers, plus 33 tent units, group campsites, trailers to 30', group picnic area, showers, Oregon Trail display, located in ponderosa pine forest, $$-$$$.
Southeast of Pendleton. I-84 26.0 southeast to campground.

RV PARK (Private)
61 campsites, 31 w/hookups for water/electricity/sewer, plus 30 w/hookups for water & electricity, trailers to 35', no pets, reservation information -(503)276-5408, showers, laundry, playground, trailer waste disposal, $$$.
In Pendleton. I-84 to exit #210, State 11 to Byers Avenue, located at 1500 SE Byers Avenue.

PHILOMATH

ALSEA FALLS (BLM)
16 units, trailers okay, picnic area, drinking water, swimming, hiking, geology, fishing, nature study, elev. 800', $.
Southwest of Philomath. State 34 19.0 miles southwest to Alsea, follow South Fork Alsea Road southeast to campground which is about 8.0 miles west of Glenbrook.

MARYS PEAK (Siuslaw National Forest)
3 tent units, picnic area, hiking, elev. 3500', $.
Southwest of Philomath. US 20 1.0 mile west, State 34 9.1 mile southwest, FSR 3010 9.2 miles northwest.

PORT ORFORD

AGATE BEACH TRAILER PARK (Private)
14 campsites, 12 w/hookups for water/electricity/sewer, plus 2 w/hookups for water & electricity, reservation information - (503)332-3031, ocean access, lake, fishing, $$.
In Port Orford. US 101 to 12th Street, west .7 mile.

CAPE BLANCO (Oregon State Park)
58 campsites w/hookups for electricity, trailers to 40', picnic area, wheelchair access, showers, trailer waste disposal, fishing, ocean access, black sand beach, beachcombing, hiking trails access the Oregon Coast Trail, historic Hughes House, $$.
Northwest of Port Orford. US 101 4.0 miles north, west 5.0 miles to campground.

EVERGREEN PARK (Private)
11 trailer sites w/hookups for water/electricity/sewer, reservation information - (503)332-5942, showers, laundry, trailer waste disposal, $$.
In Port Orford. US 101 to 9th Street, west 2 blocks.

HUMBUG MOUNTAIN (Oregon State Park)
105 campsites, 30 w/hookups for water/electricity/sewer, plus 75 tent units, trailers to 45', picnic area, wheelchair access, showers, trailer waste disposal, fishing, ocean access, beachcombing, hiking trails access the Oregon Coast Trail, $$-$$$.
South of Port Orford. US 101 6.0 miles south.

PORT ORFORD RV TRAILER VILLAGE (Private)
49 campsites, 40 w/hookups for water/electricity/sewer, plus 9 w/hookups for water & electricity, reservation information - (503)332-1041, showers, laundry, ice, trailer waste disposal, $$-$$$.
In Port Orford. US 101 to north end of town, Madrona Avenue east 1 block, Port Orford Loop .5 mile north.

PORTLAND

AINSWORTH (Oregon State Park)
45 campsites w/hookups for water/electricity/sewer, trailers to 60', picnic area, showers, trailer waste disposal, hiking, access to Columbia Gorge Trail, $$$.
East of Portland. Take the scenic route, US 30, 37.0 miles east to campground which is located just west of US 30's remerging with I-84.

JANTZEN BEACH RV PARK (Private)
165 trailer sites w/hookups for water/electricity/sewer, no tents, reservation information - (503)289-7626 or (800)443-7248, showers, laundry, ice, swimming pool, tennis, playground, rec room, $$$.
In Portland. I-5 north to Jantzen Beach exit #308, North Hayden Island Drive .5 mile west.

SOUTHGATE MOBILE HOME & RV PARK (Private)
25 trailer sites w/hookups for water/electricity/sewer, reservation information - (503)771-5262, showers, laundry, $$$.
In Portland. I-205 north to Foster Avenue exit, east to 82nd Avenue, south to 7911 SE 82nd Avenue. (Southbound on I-205 take Sunnyside exit, turn east to 82nd Avenue and head north on 82nd.)

TALL FIRS MOBILE HOME & RV PARK (Private)
7 trailer sites w/hookups for water/electricity/sewer, no tents, reservation information - (503)761-8210, showers, laundry, $$$.
In Portland. I-205 northboud to Division Avenue exit #19, east to 15656 SE Division.

TRAILER PARK OF PORTLAND (Private)
120 trailer sites, 100 w/hookups for water/electricity/sewer, plus 20 w/hookups for water & electricity, no tents, reservations - (503)692-0225, showers, laundry, groceries, trailer waste disposal, river, fishing, playground, $$-$$$.
Southeast of Portland. I-5 to exit #289, Nyberg Road (State 212) .2 mile east.

POWERS

BUCK CREEK (Siskiyou National Forest)
2 units, trailers okay, creek, primitive , $.
Southeast of Powers. Take County Road 4.2 miles southeast, FSR 333 .9 mile southeast, FSR 3292 1 mile east, FSR 3251 approximately 5 miles to campground.

DAPHNE GROVE (Siskiyou National Forest)
17 units, trailers to 18', drinking water, river, swimming, fishing, hiking, elev. 800', $.
South of Powers. CR 90 4.2 miles southeast, FSR 3300 10.4 miles south.

PIONEER CAMP (Siskiyou National Forest)
1 tent unit, primitive , $.
Southeast of Powers. Take County Road 4.2 miles southeast, FSR 333 .9 mile southeast, FSR 3292 1 mile east, FSR 3251 7.5 miles, FSR 308 3.4 miles south.

POWERS COUNTY PARK (Coos County)
60 campsites, 30 w/hookups for water & electricity, plus 30 tent sites, community kitchen, showers, playground, tennis, trailer waste disposal, lake -no motors, fishing, boat launch, $$.
In Powers, Located 1.0 miles north of city center.

WOODEN ROCK (Siskiyou National Forest)
2 units, trailers okay, primitive , $.
Southeast of Powers. Take County Road 4.2 miles southeast, FSR 333 .9 mile southeast, FSR 3292 1 mile east, FSR 3251 7.5 miles, FSR 308 3.5 miles south.

PRAIRIE CITY

DEPOT PARK (Prairie City)
21 campsites, 16 w/hookups for water/electricity/sewer, plus 9 tent sites, showers, trailer waste disposal, hiking, $$.
In Prairie City. Leave US 26 on Main Street, park is .5 mile.

PRINEVILLE

ANTELOPE RESERVOIR (Ochoco National Forest)
24 units, trailers to 32', picnic area, well, lake, boat launch, boating, swimming, fishing, elev. 4600', $.
Southeast of Prineville. CR 380 29.0 miles southeast, FSR 17 11.0 miles south, FSR 17 .3 mile east.

CRYSTAL CORRAL PARK (Private)
42 campsites, 15 w/hookups for water/electricity/sewer, 7 w/hookups for water & electricity, plus 20 tent units, reservation information - (503)447-5932, showers, laundry, groceries, lake, swimming, fishing, boat launch, elev. 3200', $-$$.
East of Prineville. US 26 6.5 miles east.

DUNNROVIN RECREATION PARK (Private)
25 campsites w/hookups for water/electricity/sewer, reservation information -(503)447-3632, showers, laundry, elev. 3500', $$.
Southeast of Prineville. US 26 1.0 mile east, Prineville Reservoir Road 9.0 miles south, Davis Road 4.0 miles west.

LAKESHORE MOTOR PARK (Private)
64 campsites, 43 w/hookups for water/electricity/sewer, 4 w/hookups for electricity, plus 17 tent units, reservation information - (503)447-5394, showers, laundry, groceries, trailer waste disposal, lake, swimming, fishing, boat launch, boat rental, lounge, playground, elev. 3100', $$-$$$.
East of Prineville. US 26 7.0 miles east.

OCHOCO DIVIDE (Ochoco National Forest)
28 units, trailers to 22', piped water, elev. 4700', $.
Northeast of Prineville. US 26 30.8 miles northeast, FSR 550 .1 mile southeast; campground is at summit of Ochoco Pass.

OCHOCO LAKE (Oregon State Park)
22 primitive campsites, trailers to 30', drinking water, picnic area, boat launch, fishing, hiking trails, $.
East of Prineville. State 26 7.0 miles east to campground.

PRINEVILLE RESERVOIR (Oregon State Park)
70 campsites, 22 w/hookups for water/electricity/sewer, plus 48 tent units, mail reservations available, trailers to 40', picnic area, showers, boat launch, fishing, swimming, $$-$$$.
Southeast of Prineville. Us 26 1.0 mile east, Prineville Reservoir Road 16.0 miles south to campground.

PRINEVILLE RESERVOIR RESORT (Private)
73 campsites, 8 w/hookups for water/electricity/sewer, plus 65 w/hookups for water & electricity, reservations - (503)447-7468, showers, laundry, groceries, trailer waste disposal, lake, swimming, fishing, boat launch, boat rental, elev. 3100', $$$.
Southeast of Prineville. US 26 1.0 mile east, Prineville Reservoir Road 18.0 miles southeast.

WALTON LAKE (Ochoco National Forest)
23 units, trailers to 22', picnic area, piped water, lake - no motors, boating, fishing, swimming, hiking trails, elev. 5000', $$.
Northeast of Prineville. US 26 16.7 miles east, CR 123 8.5 miles northeast, FSR 22 6.2 miles, FSR 2220 .3 mile to campground.

WILDCAT (Ochoco National Forest)
17 units, trailers to 32', picnic area, well, stream, hiking, adjacent to Mill Creek Wilderness, elev. 3700', $.
Northeast of Prineville. US 26 9.2 miles east, CR 122 8.9 miles northeast, FSR 33 2.0 miles, FSR 300 .2 mile east.

PROSPECT

ABBOTT CREEK (Rogue River National Forest)
21 units, 10 group sites, trailers to 22', picnic area, well, fishing, elev. 3100', $.
North of Prospect. State 62 6.8 miles north, FSR 68 3.4 miles northwest.

FAREWELL BEND (Rogue River National Forest)
61 units, trailers to 22', piped water, river, flush toilets, fishing, elev. 3400', $$.
North of Prospect. State 62 11.6 miles north.

HAMAKER (Rogue River National Forest)
10 tent units, well, river, fishing, hiking, elev. 4000', $.
North of Prospect. State 62 12.0 miles north, State 230 11.0 miles north, FSR 6530 .6 mile southeast, FSR 900 .6 mile south.

MILL CREEK (Rogue River National Forest)
3 units, trailers to 22', fishing, elev. 2800', $.
North of Prospect. State 62 2.0 miles north, FSR 30 1 mile east.

UNION CREEK (Rogue River National Forest)
72 units, trailers to 18', picnic area, piped water, fishing, hiking, elev. 3200', $.
North of Prospect. State 62 10.8 miles north, FSR 3136 .2 mile west.

WOODRUFF BRIDGE (Rogue River National Forest)
6 tent units, well, stream, fishing, elev. 2900', $.
North of Prospect 6 miles. State 62 to Woodruff Access Road #318 and campground. Located 3 miles west of Crater Lake Highway.

REDMOND

CROOKED RIVER RANCH (Private)
96 campsites, 37 w/hookups for water/electricity/sewer, 45 w/hookups for water & electricity, plus 14 tent units, reservation information - (503)923-1441, restaurant/lounge, showers, laundry, groceries, swimming pool, playground, golf course, trailer waste disposal, river, fishing, hiking, elev. 2600', $$-$$$.
Northwest of Redmond. US 97 6.0 miles north, Lower Bridge Road 7.0 miles northwest to Crooked River Ranch.

DESERT TERRACE (Private)
20 trailer sites w/hookups for water/electricity/sewer, reservation information - (503)548-2546, showers, laundry, elev. 3000', $$$.
South of Redmond. US 97 3.0 miles south.

REEDSPORT

COHO MARINA & RV PARK (Private)
49 trailer sites w/hookups for water/electricity/sewers, no tents, trailers to 35', reservations - (503)271-4676, showers, ice, trailer waste disposal, river, fishing, boat launch, boat rental, $$$.
In Reedsport. Located at center of town on US 101 at 16th Street.

ECHO MOTEL & RV PARK (Private)
12 trailer sites w/hookups for water/electricity/sewer, no tents, reservation information - (503)271-2025, showers, groceries, river, swimming, fishing, boat launch, $$.
East of Reedsport. State 38 7.5 miles east.

LOON LAKE (BLM)
59 units, trailers okay, picnic area, drinking water, boat launch, boating, swimming, hiking, berry picking, geology, fishing, nature study, elev. 700', $$-$$$.
Southeast of Reedsport. State 38 12.0 miles to Mill Road, campground is 7.0 miles.

LOON LAKE LODGE RESORT (Private)
100 campsites, 9 w/hookups for water/electricity/sewer, 28 w/hookups for water & electricity, 4 w/hookups for water, plus 59 tent units, reservations -(503)599-2244, groceries, restaurant/lounge, lake, swimming, fishing, boat launch, boat rental, hiking, $$.
Southeast of Reedsport. State 38 13.0 miles east, CR 3 8.2 miles south.

NORTH EEL CREEK (Siuslaw National Forest)
95 units, trailers to 22', piped water, stream, flush toilets, hiking, elev. 100', $$.
Southwest of Reedsport. US 101 12.1 miles southwest.

SOUTH EEL CREEK (Siuslaw National Forest)
13 units, trailers to 22', reservations required (503)271-3611, piped water, flush toilets, elev. 100', $$.
Southwest of Reedsport. US 101 12.9 miles southwest, FSR 1090 .1 mile southwest. Located 1 mile from Tenmile Lake.

SURFWOOD CAMPGROUND (Private)
163 campsites, 101 w/hookups for water/electricity/sewer, 40 w/hookups for water & electricity, plus 22 tent units, reservation information - (503)271-4020, showers, laundry, groceries, swimming pool, playground, tennis, trailer waste disposal, stream, $$.
Southwest of Reedsport. US 101 south 2.0 miles.

TAHKENITCH LAKE (Siuslaw National Forest)
35 units, trailers to 22', piped water, flush toilets, hiking, elev. 100', $$.
North of Reedsport. US 101 7.0 miles north, FSR 1090 .1 mile west.

UMPQUA BEACH RESORT (Private)
75 campsites w/hookups for water/electricity/sewer, reservation information -(503)271-3443, showers, laundry, groceries, ocean access, stream, swimming, fishing, boat launch, playground, $$-$$$.
Southwest of Reedsport. US 101 4.0 miles southwest to Winchester Bay, Salmon Harbor Drive 1.0 mile southwest.

UMPQUA LIGHTHOUSE (Oregon State Park)
63 campsites, 22 w/hookups for water/electricity/sewer, plus 41 tent units, trailers to 44', picnic area, showers, boat launch, fishing, sand dunes, hiking trails, $$-$$$.
South of Reedsport. US 101 6.0 miles south to campground.

WILLIAM M. TUGMAN (Oregon State Park)
115 campsites w/hookups for electricity, trailers to 50', picnic area, wheelchair access, showers, trailer waste disposal, boat launch, fishing, swimming, $$.
South of Reedsport. US 101 8.0 miles south to campground.

WINDY COVE COUNTY PARK (Douglas County)
93 campsites, 64 w/hookups for water/electricity/sewer, plus 29 tent units, showers, ocean access, lake, swimming, fishing, playground, wheelchair access, $$.
Southwest of Reedsport. US 101 4.0 miles southwest to Winchester Bay, Salmon Harbor Drive .3 mile west.

REMOTE

REMOTE CAMPGROUND & CABINS (Private)
17 campsites w/hookups for water/electricity/sewer, trailers to 35', reservation information - (503)572-5105, showers, laundry, groceries, river, swimming, fishing, $$.
East of Remote. Located 1.0 mile east on State 42.

RIP VAN WINKLE'S SLEEPY HOLLOW RV PARK (Private)
12 trailer sites, 9 w/hookups for water/electricity/sewer, plus 3 w/hookups for water & electricity, reservation information - (503)572-2141, showers, laundry, ice, river, swimming, fishing, $$-$$$.
West of Remote. State 42 8.5 miles west, located east of Bridge.

RHODODENDRON

CAMP CREEK (Mt. Hood National Forest)
30 units, trailers to 22', flush toilets, fishing, hiking, elev. 2200', $.
Southeast of Rhododendron. US 26 2.9 miles southeast, FSR .1 mile south to campground.

TOLLGATE (Mt. Hood National Forest)
23 units, trailers to 22', stream, wheelchair access, fishing, hiking, borders Tollgate observation site, elev. 1700', $.
Southeast of Rhododendron. US 26 .5 mile southeast.

RICHLAND

EAGLE VALLEY RV & MOBILE HOME PARK (Private)
60 campsites, 41 w/hookups for water/electricity/sewer, plus 19 w/hookups for electricity, reservation information - (503)893-6161, showers, laundry, ice, trailer waste disposal, stream, playfield, playground, wheelchair access, $$-$$$.
At Richland. State 86 east .2 mile, located near milepost #42.

ROGUE RIVER

CIRCLE W CAMPGROUND (Private)
25 campsites, 10 w/hookups for water/electricity/sewer, plus 15 w/hookups for water & electricity, reservation information - (503)582-1686, showers, laundry, ice, trailer waste disposal, river, swimming, fishing, playground, $$-$$$.
At Rogue River. I-5 to City of Rogue River exit #48, State 99 1.0 mile west.

WHISPERING PINES RV PARK (Private)
11 trailer sites, 9 w/hookups for water/electricity/sewer, plus 2 w/hookups for water & electricity, trailers to 35', reservation information - (503)582-4020, showers, laundry, river, swimming, fishing, boat launch, $$-$$$.
At Rogue River. I-5 to City of Rogue River exit #48, State 99 .1 mile west.

ROSEBURG

DOUGLAS COUNTY FAIRGROUNDS RV PARK (County)
50 trailer sites, 2 w/hookups for water & electricity, plus 48 w/hookups for electricity, no tents, reservation information - (503)440-4505, showers, trailer waste disposal, river, playground, $-$$.
In Roseburg. I-5 south to exit #123, follow signs to fairgrounds.

JOHN P. AMACHER PARK (Douglas County)
30 campsites, 20 w/hookups for water/electricity/sewer, plus 10 tent units, reservation information - (503)672-4901, showers, river, fishing boat launch, playground, hiking, wheelchair access, $$.
North of Roseburg. I-5 north to exit #129, park is .3 mile south.

NEBO TRAILER PARK (Private)
25 trailer sites w/hookups for water/electricity/sewer, no tents, reservation information - (503)673-4108, showers, laundry, ice, trailer waste disposal, $$$.
In Roseburg. I-5 to exit #125, Garden Valley Blvd. east .8 mile, NE Stephens Street (State 99) .7 mile north.

TWIN RIVERS VACATION PARK (Private)
85 campsites, 72 w/hookups for water/electricity/sewer, 8 w/hookups for water & electricity, plus 5 w/hookups for water, reservation information - (503)673-3811, showers, laundry, groceries, river, swimming, fishing, boat ramp, playground, $$-$$$.
In Roseburg. I-5 to exit #125, Garden Valley Road 5.0 miles west, Old Garden Valley Road west 1.5 miles.

WHISTLER'S BEND (Douglas County)
18 campsites, reservation information - (503)673-4863, showers, river, swimming, fishing, boat launch, playground, hiking, $$.
Northeast of Roseburg. State 138 15.0 miles northeast, Whistler's Bend Road to campground.

SALEM

ELKHORN VALLEY (BLM)
23 units, trailers okay, water, swimming, elev. 1000', $.
East of Salem. State 22 24.0 miles east, Elkhorn Road north 10.0 miles.

FOREST GLEN (Private)
100 campsites w/hookups for water/electricity/sewer, reservation information -(503)363-7616, showers, laundry, ice, therapy pool, game room, trailer waste disposal, mini-golf, hiking, $$$.
South of Salem. I-5 south 5.0 miles to Turner/Sunnyside exit #248, east over freeway, Enchanted Way .5 mile south.

KOA SALEM, INC. (Private)
204 campsites, 118 w/hookups for water/electricity/sewer, 47 w/hookups for water & electricity, 7 w/hookups for water, plus 32 tent units, reservations -(503)581-6736, showers, laundry, groceries, trailer waste disposal, lake, swimming, fishing, game room, playground, $$-$$$.
In Salem. I-5 to exit #253, State 22 .2 mile southeast, Lancaster Drive SE .05 mile south.

SILVER FALLS (Oregon State Park)
105 campsites, 53 w/hookups for electricity, plus 52 tent units, trailers to 35', group sites, picnic area, wheelchair access, showers, trailer waste disposal, waterfalls, swimming, fishing, horse camp, hiking, $$-$$$.
East of Salem. State 214 east approximately 26.0 miles; campground can also be accessed from Silverton.

TRAILER PARK VILLAGE (Private)
22 trailer sites w/hookups for water/electricity/sewer, adults only, no pets, no tents, reservations - (503)393-7424, showers, laundry, ice, $$$.
In Salem. I-5 to exit #258, State 99E .5 mile north.

SELMA

KOA RAINBOW'S END (Private)
41 campsites, 26 w/hookups for water & electricity, plus 15 w/hookups for water, reservations - (503)476-6508, showers, laundry, groceries, trailer waste disposal, stream, playfield, playground, $$$.
Northeast of Selma. US 199 7.0 miles northeast, located between mileposts #14 and #15.

THE LAST RESORT (Private)
40 campsites, 6 w/hookups for water/electricity/sewer, 18 w/hookups for water & electricity, plus 16 tent units, reservations - (503)597-4989, showers, laundry, groceries, rec room, snack bar, year-round fishing, boat rental, horse rental, $$.
East of Selma. US 199 to Lake Selmac Junction, Lake Shore Drive 2.5 miles east.

SISTERS

BIG LAKE (Willamette National Forest)
21 units, trailers to 18', piped water, flush toilets, lake, boat launch, boating, swimming, fishing, water skiing, trailheads for Mt. Washington Wilderness & Patjens Lake nearby, elev. 4600', $$.
West of Sisters. US 20 21.7 miles west, FSR 2690 3.4 miles south.

BLUE BAY (Deschutes National Forest)
19 units, 6 group sites, trailers to 22', piped water, on Suttle Lake - speed limits, boat launch, boating, swimming, fishing, water skiing, hiking, elev. 3400', $$-$$$.
Northwest of Sisters. US 20 13.0 miles northwest, FSR 2070 1.0 mile northwest.

BLUE LAKE RESORT (Private)
31 campsites, 9 w/hookups for water/electricity/sewer, 14 w/hookups for water & electricity, plus 8 w/hookups for water, reservation information - (503)595-6671, showers, ice, trailer waste disposal, lake, swimming, fishing, boat launch, boat rental, playground, hiking, elev. 3500', $$-$$$.
Northwest of Sisters. US 20/State 126 13.0 miles northwest to Blue Lake Junction, Suttle Lake Forest Road 2.5 miles west.

CIRCLE 5 TRAILER PARK (Private)
24 trailer sites, 20 w/hookups for water/electricity/sewer, plus 4 w/hookups for water & electricity, reservation information - (503)549-3861, showers, laundry, trailer waste disposal, elev. 3200', $$$.
Southeast of Sisters. US 20 .7 mile southeast.

COLD SPRING (Deschutes National Forest)
23 units, trailers to 22', well, stream, elev. 3400', $$-$$$.
West of Sisters. State 242 5.0 miles west to campground.

INDIAN FORD (Deschutes National Forest)
15 units, 10 group sites, trailers to 22', well, stream, fishing, elev. 3200', $$.
Northwest of Sisters. US 20 5.0 miles northwest to campground.

LINK CREEK (Deschutes National Forest)
25 units, 8 group sites, trailers to 22', piped water, on Suttle Lake - speed limits, boating, swimming, fishing, water skiing, hiking, elev. 3400', $$.
Northwest of Sisters. US 20 13.0 miles northwest, FSR 2070 2.0 miles northwest.

RAINBOW (Deschutes National Forest)
3 tent units, lake - no motors, boating, fishing, elev. 6400', $.
South of Sisters 18 miles. US 20 to Three Creek Lake Road #1534; campground is located at outlet of Three Creek Lake.

SCOUT LAKE (Deschutes National Forest)
6 units, 7 group sites, trailers to 22', reservations required - (503)549-2111, piped water, lake - no motors, boating, swimming, fishing, hiking, elev. 4000', $$-$$$.
West of Sisters. US 20 13 miles northwest, FSR 2070 1.0 mile southwest, FSR 2066 .5 mile south.

SISTERS KOA (Private)
57 campsites, 18 w/hookups for water/electricity/sewer, 24 w/hookups for water & electricity, plus 15 tent units, reservations - (503)549-3021, showers, laundry, groceries, trailer waste disposal, pond, swimming, fishing, mini-golf, playfield, playground, elev. 3200', $$$.
Southeast of Sisters. US 20 4.0 miles southeast.

SOUTH SHORE (Deschutes National Forest)
31 units, 8 group sites, trailers to 22', piped water, on Suttle Lake - speed limits, boat launch, boating, swimming, fishing, water skiing, hiking trails, elev. 3400', $$.
Northwest of Sisters. US 20 13.0 miles northwest, FSR 2070 1.5 miles northwest.

SUTTLE LAKE (Deschutes National Forest)
7 tent units, picnic area, community kitchen, flush toilets, boat launch, boating, fishing, swimming, water skiing, hiking, elev. 3400', $$.
Northwest of Sisters 14 miles. US 20 to Suttle Lake Area. Campground is at east end of lake.

WEST INDIAN FORD (Deschutes National Forest)
16 units, some trailers, stream, hiking, elev. 3200', $.
Northwest of Sisters. US 20 5 miles northwest to campground.

SPRAY

BULL PRAIRIE (Umatilla National Forest)
25 units, trailers to 32', piped water, trailer waste disposal, lake - no motors, bicycling, elev. 4900', $.
Northeast of Spray. State 19 2.5 miles east, State 207 12.0 miles north, FSR 2039 3.0 miles northeast, FSR 30 .5 mile southeast.

SPRINGFIELD

CHALET VILLAGE ANNEX (Private)
24 trailer sites w/hookups for water/electricity/sewer, no tents, reservation information - (503)747-8311, showers, laundry, groceries, $$$.
East of Springfield. I-5 to exit #194, State 126 7.0 miles east, Main Street west 1 block to 54th Street.

SUTHERLIN

TYEE (BLM)
9 units, water, swimming, elev. 200', $.
Northwest of Sutherlin. State 138 northwest 12.0 miles to Bullock Bridge, CR 57 north .5 mile to campground.

SWEET HOME

CAMP SHERWOOD (Private)
16 campsites, 8 w/hookups for water/electricity/sewer, plus 8 tent units, reservation information - (503)367-6284, showers, $$-$$$.
In Sweet Home. US 20 3.0 miles east, 40th Avenue 1 block north.

CASCADIA (Oregon State Park)
26 primitive sites, some trailers to 35', group picnic area, wheelchair access, fishing, hiking trails, $$.
East of Sweet Home. US 20 14.0 miles east to campground.

DIAMOND HILL RV PARK & CAMPGROUND (Private)
85 campsites, 16 w/hookups for water/electricity/sewer, 24 w/hookups for water & electricity, plus 45 w/hookups for water, reservations - (503)995-8050, showers, laundry, groceries, swimming pool, playground, trailer waste disposal, $$-$$$.
Southwest of Sweet Home. State 228 19.0 miles east to I-5, south 8.0 miles to exit #209, campground is west 1 block. (Also accessible from Harrisburg; located 5.0 miles east.)

FERNVIEW (Willamette National Forest)
11 units, trailers to 18', well, river, wheelchair access, swimming, fishing, trails, elev. 1400', $.
East of Sweet Home. US 20 23.5 miles east.

HOUSE ROCK (Willamette National Forest)
17 tent units, picnic area, well, wheelchair access, river, swimming, fishing, hiking, located in virgin old growth Douglas Fir, elev. 1600', $$.
East of Sweet Home. US 20 26.5 miles east, FSR 2044 .1 mile southeast.

LOST PRAIRIE (Willamette National Forest)
10 units, trailers to 22', well, stream, wheelchair access, historic site, hiking, elev. 3300', $$.
East of Sweet Home. US 20 39.2 miles east.

SUNNYSIDE PARK/FOSTER RESERVOIR (Linn County)
137 campsites, 63 w/hookups for water & electricity, plus 74 tent units, picnic area, showers, trailer waste disposal, lake, beach, fishing, boat launch, wheelchair access, playfield, moorage w/handicap dock, $$.
East of Sweet Home. US 20 3.0 miles east to Green Peter Dam exit, proceed north to park.

TROUT CREEK (Willamette National Forest)
24 units, trailers to 22', well, wheelchair access, swimming, fishing, trailhead to wilderness near campground, elev. 1300', $$.
East of Sweet Home. US 20 18.7 miles east.

WHITCOMB CREEK (Linn County)
34 campsites, drinking water, lake, swimming, fishing, boat launch, hiking, $.
East of Sweet Home. US 20 3.0 miles east to Green Peter Dam exit, north 9.0 miles to park.

YELLOWBOTTOM (BLM)
23 units, trailers okay, picnic area, drinking water, swimming, fishing, nature study, elev. 1500', $.
Northeast of Sweet Home. State 20 3.0 miles east to Foster; campground is 26.0 miles northeast of Foster, go past the reservoir and follow the Quartzville Road to camp.

YUKWAH (Willamette National Forest)
20 units, trailers to 32', well, river, wheelchair access, swimming, fishing, nature trail, elev. 1300', $$.
East of Sweet Home. US 20 19.3 miles east.

TALENT

HOLIDAY RV PARK (Private)
110 trailer sites w/hookups for water/electricity/sewer, no tents, reservation information - (503)535-2183, showers, laundry, groceries, swimming pool, stream, playfield, wheelchair access, $$$.
Northwest of Talent. Located on west side of I-5 at exit #24

THE DALLES

BOB'S BUDGET RV & TRAILER PARK (Private)
20 trailer sites w/hookups for water/electricity/sewer, reservations - (503)739-2829, showers, laundry, $$.
East of The Dalles. I-84 24.0 miles east to Rufus exit #109, Old Highway 30 .5 mile west, Wallace Street .2 mile south.

DESCHUTES RIVER (Oregon State Park)
34 primitive campsites, trailers to 30', fishing, hiking trails, Oregon Trail display, $.
East of The Dalles. I-84 17.0 miles east to campground.

LEPAGE PARK (Corps)
10 campsites, reservation information - (503)296-1181, showers, trailer waste disposal, on John Day River, swimming, fishing, boat launch, $$.
East of The Dalles. I-84 28.0 miles east to exit #104, follow signs .2 mile to park; located 4.0 miles east of Rufus.

LONE PINE RV PARK (Private)
22 trailer sites w/hookups for water/electricity/sewer, reservation information - (503)296-9133, showers, laundry, river, fishing, playground, $$$.
At The Dalles. I-84 to exit #87, located near north end of overpass.

MEMALOOSE (Oregon State Park)
110 campsites, 43 w/hookups for water/electricity/sewer, plus 67 tent units, trailers to 60', wheelchair access, showers, trailer waste disposal, $$-$$$.
West of The Dalles. I-84 11.0 miles west to campground; this campground is only accessible from I-84 westbound.

TIDEWATER

BLACKBERRY (Siuslaw National Forest)
31 group sites, trailers to 32', picnic area, piped water, along Alsea River, flush toilets, boat launch, boating, swimming, fishing, elev. 100', $.
Southeast of Tidewater. State 34 6.0 miles southeast.

SLIDE (Siuslaw National Forest)
6 tent units, well, stream, fishing, elev. 100', $.
Southeast of Tidewater. State 34 5.0 miles southeast.

RIVEREDGE (Siuslaw National Forest)
1 group shelter, reservations required (503)487-5811, piped water, stream, wheelchair access includes trail, boat launch, boating, swimming, fishing, hiking, elev. 200', $$.
Southeast of Tidewater. State 34 11.0 miles southeast.

TILLAMOOK

BAY SHORE TRAILER PARK (Private)
64 campsites, 49 w/hookups for water/electricity/sewer, 5 w/hookups for water & electricity, plus 10 tent units, trailer to 35', reservation information -(503)842-7774, showers, laundry, ice, ocean access, stream, fishing, boat launch, boat rental, $$-$$$.
West of Tillamook. Netarts Highway 6.0 miles west, Bilyeu Ave. .3 mile.

BIG SPRUCE TRAILER PARK (Private)
23 trailer sites w/hookups for water/electricity/sewer, no tents, trailers to 35', reservation information - (503)842-7443, showers, laundry, ocean access, stream, swimming, fishing, boat launch, $$.
West of Tillamook. Netarts Highway 6.5 miles west.

CAPE LOOKOUT (Oregon State Park)
250 campsites, 53 w/hookups for water/electricity/sewer, plus 197 tent units, trailers to 62', group campsites, mail reservations available, picnic area, wheelchair access, showers, trailer waste disposal, hiking trail, ocean beach, beachcombing, fishing, $-$$$.
Southwest of Tillamook. Leave US 101 at Tillamook and head southwest 12.0 miles to campground.

HAPPY CAMP (Private)
36 trailer sites w/hookups for water & electricity, no tents, reservations -(503)842-4012, playfield, trailer waste disposal, ocean access, swimming, fishing, boat launch, boat rental, $$.
West of Tillamook. Netarts Highway 7.0 miles west.

JETTY FISHERY (Private)
30 campsites, 15 w/hookups for water & electricity, plus 15 tent units, reservation information - (503)368-5746, groceries, ocean access, river, swimming, fishing, boat launch, boat rental, $$.
North of Tillamook. US 101 18.0 miles north.

KILCHIS RIVER PARK (Tillamook County)
40 campsites, trailer waste disposal, river, swimming, fishing, boat launch, playfield, playground, hiking, $$.
Northeast of Tillamook. US 101 .5 mile north of Tillamook Cheese Factory, Kilchis River road 7.0 miles northeast.

PACIFIC CAMPGROUND (Private)
75 campsites, 28 w/hookups for water/electricity/sewer, 4 w/hookups for water & electricity, 3 w/hookups for electricity, plus 30 tent units, reservations -(503)842-5201, showers, ice, $-$$.
North of Tillamook. US 101 2.0 miles north.

SHOREWOOD TRAVEL TRAILER VILLAGE (Private)
21 trailer sites, 6 w/hookups for water/electricity/sewer, plus 15 w/hookups for water & electricity, no tents, reservation information - (503)355-2278, showers, laundry, ice, trailer waste disposal, ocean access, swimming, fishing, playground, $$-$$$.
North of Tillamook. US 101 12.7 miles north, southwest 3 blocks at Shorewood sign.

TILLAMOOK KOA (Private)
85 campsites, 13 w/hookups for water/electricity/sewer, 65 w/hookups for water & electricity, 5 w/hookups for water, plus 2 tent units, reservations -(503)842-4779, showers, laundry, groceries, playground, trailer waste disposal, river, fishing, hiking, $$$.
South of Tillamook. US 101 6.0 miles south.

TOLLGATE

ALPINE SPRING (Umatilla National Forest)
3 tent units, no trailers, river, hiking, elev. 5000', $.
Southeast of Tollgate 7 miles. State 204 to Balloon Tree Road N30, follow this to campground.

BEAR CANYON (Umatilla National Forest)
6 tent units, river, fishing, berry picking, hiking, elev. 4900', $.
East of Tollgate 26 miles. State 204 to Eden Road N50, follow this to campground.

DEDUCK SPRINGS (Umatilla National Forest)
1 tent unit, picnic area, river, hiking, elev. 5600', $.
Northeast of Tollgate 23 miles. State 204 to Tiger Creek Road N-62, follow this to campground.

DUSTY SPRING (Umatilla National Forest)
5 tent units, piped water, picnic area, hiking, berry picking, elev. 5100', $.
East of Tollgate 9 miles. State 204 to Kendall-Skyline Road N910, follow this to campground.

INDIAN (Umatilla National Forest)
2 tent units, no trailers, picnic area, river, hiking, elev. 5800', $.
Northeast of Tollgate 27 miles. State 204 to Kendall-Skyline Road N910, follow this to campground.

LUGER SPRING (Umatilla National Forest)
5 units, some trailers, piped water, picnic area, hiking, elev. 5000', $.
East of Tollgate 17 miles. State 204 to Mottet Meadows Road N40, follow this to campground.

SQUAW SPRINGS (Umatilla National Forest)
3 tent units, no trailers, elev. 4900', $.
South of Tollgate 12 miles. State 204 to Summit Road N31, follow this to campground.

SQUAW SPRINGS (Umatilla National Forest)
10 units, some trailers, picnic area, hiking, elev. 5000', $.
Northeast of Tollgate 20 miles. State 204 to Kendall-Skyline Road N910, follow this to campground.

TIMOTHY SPRING (Umatilla National Forest)
8 units, some trailers, piped water, picnic area, hiking, berry picking, elev. 4600', $.
Northeast of Tollgate 17 miles. State 204 to Timothy Spring Road N534, follow this to campground.

TROY

ELK FLATS (Umatilla National Forest)
3 tent units, river, hiking, elev. 5000', $.
West of Troy 21 miles. State 204 to Eden Road N50, follow this to campground.

MOSIER SPRING (Umatilla National Forest)
4 units, some trailers, piped water, picnic area, hiking, berry picking, elev. 4700', $.
West of Troy 16 miles. State 204 to Eden Road N50, follow this to campground.

TYGH VALLEY

BEAVERTAIL (BLM)
21 units, trailers okay, drinking water, boating, hiking, geology, fishing, swimming, nature study, elev. 500', $.
Northeast of Tygh Valley. State 216 5.0 miles east to Sherar's Bridge, take Deschutes River Road north of Sherar's Bridge 12.0 miles to campground.

HUNT PARK/WASCO COUNTY FAIRGROUNDS (County)
150 trailer sites w/hookups for water & electricity, reservation information -(503)483-2288, showers, plaground, playfield, trailer waste disposal, stream, fishing, $-$$.
In Tygh Valley. Located on Fairground Road, 2.0 miles west of US 197.

MACKS CANYON (BLM)
16 units, trailers okay, picnic area, drinking water, boat launch, boating, hiking, geology, fishing, nature study, elev. 500', $.
Northeast of Tygh Valley. State 216 5.0 miles east to Sherar's Bridge, north to Deschutes River Road; campground is 20.0 miles north.

UKIAH

BEAR WALLOW CAMP (Umatilla National Forest)
5 units, trailers okay, elev. 4800', $.
Northeast of Ukiah. State 244 13.0 miles east, FSR 54 10.8 miles northwest to campground road, 1.0 miles southeast to campground.

BIG CREEK (Umatilla National Forest)
4 units, some trailers, fishing, hiking, elev. 5200', $.
Southeast of Ukiah 23 miles. State 244 to Ukiah-Granite Road S522, follow this to campground.

DIVIDE WELL (Umatilla National Forest)
5 units, some trailers, elev. 4500', $.
West of Ukiah 17 miles. US 395 south to Jones Prairie Road N415, follow this to campground.

DRIFT FENCE (Umatilla National Forest)
4 units, some trailers, elev. 4300', $.
Southeast of Ukiah 8 miles. State 244 to Ukiah-Granite Road S522, follow this to campground.

FOUR CORNERS (Umatilla National Forest)
4 tent units, picnic area, fishing, elev. 4300', $.
Northeast of Ukiah. State 244 19.1 miles northeast.

UKIAH-DALE FOREST (Oregon State Park)
25 primitive campsites, trailers to 25', fishing, $.
Southwest of Ukiah. US 395 3.0 miles southwest to campground.

UNION

CATHERINE CREEK (Oregon State Park)
10 primitive campsites, trailers to 30', picnic area, wheelchair access, fishing, $.
Southeast of Union. State 203 8.0 miles southeast to campground.

UNITY

UNITY LAKE (Oregon State Park)
21 campsites, 15 w/hookups for electricity, plus 6 tent units, trailers to 60', picnic area, wheelchair access, showers, trailer waste disposal, boat launch, swimming, fishing, $$.
Northwest of Unity. Campground is located approximately 2.5 miles northwest of Unity, off US 26.

UNITY MOTEL & TRAILER PARK (Private)
10 trailer sites w/hookups for water/electricity/sewer, reservation information - (503)446-3431, showers, laundry, trailer waste disposal, elev. 4000', $$.
In Unity. US 26 to east end of town.

VALE

BULLY CREEK RESERVOIR (Malheur County)
29 campsites w/hookups for electricity, reservation information - (503)473-2022, showers, trailer waste disposal, lake, swimming, fishing, boat launch, $-$$.
West of Vale. Graham Road 9.0 miles west.

LAKE OWYHEE (Oregon State Park)
40 campsites, 10 w/hookups for electricity, plus 30 tent units, trailers to 55', picnic area, showers, trailer waste disposal, boat launch, fishing, $$.
South of Vale. Head south out of Vale on the road to Lake Owyhee State Park, it's approximately 41.0 miles. This campground is also accessible from Ontario.

LAKE OWYHEE RESORT (Private)
100 campsites, 50 w/hookups for water/electricity/sewer, 16 w/hookups for water & electricity, plus 34 tent units, trailers to 35', reservations - (503)372-2444, groceries, lounge, lake, swimming, fishing, boat launch, boat rental, $$.
South of Vale. Head south out of Vale on the road to Lake Owyhee State Park, it's approximately 38.0 miles. Also accessible from Ontario.

ONTARIO RV PARK (Private)
36 campsites, reservation information - (503)889-7868, $$.
Northeast of Vale. US 20 12.0 miles east, State 201 6.0 miles northeast, SE 13th Street .2 mile south, SE 5th Avenue .3 mile west, Access Drive .3 mile south, located at 925 Access Drive in Ontario.

PROSPECTOR TRAVEL TRAILER PARK (Private)
34 campsites, 24 w/hookups for water/electricity/sewer, 4 w/hookups for water & electricity, plus 6 w/hookups for electricity, reservation information -(503)473-3879, showers, laundry, ice, trailer waste disposal, $$.
In Vale. At US 20/26 junction take US 26 .1 mile north to Hope Street, park is 1 block east.

SUCCOR CREEK (Oregon State Park)
19 primitive campsites, picnic area, hiking trails, colorful rock formations, $.
Southeast of Vale. Head south out of Vale on the road to Lake Owyhee State Park, after about 15.0 miles head east 2.0 miles to State 201, follow this 13.0 miles south to Succor Creek State Recreation Area road. Follow this southwest; you will reach the campground after 16.5 miles.

WESTERNER MOTOR HOME PARK (Private)
15 campsites, 10 w/hookups for water/electricity/sewer, plus 5 w/out hookups, reservation information - (503)473-3947, showers, laundry, trailer waste disposal, river, swimming, fishing, $$.
In Vale. Located at junction of US 20 & US 26.

VERNONIA

ANDERSON PARK (Columbia County)
24 campsites, 16 w/hookups for water/electricity/sewer, plus 8 w/hookups for water, trailer waste disposal, river, fishing, playfield, playground, $-$$.
In Vernonia. Located 2 blocks east of State 47 on Jefferson.

BIG EDDY (Columbia County)
40 campsites, 10 w/hookups for water & electricity, 10 w/hookups for electricity, plus 20 tent units, river, fishing, boat launch, playground, $.
North of Vernonia. State 47 8.0 miles north.

WALDPORT

ALSEA BAY TRAILER PARK (Private)
15 trailer sites w/hookups for water/electricity/sewer, reservation information - (503)563-2250, showers, river, swimming, fishing, hiking, $$$.
In Waldport. US 101 .5 mile north, located at northern end of bridge.

BEACHSIDE (Oregon State Park)
80 campsites, 20 w/hookups for electricity, plus 60 tent units, mail reservations available, trailers to 30', picnic area, showers, ocean access, beachcombing, fishing, $$.
South of Waldport. US 101 4.0 miles south to campground.

CHINOOK TRAILER PARK (Private)
15 trailer sites w/hookups for water/electricity/sewer, adults only, no tents, reservation information - (503)563-3485, showers, laundry, river, fishing, $$$.
East of Waldport. State 34 east 3.3 miles.

DRIFT CREEK LANDING (Private)
60 trailer sites, 52 w/hookups for water/electricity/sewer, plus 8 w/hookups for water & electricity, no tents, reservation information - (503)563-3610, showers, laundry, river, fishing, boat launch, boat rental, $$-$$$.
East of Waldport. State 34 3.7 miles east.

FISHIN' HOLE PARK & MARINA (Private)
21 campsites, 10 w/hookups for water/electricity/sewer, plus 11 w/hookups for water & electricity, reservation information - (503)563-3401, showers, laundry, river, fishing, boat launch, boat rental, $$-$$$.
East of Waldport. State 34 3.8 miles east.

HANDY HAVEN RV PARK (Private)
11 trailer sites w/hookups for water/electricity/sewer, no tents, reservation information - (503)563-4286, showers, laundry, groceries, trailer waste disposal, $$$.
In Waldport. Near city center, just east of US 101.

HAPPY LANDING RV PARK & MARINA (Private)
29 campsites, 17 w/hookups for water/electricity/sewer, plus 12 w/hookups for water & electricity, reservation information - (503)528-3300, showers, laundry, river, fishing, boat launch, boat rental, $$$.
East of Waldport. State 34 7.0 miles east.

KING SILVER TRAILER PARK (Private)
28 campsites, 14 w/hookups for water/electricity/sewer, 9 w/hookups for water & electricity, plus 5 tent units, trailers to 35', reservation information -(503)563-3502, ice, trailer waste disposal, river, fishing, boat launch, boat rental, $$-$$$.
East of Waldport. State 34 3.6 miles east.

KOZY KOVE MARINA & RV PARK (Private)
26 campsites, 8 w/hookups for water/electricity/sewer, plus 18 w/hookups for water & electricity, reservation information (503)528-3251, showers, laundry, groceries, trailer waste disposal, river, fishing, boat launch, boat rental, $$-$$$.
East of Waldport. State 34 9.5 miles east.

OAKLAND'S FISH CAMP (Private)
17 trailer sites w/hookups for water/electricity/sewer, trailers to 35', adults only, no tents, reservation information - (503)563-2122, laundry, river, fishing, boat launch, boat rental, $$.
East of Waldport. State 34 4.1 miles east.

SEAL ROCKS TRAILER COVE (Private)
44 campsites, 30 w/hookups for water/electricity/sewer, plus 14 w/hookups for electricity, trailers to 35', no pets, no tents, reservations - (503)563-3955, showers, trailer waste disposal, ocean access, swimming, fishing, $$-$$$.
North of Waldport. US 101 4.8 miles north, near Seal Rock.

TAYLORS LANDING (Private)
27 campsites, 21 w/hookups for water/electricity/sewer, plus 6 w/hookups for water & electricity, reservation information - (503)528-3388, showers, laundry, river, fishing, boat launch, boat rental, hiking, $$-$$$.
East of Waldport. State 34 7.2 miles east.

TILLICUM BEACH (Siuslaw National Forest)
57 units, trailers to 32', piped water, flush toilets, wheelchair access includes trail, ocean view campsites on shore of Pacific Ocean, fishing, elev. 100', $$.
South of Waldport. US 101 4.7 miles south.

WAMIC

CASCADE HYLANDS RESORT (Private)
120 campsites, 38 w/hookups for water/electricity/sewer, 62 w/hookups for water & electricity, plus 20 tent units, reservations - (503)544-2271, showers, laundry, groceries, trailer waste disposal, lake, swimming, fishing, boat launch, boat rental, restaurant/lounge, $$-$$$.
Northwest of Wamic. Pine Hollow Reservoir Road 3.5 miles northwest.

ROCK CREEK RESERVOIR (Mt. Hood National Forest)
33 units, trailers to 32', piped water, lake - no motors, wheelchair access, boating, fishing, elev. 2200', $$.
West of Wamic. CR 226 6.0 miles west, FSR 48 1.2 miles southwest, FSR 4820 .2 mile west, FSR 120 .2 mile north.

WARM SPRINGS

KAH-NEE-TA (Private)
80 trailer sites, 30 w/hookups for water/electricity/sewer, plus 50 w/out hookups, no tents, reservation information - (503)553-1112, showers, laundry, ice, trailer waste disposal, swimming pool, therapy pool, river, fishing boat rental, lounge, tennis, golf, mini-golf, playground, hiking, $$-$$$.
North of Warm Springs. Take Kah-Nee-Ta Road 11.0 miles north.

TROUT CREEK (BLM)
15 campsites, boating, elev. 1100', $.
Northeast of Warm Springs 10.0 miles on east bank of Deschutes River.

WELCHES

GREEN CANYON (Mt. Hood National Forest)
15 units, trailers to 32', piped water, on Salmon River, wheelchair access, fishing, hiking, elev. 1600', $$.
South of Welches. US 26 1.0 mile east, FSR 2168 4.6 miles south. Near Zigzag.

McNEIL (Mt. Hood National Forest)
34 units, trailers to 32', piped water, near Sandy River, fishing, bicycling, elev. 2000', $.
Northeast of Welches. US 26 1.0 mile east, CR 18 4.8 miles northeast, FSR 17 .8 mile east, FSR 1825 .2 mile east.

RILEY (Mt. Hood National Forest)
14 units, trailers to 22', piped water, stream, horse unloading & hitchracks, nearby horse trails, fishing, hiking, elev. 2100', $.
Northeast of Welches. US 26 1.0 mile east, CR 18 4.8 miles northeast, FSR 1825 1.2 miles east, FSR 382 .1 mile southeast.

RV WONDERLAND PRESERVE (Private)
755 campsites w/hookups for water/electricity/sewer, group campsites, reservation information - (503)622-4003, showers, laundry, groceries, hot tubs, trailer waste disposal, nearby golf & tennis, fishing, hiking, $$$.
West of Welches. US 26 west 2.0 miles.

WESTFIR

KIAHANIE (Willamette National Forest)
20 units, trailers to 18', river, fly fishing only, elev. 2200', $$.
Northeast of Westfir. FSR 19 19.3 miles northeast.

WESTON

BONE SPRING (Umatilla National Forest)
9 tent units, piped water, picnic area, elev. 5600', $.
East of Weston. State 204 17.5 miles east, FSR 64 2.1 miles east, FSR 20 .8 mile northeast, FSR 6403 11.1 miles northeast.

TARGET MEADOWS (Umatilla National Forest)
20 units, trailers to 22', picnic area, piped water, elev. 5100', $.
East of Weston. State 204 17.5 miles east, FSR 64 .3 mile east, FSR 6401 2.2 miles north, FSR 50 .7 mile northeast.

VILLADOM MOBILE HOME PARK (Private)
11 trailer sites w/hookups for water/electricity/sewer, no tents, reservation information - (503)938-7247, showers, laundry, groceries, swimming pool, $$.
North of Weston. State 11 10.0 miles north, located at junction with Crockett Road.

WOODWARD (Umatilla National Forest)
26 units, trailers to 22', picnic area, piped water, lake, elev. 5100', $.
East of Weston. State 204 17.5 miles east.

WHITE CITY

BOB'S RV PARK (Private)
37 campsites, 29 w/hookups for water/electricity/sewer, plus 8 w/hookups for water & electricity, reservation information - (503)878-2400, showers, laundry, river, fishing, boat launch, playfield, playground, hiking, $$.
Northeast of White City. State 62 19.0 miles northeast.

DOE POINT (Rogue River National Forest)
25 units, trailers to 22', piped water, lake - speed limits, flush toilets, boating, swimming, fishing, hiking, bicycling, elev. 4600', $$.
East of White City. State 140 28.2 miles southeast; on Fish Lake.

FISH LAKE (Rogue River National Forest)
17 units, trailers to 22', piped water, lake - speed limits, flush toilets, boat launch, boating, swimming, fishing, hiking, elev. 4600', $$.
East of White City. State 140 29.7 miles east; on Fish Lake.

FISH LAKE RESORT (Private)
60 trailer sites, 45 w/hookups for water/electricity/sewer, plus 15 w/out hookups, reservations - (503)949-8500, showers, laundry, groceries, fishing supplies, cafe, complete game room, trailer waste disposal, on Fish Lake, swimming, fishing, boat launch, boat rental, hiking, elev. 4600', $$.
East of White City. State 140 east 30.0 miles.

FLY-CASTERS (Private)
30 trailer sites w/hookups for water/electricity/sewer, reservations - (503)878-2749, showers, river, swimming, fishing, nearby boat launch, $$.
Northeast of White City. State 62 13.0 miles northeast, located near Rogue River bridge at milepost #20.

JOSEPH P. STEWART (Oregon State Park)
201 campsites, 151 w/hookups for electricity, plus 50 tent units, group campsites, trailers to 40', picnic area, wheelchair access, trailer waste disposal, boat launch, marina, fishing, swimming, 8 miles of hiking/bike trails, access to Upper Rogue River Trail & Pacific Crest Trail, bicycle path, $$-$$$.
Northeast of White City. State 62 25.0 miles northeast to campground.

MEDFORD OAKS CAMPARK (Private)
80 campsites, 20 w/hookups for water/electricity/sewer, 37 w/hookups for water & electricity, plus 23 tent units, reservations - (503)826-5103, showers, laundry, groceries, trailer waste disposal, swimming pool, pond, fishing, playfield, playground, $$-$$$.
East of White City. State 140 6.8 miles east.

ROGUE ELK CAMPGROUND (Jackson County)
31 campsites, trailers okay, reservation information - (503)776-7001, showers, trailer waste disposal, river, swimming, fishing, boat launch, playground, hiking, $$.
Northeast of White City. State 62 18.0 miles northeast.

SHADY TRAILS (Private)
50 campsites, 20 w/hookups for water/electricity/sewer, plus 30 w/hookups for water & electricity, reservations - (503)878-2206, showers, groceries, trailer waste disposal, river, fishing, boat launch, playground, $$-$$$.
Northeast of White City. State 62 16.0 miles northeast.

YACHATS

CAPE PERPETUA (Siuslaw National Forest)
37 units, 1 group site, reservations required (503)563-3211, trailers to 22',
piped water, stream, flush toilets, wheelchair access, trailer waste
disposal, interpretive services, fishing, hiking, Pacific Ocean access, elev.
100', $$-$$$.
South of Yachats. US 101 2.7 miles south.

ROCK CREEK (Siuslaw National Forest)
16 units, trailers to 22', piped water, flush toilets, fishing, Pacific Ocean access, elev. 100', $.
South of Yachats. US 101 10.0 miles south.

SEA PERCH RV PARK & CAMPGROUND (Private)
48 campsites, 21 w/hookups for water/electricity/sewer, plus 27 w/hookups
for water & electricity, tents okay, reservations - (503)547-3505, showers,
laundry, groceries, ocean access, swimming, fishing, $$-$$$.
South of Yachats. US 101 6.5 miles south.

WHERE TO FIND WASHINGTON'S IMPROVED CAMPGROUNDS

All campgrounds in this section are arranged alphabetically by city. The following map and area listings will help you to locate cities in your destination area. The page number is shown in parenthesis. This book should be used together with your state highway map. See page 13 for complete information on how to use this guide.

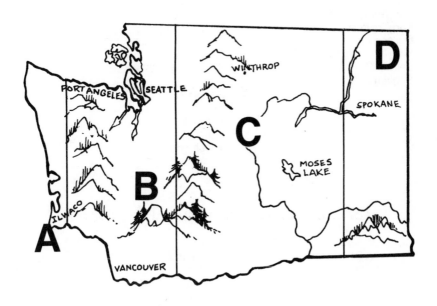

SECTION A – COASTAL TOWNS

North
Forks (138)
Queets (171)

South
Humptulips (144)
Ilwaco (144)
Long Beach (151)
Pacific Beach (164)
Quinault (172)
Raymond (173)
Westport (191)

SECTION B – I-5 & NEIGHBORING AREAS

North
Anacortes (115)
Blaine (117)
Brinnon (119)
Burlington (119)
Concrete (131)
Coupeville (133)
Darrington (135)
Eldon (136)
Everett (138)
Glacier (140)
Granite Falls (141)
Port Angeles (167)
Port Townsend (170)
Quilcene (171)
San Juan Islands (176)
Seattle (178)
Sequim (179)

South
Amboy (115)
Ashford (115)
Belfair (115)
Carson (121)
Castle Rock (122)
Chehalis (124)
Cook (133)
Cougar (133)
Elbe (136)
Enumclaw (137)
Hoodsport (143)
Kelso (147)
Montesano (153)
North Bend (160)
Olympia (161)
Packwood (165)
Puyallup (170)
Randle (172)
Shelton (180)
Tacoma (184)
Vancouver (188)
Yacolt (196)

SECTION C – CASCADES EAST/CENTRAL WASHINGTON

North
Chelan (124)
Conconully (129)
Curlew (134)
Entiat (136)
Index (146)
Leavenworth (149)
Loomis (152)
Marblemount (152)
Newhalem (159)
Okanogan (161)
Republic (174)
Skykomish (180)
Tonasket (184)
Twisp (187)
Wauconda (190)
Wilbur (192)
Winthrop (194)

South
Cle Elum (126)
Ellensburg (136)
Goldendale (141)
Moses Lake (154)
Naches (156)
Richland (175)
Trout Lake (186)
Wenatchee (190)
Yakima (197)

SECTION D – EASTERN WASHINGTON

North
Chewelah (125)
Colville (129)
Fort Spokane (140)
Hunters (144)
Ione (147)
Kettle Falls (148)
Metaline Falls (153)
Newport (159)
Orient (163)
Spokane (181)
Usk (188)

South
Asotin (115)
Colfax (128)
Dayton (135)
Pomeroy (166)

WASHINGTON CAMPGROUNDS

AMBOY

CANYON CREEK (Gifford Pinchot National Forest)
8 units, trailers to 18', picnic area, stream, fishing, elev. 1200', $.
East of Amboy. State 503 4.0 miles east, FSR 54 4.0 miles east, FSR 37 2.0 miles east.

JAKES CREEK SHELTER (Gifford Pinchot National Forest)
2 tent units, fishing, elev. 1400', $.
East of Amboy. State 503 4.0 miles east, FSR 54 4.0 miles east, FSR 37. 2.0 miles east.

ANACORTES

FERN HILL CAMPGROUND & RV PARK (Private)
102 campsites, 37 w/hookups for water/electricity/sewer, plus 65 w/out hookups, reservations - (206)293-5355, showers, laundry, ice, playfield, playground, trailer waste disposal, hiking, $$-$$$.
South of Anacortes. State 20 south to junction w/Oak Harbor, State 20 .8 mile west, Miller Road 1 block west.

WASHINGTON PARK (City of Anacortes)
79 campsites, 46 w/hookups for water & electricity, plus 33 tent units, showers, laundry, playfield, playground, trailer waste disposal, ocean access, swimming, fishing, boat launch, hiking, $$.
In Anacortes. State 20 to 12th Street, west 2.0 miles to Y, veer left .3 mile to park.

ASHFORD

BIG CREEK (Gifford Pinchot National Forest)
30 units, trailers to 22', piped water, stream, fishing, hiking, elev. 1800', $$.
Southeast of Ashford. State 706 2.3 miles east, County Road 1.4 miles south, FSR 5200 .5 mile east. Near Mt. Rainier National Park.

ASOTIN

FIELDS SPRING STATE PARK (State of Washington)
20 tent units, some trailers - no hookups, community kitchen/shelter, wheelchair access, trailer waste disposal, short hike up Puffer Butte for view of three states, birdwatching, wildflowers, winter sports, $$.
Southwest of Asotin. State 129 23.5 miles southwest to campground road.

BELFAIR

BELFAIR STATE PARK (State of Washington)
133 tent units, 47 trailer sites w/hookups for water/electricity/sewer, picnic shelter, trailer waste disposal, open play area, fishing, clamming, $$.
Southwest of Belfair. State 300 3.0 miles west to campground.

FAY BAINBRIDGE STATE PARK (State of Washington)
26 campsites w/hookups for water, picnic shelter, wheelchair access, trailer waste disposal, on Puget Sound, boat launch, scuba diving area, fishing, $$.
Northeast of Belfair. State 3 28.0 miles northeast, State 305 8.0 miles southwest to campground road, follow this to campground. Also accessible from Seattle via Winslow Ferry, then drive 5.0 miles.

FORBES LANDING (Private)
22 trailer sites w/hookups for water/electricity/sewer, reservation information - (206)638-2257, showers, groceries, ocean access, fishing, boat rental, $$-$$$.
Northeast of Belfair. State 3 north 35.0 miles, State 104 7.0 miles southeast, Hansville Road 7.0 miles north.

ILLAHEE STATE PARK (State of Washington)
25 tent units, some trailers - no hookups, group sites - reservations advised (206)478-4661, community kitchen/shelter, boat launch, pier fishing, $$-$$$.
Northeast of Belfair. State 3 12.0 miles northeast, State 304 3.0 miles east, State 303 2.0 miles north, State 306 2.0 miles east.

JARRELL COVE STATE PARK (State of Washington)
20 tent units, some trailers - no hookups, picnic shelter, wheelchair access, groceries nearby, fishing, $$.
Southwest of Belfair. State 3 17.0 miles southwest, park road 7.0 miles east and north.

KITSAP MEMORIAL STATE PARK (State of Washington)
43 tent units, some trailers - no hookups, group sites - reservations advised (206) 779-3205, community kitchen/shelter, trailer waste disposal, fishing, clamming, play fields, horseshoe pits, $$-$$$.
Northeast of Belfair. State 3 32.0 miles northeast.

MANCHESTER STATE PARK (State of Washington)
50 tent units, some trailers - no hookups, picnic shelter, wheelchair access, trailer waste disposal, historic buildings, scuba diving area, fishing, $$.
Northeast of Belfair. State 3 8.0 miles northeast, State 160 4.0 miles to Port Orchard, take the road around the point about 6.0 miles to park.

NORSELAND MOBILE ESTATES & RV PARK (Private)
21 trailer sites w/hookups for water/electricity/sewer, no tents, reservation information - (206)674-2874, showers, laundry, rec room, $$.
Northeast of Belfair. State 3 4.0 miles northeast.

PENROSE POINT STATE PARK (State of Washington)
83 tent units, some trailers - no hookups, group sites - reservations advised (206)884-2514, community kitchen, trailer waste disposal, on Carr Inlet in Puget Sound, fishing, clamming, nearby boat launch, $$-$$$.
South of Belfair. State 3 4.0 miles south, State 302 12.0 miles southeast, Longbranch road 7.0 miles south.

POINT BEACH RESORT (Private)
38 campsites w/hookup for water/electricity/sewer, trailers to 32', reservation information - (206)638-2233, showers, laundry, ice, ocean access, fishing, boat rental, $$-$$$.
Northeast of Belfair. State 3 35.0 miles north, State 104 7.0 miles southeast, Hansville Road 7.0 miles north.

R. F. KENNEDY (Dept. of Natural Resources)
8 campsites, picnic area, drinking water, boat launch, dock, $$.
South of Belfair. State 3 4.0 miles south, State 302 12.0 miles southeast,
Longbranch road approximately 5.0 miles south. Campground is located
2.0 miles northwest of Longbranch on Whiteman Cove.

ROBIN HOOD VILLAGE (Private)
14 trailer sites w/hookups for water & electricity, reservation information
-(206)898-2163, showers, laundry, ocean access, fishing, $$.
Southwest of Belfair. State 3 1.0 mile south, State 106 13.5 miles
southwest.

SCENIC BEACH STATE PARK (State of Washington)
50 tent units, some trailers - no hookups, community kitchen, wheelchair
access, trailer waste disposal, on Hood Canal, fishing, $$.
Northwest of Belfair. State 3 20.0 miles north, take road west to Scenic
Beach State Park.

SHERWOOD HILLS ADULT RV PARK (Private)
33 trailer sites w/hookups for water/electricity/sewer, adults only, reserva-
tion information - (206)275-3155, groceries, trailer waste disposal, lake,
fishing, $$$.
South of Belfair. State 3 2.2 miles south, located in Allyn near city center.

TWANOH STATE PARK (State of Washington)
30 tent units, 9 trailer sites w/hookups for water/electricity/sewer, group
sites - reservations advised (206)275-2222, community kitchen/shelter,
wheelchair access, on Hood Canal, boat launch, fishing, swimming, water
skiing, tennis court, horseshoe pits, groceries, $$-$$$.
West of Belfair. State 106 8.0 miles west.

BLAINE

BAYWOOD PARK (Private)
100 campsites w/hookups for water/electricity/sewer, reservation information -(206)371-7211, showers, laundry, lounge, playfield, playground,
trailer waste disposal, $$$.
West of Blaine. I-5 north to exit #270, Birch Bay-Lynden Road west 3.2
miles.

BIRCH BAY STATE PARK (State of Washington)
147 tent units, 20 trailer sites w/hookups for water & electricity, group sites
- reservations advised (206)366-5944, wheelchair access, picnic shelter,
trailer waste disposal, scuba diving area, fishing, birdwatching, hiking,
$$-$$$.
South of Blaine. Campground is located 8.0 miles south of Blaine along
water.

BIRCH BAY TRAILER PARK (Private)
290 trailer sites, 200 w/hookups for water/electricity/sewer, plus 90
w/hookups for water & electricity, reservation information - (206)371-7922,
showers, laundry, rec room, groceries, trailer waste disposal, ocean ac-
cess, swimming, fishing, $$$.
Southwest of Blaine. Leave I-5 at exit #270, Birch Bay-Lynden Road 4.0
miles west, south to 8080 Harborview Road.

EVERGREEN MANOR & RV PARK (Private)
16 trailer sites w/hookups for water/electricity/sewer, no tents, reservation information - (206)384-1241, laundry, $$$.
Southeast of Blaine. I-5 south to exit #266, Grandview east .5 mile, Enterprise Road .01 mile to park.

FERNDALE CAMPGROUND (Private)
23 trailer sites w/hookups for water/electricity/sewer, 22 w/hookups for water & electricity, 55 tent units, reservation information - (206)384-2622, showers, laundry, groceries, trailer waste disposal, pond, game room, playfield, playground, $$$.
Southeast of Blaine. I-5 to Ferndale exit #263, Portal Way north 1.0 mile.

HIDDEN VILLAGE RV PARK (Private)
63 campsites, 25 w/hookups for water/electricity/sewer, plus 38 w/hookups for water & electricity, reservation information - (206)398-1041, showers, laundry, rec room, trailer waste disposal, pond, fishing, $$$.
East of Blaine. Leave I-5 at exit #270, Birch Bay-Lynden Road east 10.0 miles to State 539, south 3.0 miles.

LYNDEN KOA (Private)
70 campsites, 45 w/hookups for water/electricity/sewer, plus 25 w/hookups for water & electricity, reservations - (206)354-4772, showers, laundry, groceries, playfield, playground, swimming pool, trailer waste disposal, pond, fishing, boat rental, mini-golf, $$$.
Southeast of Blaine. Leave I-5 at exit #256 on State 539, follow this north 13.0 miles to State 546, east 3.0 miles to Line Road, campground is about 1.5 miles south at 8717 Line Road in Lynden.

PLAZA RV & MOBILE HOME PARK (Private)
20 campsites, 10 w/hookups for water/electricity/sewer, 10 w/hookups for water & electricity, plus tenting area, reservations - (206)371-7822, showers, laundry, playfield, trailer waste disposal, $$-$$$.
Southwest of Blaine. Leave I-5 at exit #270, Birch Bay-Lynden Road 2.0 miles west.

SUMAS RV PARK (Private)
29 campsites, 16 w/hookups for water & electricity, plus 13 tent units, reservation information - (206)988-8875, wheelchair access, showers, rec room, trailer waste disposal, stream, fishing, $$-$$$.
East of Blaine. Leave I-5 at exit #270, Birch Bay-Lynden Road east 18.0 miles, State 9 north to Sumas, Cherry St. .01 mile.

SUNNY POINT RESORT (Private)
60 campsites, 24 w/hookups for water/electricity/sewer, 4 w/hookups for water & electricity, plus 32 tent units, reservation information - (206)945-1986, showers, ice, $$$.
Northwest of Blaine. I-5/State 99 17.0 miles north of US/Canada border, State 17 5.0 miles west, resort is 3.0 miles southwest at 1408 Gulf Road in Point Roberts.

WHALEN'S RV PARK (Private)
85 trailer sites w/hookups for water & electricity, reservation information -(206)945-2874, wheelchair access, showers, playfield, trailer waste disposal, ocean access, fishing, $$$.
Northwest of Blaine. I-5/State 99 17.0 miles north of US/Canda border, State 17 5.0 miles west, southwest 3.0 miles to Point Roberts, Roosevelt Road east 1.0 mile.

WINDMILL INN & TRAILER COURT (Private)
11 trailer sites, 8 w/hookups for water/electricity/sewer, plus 3 w/hookups for electricity, no tents, reservation information - (206)354-3424, showers, $$.
Southeast of Blaine. Leave I-5 at exit #256 on State 539, follow this north to Lynden; trailer court is located at Front Street.

BRINNON

COLLINS (Olympic National Forest)
14 units, trailers to 18', well, river, swimming, fishing, Duckabush Trailhead nearby, elev. 200', $.
West of Brinnon. US 101 2.0 miles south, FSR 2515 4.8 miles west.

COVE TRAILER PARK (Private)
35 trailer sites w/hookups for water/electricity/sewer, no tents, reservations -(206)796-4723, showers, laundry, groceries, trailer waste disposal, ocean access, fishing, $$.
North of Brinnon. US 101 3.0 miles north.

DOSEWALLIPS STATE PARK (State of Washington)
87 tent units, 40 trailer sites w/hookups for water/electricity/sewer, group sites - reservations advised (206)796-4415, wheelchair access, trailer waste disposal, access to Dosewallips River & Hood Canal, fishing, clamming, oyster gathering, $$-$$$.
South of Brinnon. Take US 101 1.0 miles south of Brinnon to campground.

ELKHORN (Olympic National Forest)
20 units, trailers to 22', well, river, swimming, fishing, hiking, elev. 600', $.
Northwest of Brinnon. US 101 1.0 mile north, FSR 261 10.0 miles west. Lake Constance Trailhead is 2 miles west of campground.

SEAL ROCK (Olympic National Forest)
35 units, trailers to 32', piped water, on Hood Canal, flush toilets, wheelchair access, boating, swimming, fishing, water skiing, elev. 100', $$.
North of Brinnon. US 101 2.0 miles north.

STEELHEAD (Olympic National Forest)
5 tent units, no trailers, well, picnic area, stream, fishing, hiking, elev. 600', $.
Northwest of Brinnon. US 101 1.0 mile north, FSR 261 8.5 miles west.

BURLINGTON

BAYVIEW STATE PARK (State of Washington)
90 tent units, 9 trailer sites w/hookups for water/electricity, sewer, community kitchen, on Padilla Bay, large children's play area, $$.
West of Burlington. State 20 west approximately 6.0 miles; campground is 1.3 miles north of highway.

BLANCHARD HILL/LILY & LIZARD LAKES (Dept. of Natural Resources)
9 campsites, trails for hikers & horses, horse facilities, $.
Northeast of Burlington. I-5 north to exit #240, Samish Lake Road .5 mile, Barrel Springs Road 1.0 mile, Road SW-C-100 1.5 miles to campground.

BURLINGTON/CASCADE KOA (Private)
87 campsites, 30 w/hookups for water/electricity/sewer, 25 w/hookups for water & electricity, 8 w/hookups for electricity, plus 24 tent units, reservations -(206)724-5511, wheelchair access, showers, laundry, groceries, indoor heated swimming pool, sauna, hot tubs, rec room, playfield, playground, trailer waste disposal, stream, fishing, $$$.
In Burlington. I-5 north to exit #232, Cook Road .2 mile east, Old Highway 99 north 3.5 miles.

CAMANO ISLAND STATE PARK (State of Washington)
87 tent units, some trailers - no hookups, group sites - reservations advised (206)387-3031, community kitchen/shelter, trailer waste disposal, boat launch, year-round saltwater fishing, clamming, scuba diving area, 5 mile nature trail, $$-$$$.
South of Burlington. I-5 17.0 miles south to Stanwood exit, west 10.0 miles to island, southwest 6.0 miles to campground.

CEDAR GROVE RESORT (Private)
26 campsites w/hookups for water/electricity/sewer, reservation information -(206)652-7083, showers, playfield, playground, lake, swimming, fishing, boat launch, boat rental, $$$.
South of Burlington. I-5 south to exit #206, Lakewood Road 5.0 miles west, 52nd Avenue NW .5 mile south.

HUTCHINSON CREEK (Dept. of Natural Resources)
15 campsites, creek, $.
Northeast of Burlington. State 20 6.5 miles east, State 9 16.0 miles north, campground is located 2.0 miles east of Acme off Mosquito Lake Road, on Hutchinson Creek.

JIM MARION'S LAKE MARTHA RV PARK (Private)
24 campsites w/hookups for water/electricity/sewer, plus 7 w/hookups for water & electricity, reservation information - (206)652-8412, showers, laundry, trailer waste disposal, swimming, fishing, boat launch, $$$.
South of Burlington. I-5 south to exit #206, 6.5 miles west on Lakewood Road, stay left at Y and follow 1.0 mile to park.

LAKE GOODWIN RESORT (Private)
85 campsites, 68 w/hookups for water/electricity/sewer, plus 17 w/hookups for water & electricity, reservation information - (206)652-8169, groceries, ice, playfield, playground, trailer waste disposal, lake, swimming, fishing, boat launch, boat rental, $$$.
South of Burlington. I-5 south to exit #206, Lakewood Road 5.0 miles west, located at 176th NW.

LARRABEE STATE PARK (State of Washington)
61 tent units, plus 26 sites w/hookups for water/electricity/sewer, group sites - reservations advised (206)676-2093, community kitchen/shelter, trailer waste disposal, on Samish Bay in Puget Sound, boat launch, fishing, tidal pools, hiking trails access two mountain lakes, $$-$$$.
Northwest of Burlington. State 11 14.0 miles northwest.

MOUNTAIN VIEW TRAILER PARK (Private)
14 trailer sites w/hookups for water/electricity/sewer, adults only, no tents, reservation information - (206)424-3775, showers, laundry, $$.
South of Burlington. I-5 south to exit #225, west to State 99S, north .01 mile.

RIVERBEND PARK (Private)
105 campsites, 75 w/hookups for water/electricity/sewer, plus 30 tent units, reservation information - (206)428-4044, wheelchair access, showers, laundry, ice, rec room, playground, trailer waste disposal, river, fishing, $$-$$$.
South of Burlington. I-5 south to exit #227, College Way west .01 mile, Freeway Drive .5 mile north to campground.

THE POTLATCH RV RESORT (Private)
73 trailer sites w/hookups for water/electricity/sewer, reservation information - (206)466-4468, wheelchair access, showers, laundry, ice, indoor heated swimming pool, spa, exercise room, rec room, lounge, trailer waste disposal, ocean access, fishing, nearby golf, $$$.
Southwest of LaConner. I-5 to exit #230, State 20 west 5.0 miles, LaConner/Whitney Road south 5.0 miles to LaConner, 3rd Street north to end and resort.

WALKER VALLEY ATV (Dept. of Natural Resources)
5 campsites, trails for hikers/horses/trailbikes/4-wheelers, $.
South of Burlington. State 20 5.5 miles east, State 9 7.5 miles south, campground is 2.5 miles east of Big Lake.

WENBERG STATE PARK (State of Washington)
65 tent units, 10 trailer sites w/hookups for water & electricity, picnic shelter, groceries, trailer waste disposal, on Lake Goodwin, boat launch, fishing, swimming, $$.
South of Burlington. I-5 17.0 miles south to Stanwood exit, west to Stanwood, south 6.0 miles, east 3.2 miles to Lake Goodwin and campground.

CARSON

BEAVER (Gifford Pinchot National Forest)
30 units, trailers to 22', group campsites, piped water, river, flush toilets, wheelchair access, swimming, fishing, mushroom hunting area, elev. 1100', $$-$$$.
Northwest of Carson. CR 92135 12.2 miles northwest to campground.

GOVERNMENT MINERAL SPRINGS (Gifford Pinchot National Forest)
44 units, trailers to 22', piped water, picnic area, flush toilets, fishing, elev. 1200', $$.
Northwest of Carson. CR 92135 13.2 miles northwest to campground.

LEWIS & CLARK CAMPGROUND/RV PARK (Private)
60 campsites, 20 w/hookups for water/electricity/sewer, plus 40 w/hookups for water & electricity, reservation information - (509)427-5559, showers, laundry, rec room, trailer waste disposal, river, fishing, hiking, $$$.
Southwest of Carson. State 14 west to milepost #37, park is located approximately 1.0 mile west of North Bonneville on Evergreen Drive.

PANTHER CREEK (Gifford Pinchot National Forest)
20 units, trailers to 22', well, stream, fishing, hiking, Pacific Crest Trail nearby, horse trails & loading ramp, elev. 1000', $-$$.
North of Carson. CR 92135 9.0 miles northwest, FSR 6517 1.5 miles east, FSR 65 .1 mile south.

PARADISE CREEK (Gifford Pinchot National Forest)
30 units, trailers to 32', well, river, wheelchair access, fishing, Lava Butte Trailhead, elev. 1500', $-$$.
North of Carson. CR 92135 13.8 miles northwest, FSR 30 6.3 miles north.

CASTLE ROCK

ANDERSON'S SILVER LAKE RESORT (Private)
35 campsites, 7 w/hookups for water/electricity/sewer, 14 w/hookups for water & electricity, plus 14 tent units, reservation information - (206)274-6141, showers, groceries, rec room, on Silver Lake, swimming, fishing, boat launch, boat rental, $$$.
East of Castle Rock. I-5 to exit #49, State 504 6.0 miles east.

BARRIER DAM CAMPGROUND (Private)
45 campsites, 26 w/hookups for water & electricity, plus 19 tent units, reservation information - (206)985-2495, showers, groceries, rec room, trailer waste disposal, river, fishing, $$.
Northeast of Castle Rock. I-5 to north to exit #68, State 12 east 14.0 miles, Fuller Road 1.0 mile south.

COWLITZ RESORT & RV PARK (Private)
50 campsites w/hookups for water/electricity/sewer, reservation information -(206)864-6611, showers, trailer waste disposal, on Cowlitz River, boat launch, fishing, $$.
Northeast of Castle Rock. I-5 north to exit #59, located at 162 Cowlitz Loop in Toledo.

ESTES RV PARK (Private)
21 trailer sites, 11 w/hookups for water/electricity/sewer, plus 10 w/hookups for water & electricity, reservation information - (206)864-2386, showers, laundry, groceries, rec room, playfield, trailer waste disposal, river, fishing, $$-$$$.
North of Castle Rock. I-5 north to exit #57, Frontage Road .3 mile to park.

FROST ROAD TRAILER PARK (Private)
25 trailer sites w/hookups for water/electricity/sewer, reservation information - (206)785-3616, showers, ice, rec room, lounge, playfield, trailer waste disposal, $$.
Northeast of Castle Rock. I-5 north to exit #63, east .8 mile, north 1.5 mile, west .5 mile to park.

HARMONY LAKESIDE RV PARK (Private)
65 campsites, 39 w/hookups for water/electricity/sewer, 12 w/hookups for water & electricity, plus 14 tent units, reservation information - (206)983-3804, wheelchair access, showers, ice, rec room, playfield, trailer waste disposal, lake, fishing, boat launch, $$.
Northeast of Castle Rock. I-5 north to exit #68, State 12 east 20.0 miles, Harmony Road 2.5 miles north.

LAKE MAYFIELD RESORT/RV PARK & MARINA (Private)
90 campsites, 8 w/hookups for water/electricity/sewer, 42 w/hookups for water & electricity, plus 40 tent units, reservation information - (206)985-2357, showers, groceries, playfield, on Lake Mayfield, swimming, fishing, boat launch, boat rental, hiking, $$-$$$.
Northeast of Castle Rock. I-5 north to exit #68, State 12 east 15.0 miles, Lake Bridge .3 mile, Winston Creek Road 1.0 mile south, Hadaller Road .5 mile west.

MAYFIELD LAKE COUNTY PARK (Lewis County)
54 campsites, reservation information - (206)985-2364, wheelchair access, showers, picnic shelter, playground, trailer waste disposal, lake, swimming, fishing, boat launch, hiking, $$$.
Northeast of Castle Rock. I-5 north to exit #68, State 12 east 17.0 miles, west at Dam .3 mile to park.

MERMAC RV PARK & STORE (Private)
10 trailer sites w/hookups for water/electricity/sewer, reservations - (206)274-6785, showers, groceries, $$.
North of Castle Rock. Leave I-5 just north of Castle Rock on exit #52, park is .6 mile.

RIVER OAKS RV PARK (Private)
53 campsites, 7 w/hookups for water/electricity/sewer, plus 46 w/hookups for water & electricity, reservation information - (206)864-2895, showers, laundry, groceries, playfield, trailer waste disposal, on Cowlitz River, fishing, boat launch, $$.
Northwest of Castle Rock. I-5 north to exit #59, State 506 .3 mile west.

SEAQUEST STATE PARK (State of Washington)
54 tent units, plus 16 trailer sites w/hookups for water/electricity/sewer, group sites - reservations advised (206)274-8633, community kitchen/shelter, trailer waste disposal, fishing, $$-$$$.
East of Castle Rock. Leave I-5 on exit #49, campground is 5.0 miles east of Castle Rock.

SCOTTS FRUIT STAND & RV PARK (Private)
50 campsites, 30 w/hookups for water/electricity/sewer, plus 20 w/out hookups, reservation information - (206)262-9220, wheelchair access, showers, laundry, groceries, sauna, stream, fishing, $$$.
Northeast of Castle Rock. I-5 to exit #68, US 12 .8 mile.

TOUTLE VILLAGE RESTAURANT & RV PARK (Private)
10 trailer sites w/hookups for water/electricity/sewer, reservation information - (206)274-7343, showers, laundry, ice, restaurant, rec room, trailer waste disposal, $$-$$$.
East of Castle Rock. I-5 to exit #49, State 504 10.0 miles east.

WINSTON CREEK (Dept. of Natural Resources)
10 campsites, wheelchair access, $$.
Northeast of Castle Rock. I-5 23.0 miles north, US 12 21.0 miles east to Mayfield Lake, campground is located 5.0 miles southeast of Mayfield Lake along Longbell County Road, on Winston Creek.

CHEHALIS

IKE KINSWA STATE PARK (State of Washington)
60 tent units, plus 41 trailer sites w/hookups for water/electricity/sewer, wheelchair access, snack bar, groceries, trailer waste disposal, boat launch, year-round fishing, swimming, horse trails, nearby fish hatcheries, $$.
Southeast of Chehalis. Take I-5 south 10.0 miles to US 12, head east approximately 10.5 miles and follow the signs leading north to Ike Kinswa State Park.

LEWIS & CLARK STATE PARK (State of Washington)
25 tent units, group sites - reservations advised (206)864-2643, community kitchen/shelter, interpretive center about Mt. St. Helens, nature trail, $$-$$$.
Southeast of Chehalis. Take I-5 south 10.0 miles to US 12, head east approximately 2.0 miles to Marys Corner, turn south to reach campground.

OFFUT LAKE RESORT & RV PARK (Private)
44 campsites, 33 w/hookups for water/electricity/sewer, plus 21 w/out hookups, reservation information - (206)264-2438, showers, laundry, groceries, rec room, playground, trailer waste disposal, lake, swimming, fishing, boat rental, $$-$$$.
Northeast of Chehalis. I-5 north to exit #99, 93rd Avenue east 3.0 miles, Old Highway 99 south 4.0 miles, Offut Lake Road east 1.0 mile, park is just north of here at 4005 120th Avenue SE, in Tenino.

RAINBOW FALLS STATE PARK (State of Washington)
47 tent units, group sites - reservations advised (206)291-3767, community kitchen, trailer waste disposal, swinging bridge over Chehalis River, nature trails through old-growth timber, play area, $$-$$$.
West of Chehalis. Take State 6 west from Chehalis approximately 18.0 miles, campground is near Doty.

STAN HEDWALL PARK (City of Chehalis)
29 campsites w/hookups for water & electricity, information - (206)748-0271, showers, playfield, playground, trailer waste disposal, river, swimming, fishing, hiking, $$.
In Chehalis. I-5 to exit #76, Rice Road .5 mile west.

TRAILER VILLAGE RV PARK (Private)
16 trailer sites w/hookups for water/electricity/sewer, no tents, pets okay, reservation information - (206)736-9260, showers, $$$.
North of Chehalis. I-5 north to Centralia exit #82, Harrison Street west .5 mile.

CHELAN

ALTA LAKE STATE PARK (State of Washington)
164 tent units, 16 trailer sites w/hookups for water & electricity, group sites - reservations advised (509)923-2473, community kitchen, wheelchair access, trailer waste disposal, fishing, swimming, trail, winter sports, $$-$$$.
North of Chelan. US 97 17.0 miles northeast, State 153 2.0 miles west, campground road south 2.0 miles.

BRIDGEPORT STATE PARK (State of Washington)
28 tent units, some trailers - no hookups, group sites - reservations advised (509)686-7231, community kitchen, trailer waste disposal, on Lake Rufus Woods, boat launch, fishing, golf nearby, $$-$$$.
Northeast of Chelan. US 97 29.0 miles northwest, State 17 6.5 miles south.

CITY OF CHELAN LAKESHORE RV PARK (City)
160 trailer sites, 151 w/hookups for water/electricity/sewer, plus 9 w/hookups for water & electricity, no tents, no dogs, information - (509)682-5031, showers, playground, trailer waste disposal, on Lake Chelan, swimming, fishing, tennis, mini-golf, $$$.
In Chelan. State 150 .1 mile northwest.

LAKE CHELAN STATE PARK (State of Washington)
127 tent units, 17 trailer sites w/hookups for water/electricity/sewer, wheelchair access, picnic shelter, on 55 mile long lake, snack bar, trailer waste disposal, boat launch, scuba diving area, fishing, swimming, water skiing, $$.
West of Chelan. Take road leading around southern side of Lake Chelan, campground is 9.0 miles west of city.

ROCK GARDEN RV PARK (Private)
20 campsites, 12 w/hookups for water/electricity/sewer, plus 8 w/hookups for water & electricity, reservation information - (509)686-5343, showers, laundry, trailer waste disposal, river, fishing, playfield, playground, $$.
Northeast of Chelan. US 97 24.0 miles northeast, State 173 9.5 miles southeast.

TWENTYFIVE MILE CREEK RESORT (Private)
95 campsites, 13 w/hookups for water/electricity/sewer, 15 w/hookups for water & electricity, plus 67 tent units, reservation information - (509)687-3610, wheelchair access, showers, groceries, swimming pool, trailer waste disposal, lake, swiming, fishing, boat launch, $$-$$$.
Southwest of Chelan. US 97 south to South Shore Road, resort is 19.0 miles west along south shore of Lake Chelan.

TWENTYFIVE MILE CREEK STATE PARK (State of Washington)
52 tent units, 33 trailer sites w/hookups for water/electricity/sewer, lake, boat launch & dock, swimming, $$.
Northwest of Chelan. Take road leading around southern side of Lake Chelan, campground is 18.0 miles northwest of city.

WATERFRONT MARINA (City of Bridgeport)
13 trailer sites w/hookups for water/electricity/sewer, playground, trailer waste disposal, river, fishing, boat launch, $$.
Northeast of Chelan. US 97 24.0 miles northeast, State 173 12.0 miles southeast to Bridgeport, located in town at Columbia Avenue & 7th Street.

CHEWELAH

FORTYNINER CAMPGROUND & MOTEL (Private)
28 campsites w/hookups for water/electricity/sewer, reservation information -(509)935-8613, showers, ice, indoor heated swimming pool, sauna, jacuzzi, rec room, trailer waste disposal, $$.
In Chewelah. Located on US 395 at south edge of town.

GRANITE POINT PARK (Private)
59 trailer sites, 53 w/hookups for water/electricity/sewer, 4 w/hookups for water & electricity, plus 2 w/out hookups, trailers to 35', no pets, no tents, reservation information - (509)233-2100, showers, laundry, groceries, rec room, playfield, playground, lake, swimming, fishing, boat launch, boat rental, $$$.
Southeast of Chewelah. US 395 southeast 17.5 miles, located about 1.5 miles south of Loon Lake.

SHORE ACRES RESORT (Private)
35 campsites, 17 w/hookups for water/electricity/sewer, 5 w/hookups for water & electricity, plus 13 tent units, trailers to 30', reservation information -(509)233-2474, showers, groceries, playground, trailer waste disposal, lake, swimming, fishing, boat launch, boat rental, $$.
South of Chewelah. US 395 southeast 16.0 miles, State 292 west 1.8 miles, Shore Acres Road south 1.8 miles.

SILVER BEACH RESORT (Private)
53 trailer sites, 33 w/hookups for water/electricity/sewer, 14 w/hookups for water & electricity, plus 6 w/hookups for electricity, trailers to 35', no tents, reservation information - (509)937-2811, showers, laundry, groceries, playground, trailer waste disposal, lake, swimming, fishing, boat launch, boat rental, $$$.
South of Chewelah. US 395 4.0 miles, State 231 2.0 miles south to Waitts Lake Road, west 3.0 miles.

STYMANS RESORT (Private)
30 trailer sites w/hookups for water/electricity/sewer, trailers to 35', reservation information - (509)233-2233, wheelchair access, showers, laundry, groceries, rec room, playground, trailer waste disposal, on Deer Lake, swimming, fishing, boat launch, boat rental, $$$.
Southeast of Chewelah. US 395 southeast 15.5 miles, Deer Lake Road east 2.0 miles.

CLE ELUM

BAKER (Wenatchee National Forest)
3 tent units, no trailers, fishing, hiking, elev. 2600', $.
Northeast of Cle Elum. US 97 12.0 miles east, US 97 4.0 miles north.

CLE ELUM RIVER (Wenatchee National Forest)
3 units, 20 group sites, trailers to 22', well, fishing, elev. 2200', $.
Northwest of Cle Elum. State 903 11.2 miles northwest, CR 903 7.0 miles northwest.

CRYSTAL SPRINGS (Wenatchee National Forest)
28 units, 2 group sites, trailers to 22', picnic area w/open-sided group picnic shelter, piped water, fishing, elev. 2400', $.
Northwest of Cle Elum. I-90 20.7 miles northwest, FSR 212 .4 mile northwest.

FRENCH CABIN CREEK (Wenatchee National Forest)
7 tent units, fishing, berry picking, elev. 2100', $.
North of Cle Elum 16 miles via State 903.

KACHESS (Wenatchee National Forest)
159 units, 23 group sites, trailers to 32', picnic area, piped water, flush toilets, groceries, gasoline, trailer waste disposal, lake, boat launch, boat rental, swimming, fishing, water skiing, hiking, bicycling, elev. 2300', $$.
Northwest of Cle Elum. I-90 20.7 miles northwest, FSR 49 5.4 miles northeast. Sometimes closed late in season due to low water.

LAKE EASTON STATE PARK (State of Washington)
91 tent units, 45 trailer sites w/hookups for water/electricity/sewer, group sites - reservations advised (509)656-2230, wheelchair access, trailer waste disposal, boat launch, fishing, swimming, winter sports, $$-$$$.
Northwest of Cle Elum. I-90 12.0 miles northwest, campground is located 1.0 mile west of Easton.

MINERAL SPRINGS (Wenatchee National Forest)
12 units, trailers to 22', piped water, stream, groceries, gasoline, showers, laundry, cafe/snack bar, fishing, elev. 2700', $$.
Northeast of Cle Elum. US 97 12.0 miles east, US 97 6.0 miles north.

PARK (Wenatchee National Forest)
3 tent units, no trailers, elev. 3000', $.
Northeast of Cle Elum. US 97 12.0 miles east, US 97 9.0 miles north, FSR 2208 .5 mile to campground.

RED TOP (Wenatchee National Forest)
3 tent units, no trailers - rough road, agate beds, horse trails, elev. 5100', $.
Northeast of Cle Elum. US 97 12.0 miles east, US 97 6.1 miles north, FSR 2106 approximately 10 miles to campground.

ROCKY RUN (Wenatchee National Forest)
18 tent units, picnic area, piped water, at Lake Keechelus, boat launch, fishing, water skiing, hiking, berry picking, elev. 2600', $$.
West of Cle Elum 29 miles via I-90, campground is located 5.0 miles east of Snoqualmie Pass.

RV TOWN INC. (Private)
72 trailer sites, 20 w/hookups for water/electricity/sewers, plus 52 w/hookups for water & electricity, reservation information - (509)656-2360, showers, laundry, groceries, rec room, playground, restaurant, swimming pool, trailer waste disposal, stream, fishing, $$-$$$.
Northwest of Cle Elum. I-90 west to exit #70; in Easton.

SALMON LA SAC (Wenatchee National Forest)
70 units, 14 group sites, trailers to 22', picnic area w/open-sided group picnic shelter, piped water, river, flush toilets, wheelchair access, swimming, fishing, hiking, trailhead to Cascade Crest Trail & Alpine Lakes Wilderness, elev. 2400', $-$$.
Northwest of Cle Elum. State 903 11.2 miles northwest, CR 903 10.7 miles northwest.

STAFFORD (Wenatchee National Forest)
10 units, some trailers, stream, fishing, elev. 2800', $.
Northeast of Cle Elum. US 97 12.0 miles east, US 97 approximately 9.8 miles north, FSR 2226 to campground.

SUN COUNTRY GOLF RESORT & RV PARK (Private)
23 trailer sites w/hookups for water/electricity/sewer, reservations - (509)674-2226, showers, rec room, on Yakima River, fishing, golf, $$. Northwest of Cle Elum. I-90 west to exit #78, .5 mile south to resort road, .5 mile south.

SWAUK (Wenatchee National Forest)
23 units, trailers to 22', picnic area, piped water, stream, flush toilets, fishing, hiking, elev. 3200', $$. Northeast of Cle Elum. US 97 12.0 miles east, US 97 10.0 miles north.

TANEUM (Wenatchee National Forest)
13 units, trailers to 22', picnic area, piped water, stream, wheelchair access, fishing, elev. 2400', $. Southeast of Cle Elum. I-90 12.0 miles southeast, CR 9123 3.0 miles south, CR 51 2.0 miles west, FSR 33 4.2 miles northwest.

TEANAWAY (Dept. of Natural Resources)
6 campsites, $. East of Cle Elum. Campground is 8.0 miles northwest of junction of Teanaway River Road and US 97.

TRAILER CORRAL RV PARK (Private)
30 campsites, 18 w/hookups for water/electricity/sewer, 6 w/hookups for water & electricity, plus 6 w/out hookups, reservations - (509)674-2433, showers, laundry, trailer waste disposal, $$. East of Cle Elum. I-90 east to exit #85, State 970 1.0 mile east.

WISH POOSH (Wenatchee National Forest)
10 units, 5 group sites, trailers to 22', picnic area, piped water, lake, flush toilets, groceries, gasoline, ice, boat launch, cafe-snack bar, boating, swimming, fishing, water skiing, elev. 2400', $$. Northwest of Cle Elum. State 903 10.2 miles northwest, FSR 112 .1 mile west. Sometimes closed late in season due to low water.

COLFAX

BOYER PARK & MARINA (Private)
28 campsites, 14 w/hookups for water/electricity/sewer, plus 14 w/hookups for water & electricity, reservations - (509)397-3208, showers, laundry, ice, restaurant, groceries, trailer waste disposal, on Snake River, swimming, fishing, boat launch, boat rental, $$. Southwest of Colfax. State 26 west to CR 8000, follow this to CR 8250, park is located 23.0 miles south of Colfax; on Little Goose Pool 2.0 miles downstream from Lower Granite Dam. (Follow any signs directing you to Marina, Almota, Snake River or Lower Granite Dam.)

CITY OF PULLMAN RV PARK (City)
24 trailer sites w/hookups for water/electricity/sewer, reservation information - (509)334-4555, swimming pool, playfield, playground, $$. Southeast of Colfax. US 195 13.0 miles southeast to Pullman, Grand 2 blocks northeast to Paradise Street, east to Spring Street where you will find signs directing you to City Playfield, park is at south end of Playfield.

COLVILLE

BEAVER LODGE RV PARK (Private)
34 campsites, 8 w/hookups for water/electricity/sewer, 4 w/hookups for water & electricity, plus 22 w/out hookups, tents okay, reservation information -(509)684-5657, showers, deli/snack bar, groceries, on Little Pend Oreille Lake, swimming, fishing, boat launch, boat rental, elev. 3300', $$.
East of Colville. State 20 25.0 miles east.

COLVILLE FAIRGROUNDS RV PARK (Stevens County)
40 trailer sites w/hookups for water/electricity/sewer, wheelchair access, showers, playfield, trailer waste disposal, $$.
In Colville. US 395 to Fairgrounds exit, follow signs.

DOUGLAS FALLS (Dept. of Natural Resources)
19 campsites, drinking water, wheelchair access, waterfalls, hiking trails, $$.
East of Colville. State 20 .5 mile east, Aladdin Road & Douglas Falls County Road 5.0 miles north to campground.

FLODELLE CREEK (Dept. of Natural Resources)
8 campsites, drinking water, $$.
East of Colville. State 20 21.0 miles east, Flodell Creek Road .2 mile to campground.

ROCKY LAKE (Dept. of Natural Resources)
8 campsites, drinking water, boat launch, $$.
Southeast of Colville. Campground is located 3.0 miles southeast of Colville, off State 395, on Rocky Lake.

WILDERNESS WEST RESORT (Private)
65 campsites, 25 w/hookups for water/electricity/sewer, plus 40 tent units, reservation information - (509)732-4263, showers, laundry, groceries, rec room, playfield, trailer waste disposal, on Deep Lake, swimming, fishing, boat launch, boat rental, hiking, elev. 3200', $$.
Northeast of Colville. State 20 east 1.0 mile, Aladdin Road 30.0 miles north to Deep Lake, located on northeast shore.

WILLIAMS LAKE (Dept. of Natural Resources)
10 campsites, drinking water, $$.
North of Colville. Campground is 16.0 miles north of Colville along Echo County Road, on Williams Lake.

CONCONULLY

ALDER (Okanogan National Forest)
5 tent units, fishing, hiking, elev. 3200', $.
North of Conconully. CR 2361 1.8 miles north, FSR 38 2.3 miles northwest.

ANDY'S RV PARK (Private)
35 trailer sites w/hookups for water/electricity/sewer, companion tents okay, reservations - (509)826-0326, showers, laundry, swimming pool, on Upper & Lower Conconnully Reservoir, fishing, $$.
In Conconully. Located 1 block east of Main Street in Conconully.

COTTONWOOD (Okanogan National Forest)
4 units, trailers to 22', artesian well, stream, fishing, elev. 2700', $.
North of Conconully. CR 2361 1.8 miles north, FSR 38 .3 mile north.

FLEMING'S HAVEN RESORT (Private)
11 trailer sites w/hookups for water/electricity/sewer, no tents, reservations
-(509)826-0813, showers, ice, on Conconully Lake, swimming, fishing, boat
launch, boat rental, $$$.
East of Conconully. Upper Conconully Lake Road east 1.0 mile.

JACK'S RV PARK (Private)
66 trailer sites w/hookups for water/electricity/sewer, reservations -
(509)826-0132, showers, laundry, trailer waste disposal, on Upper & Lower
Conconully Reservoir, stream, fishing, boat rental, $$.
In Conconully. Located 1 block east of Main Street in Conconully.

KOZY CABINS & RV PARK (Private)
12 campsites w/hookups for water/electricity/sewer, tents okay, reserva-
tions -(509)826-6780, showers, stream, fishing, $$.
In Conconully. Turn right, located at 111 Broadway.

LIARS COVE RESORT (Private)
30 trailer sites w/hookups for water/electricity/sewer, no tents, reservations
-(509)826-1288, showers, ice, lake, swimming, fishing, boat launch, boat
rental, $$$.
In Conconully. Located at east end of town.

ORIOLE (Okanogan National Forest)
8 units, well, stream, fishing, elev. 2900', $-$$.
Northwest of Conconully. CR 2361 1.8 miles northwest, FSR 38 .7 mile
northwest, FSR 25 .4 mile northwest. Located 3 miles northwest of Conconully State Park.

ROGER LAKE (Okanogan National Forest)
1 unit, trailer to 18', boating, fishing, elev. 6000', $.
Northwest of Conconully. CR 2017 2.3 miles southwest, FSR 364 21.2
miles northwest, FSR 370 1.6 miles northeast.

SALMON MEADOWS (Okanogan National Forest)
11 units, trailers to 22', picnic area, well, stream, hiking trails, elev. 4500',
$-$$.
Northwest of Conconully. CR 2361 1.8 miles northwest, FSR 38 6.9 miles
northwest.

SALMON MEADOWS GROUP CAMP (Okanogan National Forest)
Group sites, trailers to 22', reservations required - (509)422-3811, stream,
hiking trails, elev. 4500', $$$.
Northwest of Conconully. CR 2361 1.9 miles north, FSR 38 8.0 miles north-
west, FSR 3918 .7 mile north.

SHADY PINES RESORT (Private)
24 campsites, 13 w/hookups for water/electricity/sewer, plus 11 w/hookups
for water & electricity, reservations - (509)826-2287, showers, ice, on Con-
conully Reservoir, stream, swimming, fishing, boat rental, $$$.
West of Conconully. Located on west shore of Conconully Reservoir 1.0
mile west of town.

STATE ROAD CABIN (Okanogan National Forest)
2 units, trailers to 18', stream, elev. 3400', $.
Southwest of Conconully. CR 2017 2.3 miles southwest, FSR 364 .9 mile
southwest, FSR 42 3.5 miles southwest.

"THE OTHER PLACE" RV PARK (Private)
25 trailer sites w/hookups for water/electricity/sewer, no tents, reservations
-(509)826-4231, wheelchair access, showers, nearby lake & fishing, $$.
In Conconully. Located in Conconully east of Main, on A Street.

THIRTYMILE MEADOWS (Okanogan National Forest)
1 tent unit, hiking, elev. 6200', $.
Northwest of Conconully. CR 2361 1.8 miles north, FSR 38 27.3 miles
northwest.

TIFFANY MEADOWS (Okanogan National Forest)
1 tent unit, stream, elev. 6800', $.
Northwest of Conconully. CR 2017 1.8 miles southwest, FSR 364 21.2
miles northwest, FSR 370 7.0 miles northeast.

WAGON CAMP (Okanogan National Forest)
3 tent units, stream, fishing, elev. 3900', $.
West of Conconully. CR 2017 1.8 miles southwest, FSR 364 5.9 miles
northwest, FSR 3619 1.6 miles northwest.

CONCRETE

BAKER LAKE (Mt. Baker-Snoqualmie National Forest)
12 tent units, picnic area, well, boat launch, fishing, water skiing, hiking,
elev. 730', $.
Northeast of Concrete. CR 25 9.6 miles north, FSR 11 9.2 miles north.

CASCADE ISLANDS (Dept. of Natural Resources)
19 campsites, drinking water, river, $$.
East of Concrete. State 20 19.0 miles east, on Cascade River.

CLARK'S SKAGIT RIVER RV PARK (Private)
12 trailer sites w/hookups for water/electricity/sewer, reservation informa-
tion - (206)873-2250, showers, laundry, river, fishing, on Cascade Loop, $$.
East of Concrete. State 20 14.5 miles east.

CREEKSIDE CAMPING (Private)
27 campsites, 11 w/hookups for water/electricity/sewer, 13 w/hookups for
water & electricity, plus 3 w/out hookups, pets okay, reservations -
(206)826-3566, showers, laundry, groceries, playground, trailer waste
disposal, stream, fishing, on Cascade Loop, $$.
West of Concrete. State 20 west 7.0 miles, Baker Lake Road .2 mile north.
(Also accessible off I-5, take exit #232 and follow State 20 east 17.0 miles
to Baker Lake Road.)

DEPRESSION LAKE (Mt. Baker-Snoqualmie National Forest)
3 units, trailers to 18', lake - no motors, boating, fishing, elev. 700', $.
North of Concrete. CR 25 9.6 miles north, FSR 11 2.1 miles northeast, FSR
1106 1.3 miles east, FSR 3720A 5. mile north. Campground is two miles
from Baker Lake.

GRANDY CREEK KOA (Private)
75 campsites, 10 w/hookups for water/electricity/sewer, 23 w/hookups for water & electricity, plus 42 tent units, reservations - (206)826-3554, showers, laundry, groceries, rec room, playground, swimming pool, trailer waste disposal, stream, hiking, on Cascade Loop, $$$.
West of Concrete. State 20 5.5 miles west, Russell Road .3 mile north.

HORSESHOE COVE (Mt. Baker-Snoqualmie National Forest)
8 units, trailers to 22', picnic area, piped water, on Baker Lake, flush toilets, boat launch, boating, swimming, fishing, water skiing, elev. 700', $$.
North of Concrete. CR 25 9.6 miles north, FSR 11 2.4 miles north, FSR 1118 2.0 miles east.

LOWER PARK CREEK (Mt. Baker-Snoqualmie National Forest)
2 campsites, trailers to 18', elev. 800', $.
North of Concrete. CR 25 9.6 miles north, FSR 11 7.4 miles north.

MOROVITS (Mt. Baker-Snoqualmie National Forest)
Campsites, trailers to 18', stream, elev. 900', $.
North of Concrete. CR 25 9.6 miles north, FSR 11 7.4 miles north, FSR 1144 1.0 mile northwest. Campground is 5 miles east of Mt. Baker.

PANORAMA POINT (Mt. Baker-Snoqualmie National Forest)
16 units, trailers to 22', well, on Baker Lake, boat launch, swimming, fishing, water skiing, elev. 700', $$.
North of Concrete. CR 25 9.6 miles north, FSR 11 6.4 miles north. Campground is 5.0 miles east of Mt. Baker.

ROCKPORT STATE PARK (State of Washington)
8 tent units, plus 50 trailer sites w/hookups for water/electricity/sewer, group sites - reservations advised (206)853-4705, picnic shelter, wheelchair access includes trail, trailer waste disposal, fishing, hiking, $$-$$$.
East of Concrete. State 20 8.0 miles east.

SKAGIT COUNTY STEELHEAD PARK (County)
60 campsites, 40 w/hookups for water & electricity, plus 20 w/hookups for electricity, reservation information - (206)853-8808, wheelchair access, showers, groceries, playground, trailer waste disposal, river, swimming, fishing, boat launch, hiking, on Cascade Loop, $$.
East of Concrete. State 20 10.0 miles east past Rockport to Alfred Street and park.

TIMBERLINE TRAVELERS RV PARK (Private)
35 trailer sites w/hookups for water/electricity/sewer, reservation information - (206)826-3131, wheelchair access, showers, laundry, groceries, rec room, playfield, playground, on Cascade Loop, $$.
West of Concrete. State 20 5.0 miles west, Russell Road north to Challenger Road, east .3 mile to park at 736 Wilde Road.

WILDERNESS VILLAGE (Private)
45 trailer sites w/hookups for water/electricity/sewer, reservation information - (206)873-2571, showers, laundry, ice, rec room, river, fishing, on Cascade Loop, $$.
East of Concrete. State 20 14.0 miles east.

COOK

BUCK CREEK RIDGE (Dept. of Natural Resources)
6 campsites, trails for hikers & horses, $.
Northeast of Cook, State 14 east to White Salmon, campground is 3.0
miles north of White Salmon on west side of White Salmon River.

OKLAHOMA (Gifford Pinchot National Forest)
21 units, trailers to 22', well, on Little White Salmon River, wheelchair access, swimming, fishing, elev. 1700', $.
North of Cook. CR 1800 14.4 miles north to campground.

MOSS CREEK (Gifford Pinchot National Forest)
18 units, trailers to 32', piped water, on Little White Salmon River,
wheelchair access, fishing, elev. 1400', $.
North of Cook. CR 1800 8.0 miles north to campground.

COUGAR

CLEARWATER (Gifford Pinchot National Forest)
33 units, trailers to 22', piped water, stream, fishing, elev. 1500', $.
Northeast of Cougar. State 503 to Muddy River Road #90, campground is 4
miles north of Swift Creek Reservoir.

KALAMA SPRING (Gifford Pinchot National Forest)
18 units, trailers to 22', picnic area, fishing, hiking, elev. 2800', $.
North of Cougar 12 miles. State 503 to Merrill Lake Road #81, follow this to
campground.

LAKE MERRILL (Dept. of Natural Resources)
7 campsites, picnic area, drinking water, boat launch, $$.
North of Cougar. Located on the east shore of Lake Merrill, 6.0 miles north
of Cougar.

LONE FIR RESORT (Private)
32 campsites w/hookups for water/electricity/sewer, reservations -
(206)238-5210, showers, laundry, ice, swimming pool, $$-$$$.
In Cougar. Located on Lewis River Road in Cougar.

COUPEVILLE

DECEPTION PASS STATE PARK (State of Washington)
246 tent units, some trailers - no hookups, community kitchen/shelter,
wheelchair access, trailer waste disposal, boat launch/buoys/floats,
fishing, scuba diving area, swimming, $$.
North of Coupeville. Deception State Park is located at the northern end of
Whidbey Island, approximately 16.0 miles north of Coupeville.

FORT CASEY STATE PARK (State of Washington)
35 tent units, some trailers - no hookups, wheelchair access, located in historic US Defense Post, boat launch, fishing, scuba diving area, beach access, $$.
South of Coupeville. Located about 3.5 miles south of Coupeville along County Road; or follow State 20 south out of Coupeville and then west to water's edge and campground, approximately 8.0 miles.

FORT EBEY STATE PARK (State of Washington)
50 tent units, some trailers - no hookups, historic WWII defense bunker, beach access, fishing, $$.
Northwest of Coupeville. Located on west side of Whidbey Island, approximately 6.0 miles northwest of Coupeville.

MUTINY BAY RESORT (Private)
25 trailer sites w/hookups for water/electricity/sewer, trailers to 30', no tents, no pets, reservation information - (206)321-4500, showers, ice, tennis, playfield, playground, trailer waste disposal, ocean access, swimming, fishing, $$$.
South of Coupeville. Located in Freeland, 10.0 miles from Clinton Ferry Landing via State 525, Fish Road 1.0 mile south, Mutiny Bay Road to resort.

OAK HARBOR CITY BEACH (City)
55 campsites w/hookups for water & electricity, showers, tennis, playground, trailer waste disposal, ocean access, swimming, fishing, boat launch, $$.
North of Coupeville. State 20 north toward Oak Harbor, campground is located just south of Oak Harbor at Pioneer Road.

POINT PARTRIDGE (Dept. of Natural Resources)
6 campsites, hiking trails, $$.
West of Coupeville. Campground is 2.5 miles west of Coupeville.

RHODODENDRON (Dept. of Natural Resources)
8 campsites, drinking water, hiking trails, $$.
Southeast of Coupeville. State 525 2.0 miles southeast.

SOUTH WHIDBEY STATE PARK (State of Washington)
54 tent sites, some trailers - no hookups, group sites - reservations advised (206)321-4559, wheelchair access, trailer waste disposal, scuba diving area, fishing, beachcombing, clamming, $$-$$$.
South of Coupeville. Leave Coupeville on State 20 to State 525, follow this about 6.0 miles where you will find a road leading southwest toward the water and campground.

CURLEW

DEER CREEK SUMMIT (Colville National Forest)
4 units, trailers to 18', hiking trails, elev. 4600', $.
East of Curlew. CR 602 11.5 miles east.

DARRINGTON

CRYSTAL CREEK (Mt. Baker-Snoqualmie National Forest)
Campsites, fishing, elev. 1700', $.
Southeast of Darrington. Take County Road 1.3 miles north, FSR 22 10.3 miles southeast, FSR 23 5.3 miles east.

HYAKCHUCK (Mt. Baker-Snoqualmie National Forest)
2 units, trailers to 18', stream, elev. 600', $.
Southeast of Darrington. Take County Road 1.3 miles north, FSR 22 3.6 miles southeast.

OWL CREEK (Mt. Baker-Snoqualmie National Forest)
4 tent units, picnic area, fishing, hiking, horse trails, geology, elev. 1800', $.
Southeast of Darrington. Take County Road 1.3 miles north, FSR 22 10.3 miles southeast, FSR 23 10.3 miles east.

TEXAS POND (Mt. Baker-Snoqualmie National Forest)
3 tent units, lake - no motors, good fishing, elev. 1400', $.
North of Darrington. Take County Road 6.2 miles north, FSR 29 6.0 miles northwest.

WILLIAM C. DEARINGER (Dept. of Natural Resources)
16 campsites, wheelchair access, $.
Northeast of Darrington. Sauk Prairie Road 2.0 miles northeast, East Sauk Prairie Road 4.0 miles to campground.

DAYTON

EDMISTON (Umatilla National Forest)
9 units, some trailers, picnic area, elev. 5300', $.
Southeast of Dayton 21 miles. US 12 to Kendall-Skyline Road N910, follow this to campground.

FORT PARK/WALLA WALLA CAMPGROUND (City of Walla Walla)
70 campsites, 26 w/hookups for water & electricity, plus 44 tent units, reservation information - (509)525-3700, wheelchair access, showers, groceries, playfield, playground, trailer waste disposal, stream, hiking, $$.
Southwest of Dayton. US 12 southwest 30.0 miles to Walla Walla, State 125 southwest 4.0 miles, Dalles Military Road west .5 mile.

LEWIS & CLARK TRAIL STATE PARK (State of Washington)
30 tent units, some trailers - no hookups, community kitchen/shelter, trailer waste disposal, on historic Lewis & Clark Trail, campfire programs in summer, fishing, winter sports, $$.
Southwest of Dayton. US 12 5.0 miles southwest.

STOCKADE SPRING (Umatilla National Forest)
2 tent units, no trailers, piped water, picnic area, elev. 4600', $.
Southeast of Dayton 18 miles. US 12 to Kendall-Skyline Road N910, follow this to campground.

ELBE

COUGAR ROCK CAMPGROUND (Mt. Rainier National Park)
200 campsites, trailers to 30', information - (206)569-2211, trailer waste disposal, hiking, $$.
East of Elbe. State 706 east 22.2 miles, located 8.0 miles east of Nisqually Entrance.

SUNSHINE POINT (Mt. Rainier National Park)
18 campsites, trailers to 25', on Nisqually River, fishing, $.
East of Elbe. State 706 east 22.6 miles, located .5 mile east of Nisqually Entrance.

ELDON

HAMMA HAMMA (Olympic National Forest)
15 units, trailers to 22', well, river, swimming, fishing, hiking, bicycling, elev. 600', $.
Northwest of Eldon. US 101 1.7 miles north, FSR 249 6.5 miles west. Lena Lakes Trailhead is 2.5 miles west of campground.

LENA CREEK (Olympic National Forest)
14 units, trailers to 22', well, swimming, fishing, Lena Lakes Trailhead, elev. 700', $.
Northwest of Eldon. US 101 1.7 miles north, FSR 249 9.0 miles west.

ELLENSBURG

ELLENSBURG KOA (Private)
100 campsites, 12 w/hookups for water/electricity/sewer, plus 88 w/hookups for water & electricity, reservations - (509)925-9319, showers, laundry, groceries, rec room, playfield, playground, swimming pool, trailer waste disposal, river, fishing, $$$.
At Ellensburg. I-90 to exit #106 and campground.

GINKGO/WANAPUM STATE PARK (State of Washington)
50 trailer sites w/hookups for water/electricity/sewer, Ginkgo Petrified Forest Interpretive Center, boat launch, fishing, beach access, trail, $$.
East of Ellensburg. I-90 29.0 miles east.

VANTAGE KOA (Private)
150 campsites, 100 w/hookups for water/electricity/sewer, plus 50 tent units, reservation information - (509)856-2230, showers, laundry, groceries, rec room, playground, swimming pool, therapy pool, trailer waste disposal, lake, swimming, fishing, $$$.
Southeast of Ellensburg. I-90 east 28.0 miles to Vantage exit #136, north 2 blocks to campground.

ENTIAT

BIG HILL (Wenatchee National Forest)
1 tent unit, shelter, no water, elev. 6800', $.
Northwest of Entiat. US 97 1.4 miles southwest, CR 371 25.2 miles northwest, FSR 317 4.2 miles northwest, FSR 298 7.9 miles north, FSR 298A 1.5 miles north.

COTTONWOOD (Wenatchee National Forest)
25 units, 1 group site, trailers to 22', well, river, fishing, hiking, elev. 3100', $.
Northwest of Entiat. US 97 1.4 miles southwest, CR 371 25.2 miles northwest, FSR 317 12.7 miles northwest.

ENTIAT CITY PARK (City)
31 campsites w/hookups for electricity, showers, playground, trailer waste disposal, lake, swimming, fishing, boat launch, $$-$$$.
In Entiat. Leave US 97 at Entiat on Lakeshore Drive and follow to park.

FOX CREEK (Wenatchee National Forest)
9 units, trailers to 18', well, fishing, elev. 2300', $.
Northwest of Entiat. US 97 1.4 miles southwest, CR 371 25.2 miles northwest, FSR 317 1.8 miles northwest.

HALFWAY SPRING (Wenatchee National Forest)
5 tent units, no trailers, piped water, hiking, elev. 5000', $.
Northwest of Entiat. US 97 1.4 miles southwest, CR 371 25.2 miles northwest, FSR 317 3.5 miles northwest, FSR 298 2.1 miles to campground.

LAKE CREEK (Wenatchee National Forest)
12 units, trailers to 18', well, fishing, hiking, elev. 2400', $.
Northwest of Entiat. US 97 1.4 miles southwest, CR 371 25.2 miles northwest, FSR 317 3.0 miles northwest.

NORTH FORK (Wenatchee National Forest)
7 units, 1 group site, trailers to 22', river, fishing, elev. 2700', $.
Northwest of Entiat. US 97 1.4 miles southwest, CR 371 25.2 miles northwest, FSR 317 8.3 miles northwest.

SHADY PASS (Wenatchee National Forest)
1 tent unit, no trailers, elev. 5400', $.
Northwest of Entiat. US 97 1.4 miles southwest, CR 371 25.2 miles northwest, FSR 317 3.5 miles northwest, FSR 298 5.1 miles to campground.

SILVER FALLS (Wenatchee National Forest)
71 units, trailers to 22', picnic area, well, stream, fishing, hiking, elev. 2400', $$-$$$.
Northwest of Entiat. US 97 1.4 miles southwest, CR 371 25.2 miles northwest, FSR 317 5.2 miles northwest.

ENUMCLAW

GREEN RIVER GORGE (Dept. of Natural Resources)
9 campsites, picnic area, drinking water, hiking trails, $$.
North of Enumclaw. State 169 6.0 miles north.

IPSUT CREEK (Mt. Rainier National Park)
29 campsites, trailers to 20', hiking, elev. 4400', $.
South of Enumclaw. State 165 south approximately 12.0 miles to Carbonado, located 5.0 miles east of Mt. Rainier National Park's Carbon River Entrance on park access road.

KANASKAT/PALMER STATE PARK (State of Washington)
31 tent units, 19 trailer sites w/hookups for electricity, group sites -reservations advised (206)886-0148, community kitchen/shelter, wheelchair access, on Green River, boating, fishing, $$-$$$.
Northeast of Enumclaw. State 410 east 1.0 miles, Palmer Road 9.0 miles northeast.

SILVER SPRINGS (Mt. Baker-Snoqualmie National Forest)
52 units, 4 group sites, trailers to 22', picnic area, piped water, wheelchair access, fishing, elev. 2600', $.
Southeast of Enumclaw. State 410 31.3 miles southeast. Campground is located 1 mile northwest of Mt. Rainier National Park Boundary.

WHITE RIVER CAMPGROUND (Mt. Rainier National Park)
117 campsites, trailers to 20', on White River, hiking, $$.
West of Enumclaw. State 410 east, located 5.0 miles west of White River Entrance.

EVERETT

FERGUSON PARK (City of Snohomish)
11 trailer sites w/hookups for water & electricity, trailers to 34', reservation information - (206)568-3115, wheelchair access, showers, laundry, rec room, playground, trailer waste disposal, lake, swimming, fishing, boat launch, $$$.
Southeast of Everett. I-5 north to exit #194, US 2 southeast 6.0 miles to Snohomish, located near junction of US 2 and State 9.

SILVER SHORES RV PARK (Private)
83 trailer sites, 57 w/hookups for water/electricity/sewer, 11 w/hookups for water & electricity, plus 15 w/out hookups, reservations - (206)337-8741, showers, laundry, ice, rec room, tennis, trailer waste disposal, on Silver Lake, swimming, fishing, $$$.
In Everett. I-5 to exit #186 to 128th Street, west to 4th Avenue, north to 112th Steet, take this east across freeway, 14th Avenue/Silver Lake Road south to 11621 West Silver Lake Road.

SMOKEY POINT RV PARK (Private)
96 trailer sites w/hookups for water/electricity/sewer, reservation information - (206)652-7300, showers, laundry, therapy pool, rec room, trailer waste disposal, $$-$$$.
Northeast of Everett. I-5 north 14.0 miles to exit #206.

FORKS

BEAR CREEK (Dept. of Natural Resources)
6 campsites, drinking water, $.
Northeast of Forks. US 101 northeast, campground is located 2.0 miles east of Sappho on Hoh River Road.

BEAR CREEK RV PARK & MOTEL (Private)
18 trailer sites w/hookups for water/electricity/sewer, reservation information - (206)327-3558, showers, laundry, ice, river, swimming, fishing, $$-$$$.
North of Forks. US 101 15.0 miles north, located near milepost #206.

BOGACHIEL STATE PARK (State of Washington)
41 tent units, some trailers, community kitchen/shelter, trailer waste disposal, on Bogachiel River, good fishing, $-$$.
South of Forks. Highway 101 6.0 miles south to campground.

FORKS MOBILE HOME & RV PARK (Private)
7 trailer sites w/hookups for water/electricity/sewer, reservations - (206)374-5510, laundry, $$.
In Forks. US 101 to Calawah Way, east about 3 blocks park.

HOH RIVER (Olympic National Park)
89 campsites, trailers to 21', trailer waste disposal, river, fishing, hiking, $$.
South of Forks. US 101 south 14.0 miles, Hoh River Road east 19.0 miles.

HOH RIVER RESORT & RV PARK (Private)
25 trailer sites w/hookups for water/electricity/sewer, reservations - (206)374-5566, showers, laundry, groceries, on Hoh River, fishing, $$$.
South of Forks. US 101 south 15.0 miles.

HUELSDONK (Dept. of Natural Resources)
5 campsites, $.
South of Forks. US 101 14.0 miles south to Hoh River, campground is 10.0 miles east on Hoh River.

KLAHANIE (Olympic National Forest)
15 units, trailers to 22', river, fishing, elev. 300', $.
East of Forks. US 101 1.7 miles northwest, FSR 300 5.4 miles east. Campground offers excellent example of Olympic Rain Forest.

KLAHOWYA (Olympic National Forest)
44 units, trailers to 32', picnic area, piped water, river, wheelchair access, boat launch, interpretive service, boating, good fishing, hiking trails, elev. 800', $$.
East of Forks. US 101 20.0 miles northeast.

MORA CAMPGROUND (Olympic National Park)
94 campsites, trailers to 21', trailer waste disposal, ocean access, on Quinault River, swimming, fishing, hiking, $$.
West of Forks. LaPush Road 15.0 miles west.

SHORELINE RESORT & TRAILER COURT (Private)
61 trailer sites w/hookups for water/electricity/sewer, no tents, reservation information - (206)374-6488, showers, laundry, trailer waste disposal, ocean access, swimming, fishing, $$.
Southwest of Forks. US 101 north to La Push Road, southwest to La Push and resort.

SPRUCE CREEK (Dept. of Natural Resources)
5 campsites, $.
Southeast of Forks. US 101 13.0 miles south to Valley Road. Campground is 7.0 miles.

THREE RIVERS RESORT (Private)
11 campsites, 5 w/hookups for water/electricity/sewer, 4 w/hookups for water & electricity, plus 2 w/out hookups, tents okay, reservations - (206)374-5300, laundry, groceries, gasoline, propane, restaurant, $$.
West of Forks. LaPush Road 8.0 miles west.

YAHOO LAKE (Dept. of Natural Resources)
6 walk-in campsites, hiking trails, $.
South of Forks. US 101 14.0 miles south to Hoh River, campground is 24.0 miles east, past the Clearwater Honor Camp.

FORT SPOKANE

FORT SPOKANE (Coulee Dam Recreation Area)
Campsites, trailers okay - no hookups, group campsites, picnic area, drinking water, handicap access, trailer & boat waste disposal, boat ramp & dock, swimming/lifeguard, summer amphitheater programs, elev. 1400', $$-$$$.
North of Fort Spokane. Campground is located just north of historic Fort Spokane on State 25.

PORCUPINE BAY (Coulee Dam Recreation Area)
Campsites, trailers okay - no hookups, group campsites, picnic area, drinking water, cafe/snack bar, trailer waste disposal, boat dock & ramp, swimming/lifeguard, $$.
Southeast of Fort Spokane. State 25 southeast 8.1 miles, Porcupine Bay Road 4.3 miles north to campground.

SEVEN BAYS MARINA (Coulee Dam Recreation Area)
Campsites, trailers okay - no hookups, group campsites, picnic area, drinking water, groceries, trailer & boat waste disposal, boat ramp & fee dock, boat fuel, $$-$$$.
Southwest of Fort Spokane. Just south of Fort Spokane leave highway and head south; campground is approximately 5.0 miles.

GLACIER

BRIDGE (Mt. Baker-Snoqualmie National Forest)
12 units, trailers to 18', river, interpretive services, fishing, elev. 1300', $.
Northeast of Glacier. State 542 1.0 mile east, FSR 37 5.0 miles east.

DOUGLAS FIR (Mt. Baker-Snoqualmie National Forest)
30 units, trailers to 32', picnic area, community kitchen, piped water, on Nooksack River, fishing, hiking, elev. 1000', $$.
Northeast of Glacier. State 542 2.0 miles northeast. Campground is located 8 miles north of trailhead to Mt. Baker.

SILVER FIR (Mt. Baker-Snoqualmie National Forest)
21 units, trailers to 32', picnic area, community kitchen, piped water, along Nooksack River, wheelchair access, fishing, elev. 2000', $$.
East of Glacier. State 542 12.5 miles east. Campground located 8 miles north of Heather Meadows Recreation Area.

TWIN LAKES (Mt. Baker-Snoqualmie National Forest)
10 tent units, hike-in, fishing, hiking, elev. 5100', $.
Northeast of Glacier. State 542 12.3 miles east, FSR 3065 4.0 miles north, Trail 672 2.5 miles northeast. Campground is located 1 mile south of Winchester Mt. Lookout.

GOLDENDALE

BROOKS MEMORIAL STATE PARK (State of Washington)
22 tent units, plus 23 trailer sites w/hookups for water & electricity, group sites - reservations advised (509)773-4611, community kitchen, nearby groceries, trailer waste disposal, fishing, hiking trails, winter sports, $$-$$$.
North of Goldendale. State 97 15.0 miles north.

CROW BUTTE STATE PARK (State of Washington)
50 trailer sites w/hookups for water/electricity/sewer, group sites -reservations advised (509)875-2644, picnic shelter, wheelchair access, trailer waste disposal, boat launch, fishing, water skiing, $$-$$$.
East of Goldendale. US 97 10.0 miles south, State 14 49.0 miles east.

HORSETHIEF LAKE STATE PARK (State of Washington)
12 tent units, some trailers - no hookups, trailer waste disposal, 2 boat launches - lake & Columbia River, scuba diving area, fishing, $$.
West of Goldendale. US 97 10.0 miles south, State 14 18.0 miles west.

MARYHILL STATE PARK (State of Washington)
50 trailer sites w/hookups for water/electricity/sewer, community kitchen, wheelchair access, trailer waste disposal, on Columbia River, boat launch, fishing, swimming, wind surfing, water skiing, $$.
Southeast of Goldendale. US 97 10.0 miles south, State 14 2.0 miles east.

GRANITE FALLS

BEAVER BAR (Mt. Baker-Snoqualmie National Forest)
3 units, trailers to 18', group sites, river, fishing, elev. 1600', $.
East of Granite Falls. CR 7 24.3 miles east.

BEAVER CREEK (Mt. Baker-Snoqualmie National Forest)
4 tent units, fishing, elev. 1600', $-$$$.
East of Granite Falls. CR 7 24.4 miles east.

BIG FOUR (Mt. Baker-Snoqualmie National Forest)
6 tent units, fishing, hiking, elev. 1700', $.
East of Granite Falls. CR 7 26.0 miles east.

BOARDMAN CREEK (Mt. Baker-Snoqualmie National Forest)
8 tent units, group sites, fishing, elev. 1200', $-$$$.
East of Granite Falls. CR 7 16.6 miles east.

COAL CREEK (Mt. Baker-Snoqualmie National Forest)
7 units, some trailers, fishing, elev. 1600', $.
East of Granite Falls. CR 7 23.7 miles east.

COAL CREEK BAR (Mt. Baker-Snoqualmie National Forest)
5 units, group sites, trailers to 18', fishing, elev. 1600', $-$$$.
East of Granite Falls. CR 7 23.5 miles east.

GOLD BASIN (Mt. Baker-Snoqualmie National Forest)
93 units, trailers to 32', group sites, piped water, river, wheelchair access, fishing, elev. 1100', $$.
East of Granite Falls. CR 7 13.4 miles east.

HAPS HILL (Mt. Baker-Snoqualmie National Forest)
4 tent units, river, fishing, elev. 2500', $.
Southeast of Granite Falls. CR 7 30.1 miles east, CR MC 2.2 miles southeast.

HEMPLE CREEK (Mt. Baker-Snoqualmie National Forest)
3 units, trailers to 22', picnic area, piped water, fishing, hiking, elev. 1000', $.
East of Granite Falls. CR 7 13.0 miles.

MARTEN CREEK (Mt. Baker-Snoqualmie National Forest)
4 units, trailers to 18', group site, fishing, elev. 1400', $-$$$.
East of Granite Falls. CR 7 20.6 miles east.

MT. PILCHUCK RECREATION AREA (Mt. Baker-Snoqualmie National Forest)
12 units, trailers to 32', group sites, picnic area, piped water, hiking, elev. 3000', $$.
East of Granite Falls. CR 7 12.0 miles east, FSR 42 6.9 miles southwest.

OLD TRAIL (Mt. Baker-Snoqualmie National Forest)
3 tent units, river, fishing, elev. 1500', $.
East of Granite Falls. CR 7 30.1 miles east, FSR 20 4.1 miles northeast.

SAUK RIVER (Mt. Baker-Snoqualmie National Forest)
4 tent units, fishing, elev. 2600', $.
Southeast of Granite Falls. CR 7 30.1 miles east, CR MC 2.9 miles southeast.

SILVER TIP (Mt. Baker-Snoqualmie National Forest)
3 tent units, river, fishing, elev. 2600', $.
Southeast of Granite Falls. CR 7 30.1 miles east, CR MC 2.6 miles southeast.

SOUTH FORK CANYON CREEK CROSSING (Mt. Baker-Snoqualmie National Forest)
6 tent units, fishing, elev. 1600', $.
Northeast of Granite Falls. CR 7 6.5 miles east, FSR 41 8.4 miles northeast.

SUNNYSIDE (Mt. Baker-Snoqualmie National Forest)
7 tent units, fishing, hiking, elev. 1300', $.
East of Granite Falls. CR 7 18.0 miles east.

TULALIP MILLSITE (Mt. Baker-Snoqualmie National Forest)
12 units, trailers to 32', group sites, reservations required (206)436-1155, elev. 1400', $$$.
East of Granite Falls. CR 7 18.6 miles east.

TURLO (Mt. Baker-Snoqualmie National Forest)
19 units, trailers to 32', piped water, river, swimming, fishing, elev. 900', $$.
East of Granite Falls. CR 7 10.8 miles east.

TWIN PEAKS (Mt. Baker-Snoqualmie National Forest)
6 tent units, river, fishing, elev. 1500', $.
East of Granite Falls. CR 7 30.1 miles east, FSR 20 4.3 miles northeast.

TYEE POOL (Mt. Baker-Snoqualmie National Forest)
2 tent units, river, fishing, elev. 1600', $.
East of Granite Falls. CR 7 30.1 miles east, FSR 20 3.8 miles northeast.

VERLOT (Mt. Baker-Snoqualmie National Forest)
18 units, trailers to 32', piped water, river, flush toilets, swimming, fishing, elev. 900', $$.
East of Granite Falls. CR 7 11.0 miles east.

WHITE DEER (Mt. Baker-Snoqualmie National Forest)
2 units, trailers to 18', river, fishing, elev. 1800', $.
East of Granite Falls. CR 7 30.1 miles east, FSR 20 2.8 miles northeast.

WILEY CREEK (Mt. Baker-Snoqualmie National Forest)
3 group sites, reservations required - (206)436-1155, no trailers, shelters, fishing, elev. 1200', $$$.
East of Granite Falls. CR 7 15.0 miles east.

HOODSPORT

BIG CREEK (Olympic National Forest)
18 units, trailers to 20', swimming, fishing, hiking trail, elev. 700', $.
West of Hoodsport. CR 9420 8.0 miles west, FSR 24 .1 mile south. Just north of Lake Cushman.

GLEN AYR RV PARK (Private)
54 trailer sites w/hookups for water/electricity/sewer, no tents, reservation information - (206)877-9522, showers, laundry, picnic shelter, therapy pool, rec room, lounge, ocean access, swimming, fishing, hiking, on Hood Canal, $$$.
North of Hoodsport. US 101 1.0 mile north.

LAKE CUSHMAN RESORT (Private)
40 campsites, 10 w/hookups for water & electricity, plus 30 w/out hookups, reservation information - (206)877-9630, groceries, lake, swimming, fishing boat launch, boat rental, hiking, $-$$.
Northwest of Hoodsport. US 101 north to Lake Cushman Road, west 5.0 miles.

LAKE CUSHMAN STATE PARK (State of Washington)
51 tent units, 30 trailer sites w/hookups for water/electricity/sewer, group sites - reservations advised (206)877-5491, community kitchen, wheelchair access, trailer waste disposal, boat launch, on Lake Cushman, fishing, hiking trails, $$-$$$.
Northwest of Hoodsport. Leave US 101 at Hoodsport on the road to Lake Cushman, campground is 7.0 miles west.

LILLIWAUP (Dept. of Natural Resources)
6 campsites, creek, drinking water, $.
Northwest of Hoodsport. Take Cushman-Jorstad Road 4.0 miles northeast of Lake Cushman to Lilliwaup Creek and campground.

MELBOURNE (Dept. of Natural Resources)
5 units, lake, $.
Northwest of Hoodsport. US 101 north, Jorsted Creek Road 5.5 miles northwest, west 2.5 miles keeping left at Y.

MINERVA BEACH (Private)
36 trailer sites w/hookups for water/electricity/sewer, no tents, reservation information - (206)877-5145, showers, laundry, heated swimming pool, on Hood Canal, scuba diving, fishing, $$-$$$.
South of Hoodsport. US 101 3.2 miles south.

POTLATCH STATE PARK (State of Washington)
17 tent units, plus 18 trailer sites w/hookups for water/electricity/sewer, picnic shelter, trailer waste disposal, on Hood Canal, scuba diving area, fishing, crabbing, clamming, $$.
South of Hoodsport. Follow US 101 south, past Potlatch, to Potlatch State Park and campsites.

REST A WHILE RV PARK (Private)
92 campsites w/hookups for water/electricity/sewer, reservations - (206)877-9474, showers, laundry, groceries, ocean access, swimming, fishing, boat launch, $$$.
North of Hoodsport. US 101 2.5 miles north.

STAIRCASE CAMPGROUND (Olympic National Park)
59 campsites, trailers to 16', on Elk Creek, near Lake Cushman, swimming, fishing, hiking, $$.
Northwest of Hoodsport. US 101 north to Lake Cushman Road, west 16.0 miles.

HUMPTULIPS

RIVERVIEW RV PARK (Private)
21 campsites, 6 w/hookups for water/electricity/sewer, 6 w/hookups for water & electricity, plus 9 w/out hookups, reservation information - (206)987-2216, showers, on Humptulips River, swimming, fishing, $$.
At Humptulips. West of US 101 .3 mile.

HUNTERS

GIFFORD (Coulee Dam Recreation Area)
Campsites, trailers okay - no hookups, picnic area, drinking water, trailer waste disposal, boat ramp & dock, $.
North of Hunters on State 25, just south of Gifford.

HUNTERS (Coulee Dam Recreation Area)
Campsites, trailers okay - no hookups, picnic area, drinking water, trailer waste disposal, boat ramp & dock, $.
West of Hunters. Leave State 25 at Hunters and head west to campground and water.

ILWACO

CHINOOK COUNTY PARK (Pacific County)
100 campsites, reservation information - (206)777-8442, showers, playground, river, fishing, $$.
Southeast of Ilwaco. US 101 Southeast 5.0 miles to Chinook, park is located at east end of town.

COVE RV PARK (Private)
35 campsites, 25 w/hookups for water/electricity/sewer, plus 10 w/hookups for water & electricity, pets welcome, reservation information - (206)642-3689, showers, laundry, trailer waste disposal, ocean access, on Columbia River, fishing, $$.
In Ilwaco. Located at west end of port area.

FORT CANBY STATE PARK (State of Washington)
190 tent units, 60 trailer sites w/hookups for water/electricity/sewer, wheelchair access, groceries, trailer waste disposal, boat launch, fishing, Interpretive Center, ocean access, trails, $$-$$$.
Southwest of Ilwaco. Campground is 2.5 miles southwest of Ilwaco.

ILWACO KOA (Private)
114 campsites, 34 w/hookups for water/electricity/sewer, 46 w/hookups for water & electricity, plus 34 tent units, reservations - (206)642-3292, showers, laundry, groceries, playground, trailer waste disposal, ocean access, on Columbia River, fishing, $$$.
Southeast of Ilwaco. US 101 southeast; located between Ilwaco and Chinook.

MAUCH'S SUNDOWN RV PARK (Private)
50 campsites, 42 w/hookups for water/electricity/sewer, plus 8 w/hookups for water & electricity, reservation information - (206)777-8713, showers, laundry, ice, trailer waste disposal, river, fishing, $$.
Southeast of Ilwaco. US 101 southeast 8.5 miles, located just west of Astoria Bridge.

NASALLE TRAILER COURT (Private)
24 trailer sites w/hookups for water/electricity/sewer, no tents, reservation information - (206)484-3351, showers, laundry, $$.
Northeast of Ilwaco. US 101 southeast 10.0 miles, State 401 north 12.0 miles, State 4 southeast 1.5 miles.

OLSEN'S CAMPGROUND (Private)
60 campsites, 58 w/hookups for water & electricity, plus 2 w/out hookups, reservation information - (206)777-8475, showers, groceries, trailer waste disposal, river, fishing, $$.
East of Ilwaco. US 101 9.0 miles to junction with State 401, State 401 north 3.0 miles to campground.

RIVER'S END CAMPGROUND (Private)
60 campsites, 20 w/hookups for water/electricity/sewer, plus 40 w/hookups for water & electricity, reservation information - (206)777-8317, showers, laundry, ice, rec room, playground, trailer waste disposal, river, fishing, $$.
Southeast of Ilwaco. US 101 4.3 miles east, located this side of Chinook.

SOU'WESTER LODGE & TRAILER PARK (Private)
60 campsites w/hookups for water/electricity/sewer, reservation information -(206)642-2542, showers, laundry, ocean access, fishing, $$$.
North of Ilwaco. US 101 north, just before Seaview take Seaview Beach Road west 1 block to park.

THE BEACON RV PARK (Private)
60 campsites, 40 w/hookups for water/electricity/sewer, 10 w/hookups for electricity, plus 10 w/out hookups, reservation information - (206)642-2138, showers, ice, river, fishing - salmon charters, $$-$$$.
In Ilwaco. Located at east end of docks.

INDEX

BIG GREIDER LAKE (Dept. of Natural Resources)
5 campsites, hike-in only, trails, $.
Northwest of Index. US 2 west to Sultan; Sultan Basin Road northeast to Greider Creek and Relection Ponds, hike-in 3.0 miles to Big Greider Lake.

BOULDER LAKE (Dept. of Natural Resources)
9 campsites, hike-in only, trails, $.
Northwest of Index. US 2 west to Sultan; Sultan Basin Road northeast 20.0 miles to Elk Creek, hike 3.2 miles to lake and campsites.

CUTTHROAT LAKES (Dept. of Natural Resources)
10 campsites, hike-in only, trails, $.
Northwest of Index. US 2 west to Sultan; Sultan Basin Road northeast 22.0 miles to Gilbert Creek Trailhead #37, hike-in 3.0 miles to lake and campsites.

ELWELL (Dept. of Natural Resources)
19 campsites, drinking water, $$.
Southwest of Index. US 2 west to State 203, south to Harris Creek road, 5.0 miles to Stossel Creek Road, follow this 6.0 miles to campground.

LITTLE GREIDER LAKE (Dept. of Natural Resources)
9 campsites, hike-in only, trails, $.
Northwest of Index. US 2 west to Sultan; Sultan Basin Road northeast to Greider Creek and Reflection Ponds, hike-in 5.5 miles to Little Greider Lake.

OLNEY PARK (Dept. of Natural Resources)
14 campsites, $.
Northwest of Index. US 2 west to Sultan; campground is 7.0 miles northeast of Sultan on Sultan Basin Road.

THUNDERBIRD PARK (Private)
100 campsites, 52 w/hookups for water/electricity/sewer, 16 w/hookups for water & electricity, plus 32 tent sites, reservation information - (206)794-8987, showers, laundry, groceries, swimming pool, picnic shelter, playfield, playground, trailer waste disposal, river, fishing, boat launch, $$$.
Northwest of Index. US 2 west 26.0 miles, State 203 south 1.0 mile, Ben Howard Road east 5.0 miles.

TROUBLESOME CREEK GROUP CAMP (Mt. Baker-Snoqualmie National Forest)
Group sites, picnic area, fishing, trailhead to Troublesome Creek Interpretive Trail, elev. 1300', $$$.
Northeast of Index. CR 63 12.0 miles northeast.

WALLACE FALLS STATE PARK (State of Washington)
6 tent units, no trailers, picnic shelter, wheelchair access, along Wallace River, series of waterfalls, $$.
Northwest of Index. US 2 west 6.0 miles to Gold Bar, campground is 2.0 miles northeast of Gold Bar.

IONE

EAST GILLETTE (Colville National Forest)
30 units, trailers to 32', piped water, flush toilets, wheelchair access, trailer waste disposal, hiking trails, nearby motorcycle trails, bicycling, elev. 3200', $$-$$$.
Southwest of Ione. State 31 4.0 miles south, State 20 11.0 miles southwest, CR 4987 .5 mile east.

IONE MOTEL & RV PARK (Private)
19 campsites w/hookups for water/electricity/sewer, tents okay, reservations -(509)442-3213, showers, laundry, on Pend Oreille River, swimming, fishing, boat launch, water skiing, $$-$$$.
In Ione. Located at south end of town.

LAKE LEO (Colville National Forest)
8 units, trailers to 18', well, boat launch, boating, swimming, fishing, elev. 3200', $$.
Southwest of Ione. State 31 4.0 miles south, State 30 7.0 miles southwest.

LAKE THOMAS (Colville National Forest)
15 tent units, piped water, boating, swimming, fishing, water skiing, nearby motorcycle trails, bicycling, elev. 3200', $$.
Southwest of Ione. State 31 4.0 miles south, State 20 11.0 miles southwest, CR 4987 1.2 miles east.

NOISY CREEK (Colville National Forest)
19 units, trailers to 32', piped water, boat launch, boating, swimming, fishing, water skiing, hiking trails, elev. 2600', $$.
Northeast of Ione. State 31 1.0 miles south, CR 9345 9.0 miles northeast.

KELSO

CAMP KALAMA RV PARK (Private)
100 campsites, 50 w/hookups for water/electricity/sewer, 20 w/hookups for water & electricity, plus 30 w/out hookups, reservation information - (206)673-2456, showers, laundry, groceries, playfield, playground, trailer waste disposal, on Kalama River, swimming, fishing, boat launch, $$-$$$.
South of Kelso. I-5 south to Kalama exit #32, Kalama River Road east .1 mile, south to park.

MARV'S RV PARK (Private)
20 trailer sites w/hookups for water/electricity/sewer, reservation information - (206)795-3453, showers, rec room, trailer waste disposal, fishing, $$$.
West of Kelso. State 4 west 23.5 miles, just this side of Cathlamet.

PORT OF KALAMA RV PARK (Port)
22 trailer sites w/hookups for water/electricity/sewer, reservation information - (206)673-2325, showers, playfield, playground, trailer waste disposal, river, fishing, boat launch, boat rental, $$.
South of Kelso. I-5 south to Kalama exit #32, park is west 1 block.

RAINBOW PARK CAMPGROUND (Private)
46 campsites, 10 w/hookups for water/electricity/sewer, 34 w/hookups for water & electricity, plus 2 w/hookups for water, reservation information - (206)673-4574, showers, groceries, playground, trailer waste disposal, river, swimming, fishing, $$-$$$.
South of Kelso. I-5 south to Kalama exit #32, Kalama River Road east 1.0 mile, head south across bridge to Modrow Road, campground is .3 mile.

SKAMOKAWA VISTA PARK (Public)
15 trailer sites w/hookups for electricity, reservation information - (206)795-8605, wheelchair access, showers, tennis, playfield, playground, trailer waste disposal, river, swimming, fishing, boat launch, hiking, $$.
East of Kelso. State 4 28.5 miles east, located just west of Skamokawa.

THE CEDARS RV PARK (Private)
25 campsites, 23 w/hookups for water & electricity, plus 2 w/out hookups, trailers to 40', reservations - (206)274-7019, showers, laundry, trailer waste disposal, $$.
North of Kelso. I-5 north to exit #46, Access Road .3 mile north to park.

KETTLE FALLS

CANYON CREEK (Colville National Forest)
12 units, trailers okay, piped water, fishing, hiking, horse trails, elev. 2200', $.
West of Kettle Falls. US 395 3.5 miles northwest, State 20 west 5.5 miles, FSR 2000 5.0 miles northwest.

EVANS (Coulee Dam Recreation Area)
Campsites, trailers okay - no hookups, picnic area, drinking water, trailer waste disposal, boat ramp & dock, swimming/lifeguard, $$.
North of Kettle Falls. State 25 approximately 9.0 miles north to campground.

KETTLE FALLS (Coulee Dam Recreation Area)
Campsites, trailers okay - no hookups, group campsites, drinking water, picnic area, wheelchair access, cafe/snack bar, groceries, boat dock & ramp, boat fuel, swimming/lifeguard, summer amphitheater programs, elev. 1300', $$-$$$.
West of Kettle Falls. Leave Kettle Falls heading due west toward water and campground.

MARCUS ISLAND (Coulee Dam Recreation Area)
24 campsites, trailers okay, boat dock & ramp, $.
North of Kettle Falls approximately 5 miles via Hwy. 25.

SHEEP CREEK (Dept. of Natural Resources)
20 campsites, picnic area, drinking water, $$.
Northeast of Kettle Falls. State 25 33.0 miles northeast to Northport, campground is 4.0 miles northwest of Northport on Sheep Creek.

SHERMAN PASS (Colville National Forest)
9 units, trailers okay, picnic area, piped water, hiking, horse trails, elev. 5300', $.
West of Kettle Falls 22 miles on State 20 at Sherman Pass.

WHISPERING PINES RV PARK (Private)
40 campsites w/hookups for water/electricity/sewer, reservation information -(509)738-2593, showers, laundry, ice, playground, river, lake, fishing, $-$$.
Northwest of Kettle Falls. US 395 north 6.5 miles, watch for signs.

LEAVENWORTH

BLACKPINE CREEK HORSECAMP (Wenatchee National Forest)
9 units, trailers to 22', well, fishing, hiking, elev. 2900', $.
West of Leavenworth. US 2 .5 mile southeast, CR 71 2.9 miles south, FSR 2451 15.0 miles northwest.

BLUE SHASTIN TRAILER & RV PARK (Private)
60 campsites w/hookups for water/electricity/sewer, reservation information -(509)548-4184, showers, laundry, lounge, swimming pool, trailer waste disposal, river, fishing, hiking, $$$.
Southeast of Leavenworth. US 2 southeast 4.0 miles, US 97 south 7.0 miles.

BONANZA (Wenatchee National Forest)
5 units, trailers to 18', well, stream, hiking, elev. 3000', $.
South of Leavenworth. US 2 4.5 miles southeast, US 97 13.1 miles south.

BRIDGE CREEK (Wenatchee National Forest)
6 units, trailers to 22', well, fishing, hiking, elev. 1900', $.
Southwest of Leavenworth. US 2 .5 mile southwest, CR 71 2.9 miles south, FSR 2451 5.4 miles west.

CHALET PARK (Private)
24 campsites, 12 w/hookups for water/electricity/sewer, 3 w/hookups for water, plus 9 w/out hookups, reservations - (509)548-4578, showers, walking distance to town, $$-$$$.
East of Leavenworth, US 2 .5 mile east.

CHATTER CREEK (Wenatchee National Forest)
13 units, trailers to 22', picnic area, well, fishing, hiking, elev. 2800', $-$$$.
West of Leavenworth. US 2 .5 mile southwest, CR 71 2.9 miles south, FSR 2451 12.3 miles northwest.

CHIWAUKUM CREEK (Wenatchee National Forest)
7 units, some trailers, fishing, hiking, elev. 2400', $.
Northwest of Leavenworth 11 miles. Take US 2 to Chiwaukum Creek Road #265, follow this to campground.

EIGHTMILE (Wenatchee National Forest)
22 units, trailers to 22', well, stream, corral on site, fishing, hiking, elev. 1800', $-$$$.
Southwest of Leavenworth. US 2 .5 mile southwest, CR 71 2.9 miles south, FSR 2451 4.2 miles west.

GLACIER VIEW (Wenatchee National Forest)
20 tent units, picnic area, piped water, lake, boating, swimming, fishing, water skiing, elev. 1900', $.
Northwest of Leavenworth. US 2 15.9 miles northwest, State 207 3.4 miles northeast, CR 290 3.9 miles west, FSR 290 1.5 miles west.

ICICLE RIVER RANCH (Private)
80 campsites, 36 w/hookups for water/electricity/sewer, 6 w/hookups for water & electricity, plus 38 tent sites, reservation information - (509)548-5420, showers, river, swimming, fishing, $$-$$$.
Southwest of Leavenworth. US 2 west to Icicle Road, follow this 3.0 miles to ranch.

JOHNNY CREEK (Wenatchee National Forest)
16 units, trailers to 22', well, fishing, hiking, elev. 2300', $.
West of Leavenworth. US 2 .5 mile southwest, CR 71 2.9 miles south, FSR 2451 8.1 miles northwest.

LAKE WENATCHEE STATE PARK (State of Washington)
197 tent units, some trailers - no hookups, group sites - reservations advised (509)763-3101, picnic shelter, wheelchair access, groceries, trailer waste disposal, summer interpretive programs, boat launch, boating, fishing, swimming, horse trails, horse rental, winter sports, $$-$$$.
North of Leavenworth. US 2 16.0 miles north to junction with State 207, campground is approximately 6.0 miles north.

MAPLE CREEK (Wenatchee National Forest)
7 units, trailers to 22', fishing, entrance to Glacier Peak Wilderness via Little Giant Trailhead, elev. 2600', $.
Northwest of Leavenworth. US 2 15.9 miles northwest, State 207 4.0 miles north, CR 22 1.0 miles east, FSR 311 19.0 miles northwest.

NASON CREEK (Wenatchee National Forest)
67 units, 1 group site, trailers to 32', picnic area, piped water, flush toilets, fishing, Nason Ridge Trailhead, elev. 1800', $$.
Northwest of Leavenworth. US 2 15.9 miles northwest, State 207 3.4 miles northeast, CR 290 .1 mile west.

PINE VILLAGE KOA (Private)
112 campsites, 40 w/hookups for water/electricity/sewer, 24 w/hookups for water & electricity, plus 48 tent sites, reservations - (509)548-7709, showers, laundry, groceries, picnic shelter, playground, trailer waste disposal, swimming pool, river, swimming, fishing, hiking, $$$.
East of Leavenworth. US 2 .3 mile east, River Bend Drive .5 mile north.

ROCK ISLAND (Wenatchee National Forest)
19 units, trailers to 22', well, stream, fishing, hiking, elev. 2900', $.
West of Leavenworth. US 2 .5 mile southwest, CR 71 2.9 miles south, FSR 2451 13.7 miles northwest.

TRONSEN (Wenatchee National Forest)
20 units, trailers to 22', well, stream, hiking, elev. 3900', $.
South of Leavenworth. US 2 4.5 miles southeast, US 97 18.1 miles south.

TUMWATER (Wenatchee National Forest)
80 units, 2 group sites, trailers to 22', picnic area, piped water, stream, flush toilets, fishing, hiking, elev. 2000', $$-$$$.
Northwest of Leavenworth. US 2 9.9 miles northwest.

LONG BEACH

ANDERSEN'S TRAILER COURT (Private)
56 campsites w/hookups for water/electricity/sewer, reservations - (206)642-2231, showers, laundry, trailer waste disposal, ocean access, fishing, playground, $$.
North of Long Beach. State 103 north 3.5 miles.

ANTHONY'S HOME COURT (Private)
21 campsites w/hookups for water/electricity/sewer, reservation information -(206)642-2802, showers, laundry, ice & pop, fish cleaning area, fish smoker, $$.
In Long Beach. State 103 north .6 mile; located at 1310 Pacific Highway North.

CRANBERRY TRAILER PARK (Private)
24 trailer sites w/hookups for water/electricity/sewer, no tents, adults only, reservations - (206)642-2027, showers, $$.
North of Long Beach. State 103 north 3.0 miles, Cranberry Road east .3 mile.

DRIFTWOOD RV TRAV-L-PARK (Private)
50 campsites w/hookups for water/electricity/sewer, reservations - (206)642-2711, showers, ice, $$$.
In Long Beach. State 103 north .8 mile.

EVERGREEN COURT (Private)
18 campsites, 16 w/hookups for water/electricity/sewer, plus 2 tent units, reservation information - (206)665-5100, showers, playground, trailer waste disposal, $-$$.
North of Long Beach. State 103 north 7.9 miles.

FOUR PINES RV COURT (Private)
34 campsites w/hookups for water/electricity/sewer, reservations - (206)642-3990, showers, $$-$$$.
North of Long Beach. State 103 north 1.0 mile.

OCEAN AIRE TRAILER PARK (Private)
50 trailer sites w/hookups for water/electricity/sewer, no tents, trailers to 35', reservation information - (206)665-4027, showers, laundry, ice, $$.
North of Long Beach. State 103 north 9.0 miles to Ocean Park, 260th Street east .1 mile.

OCEAN PARK RESORT (Private)
100 campsites, 94 w/hookups for water/electricity/sewer, plus 6 w/hookups for water & electricity, reservation information - (206)665-4585, showers, laundry, ice, heated swimming pool, spa, playground, $$.
North of Long Beach. State 103 north 9.0 miles to Ocean Park, 259th Street east .1 mile.

PACIFIC PARK TRAILER PARK (Private)
53 trailer sites, 40 w/hookups for water/electricity/sewer, plus 13 w/hookups for water & electricity, reservation information - (206)642-3253, showers, laundry, ocean access, $$.
North of Long Beach. State 103 2.0 miles north.

PEGG'S OCEANSIDE RV PARK (Private)
30 campsites w/hookups for water/electricity/sewer, reservation information -(206)642-2451, showers, ice, ocean access, swimming, fishing, $$.
North of Long Beach. State 103 4.5 miles north.

SAND-LO MOTEL & TRAILER PARK (Private)
14 campsites w/hookups for water/electricity/sewer, reservations - (206)642-2600, showers, laundry, restaurant, groceries, fish cleaning area, $$.
North of Long Beach. State 103 1.0 mile north.

WESTGATE RV PARK & MOTEL (Private)
36 trailer sites, 32 w/hookups for water/electricity/sewer, plus 4 w/out hookups, no tents, reservation information - (206)665-4211, showers, ice, rec room, ocean access, fishing, $$.
North of Long Beach. State 103 north 7.0 miles; at Klipsan Beach.

WHITMAN'S RV PARK & CAMPGROUND (Private)
39 campsites, 29 w/hookups for water/electricity/sewer, plus 10 tent units, reservations - (206)642-2174, showers, laundry, ice, $$.
In Long Beach. State 103 north .5 mile.

WILDWOOD SENIOR RV PARK (Private)
50 campsites, 30 w/hookups for water/electricity/sewer, plus 20 w/out hookups, seniors only - over 50, reservation information - (206)642-2131, showers, trailer waste disposal, lake, fishing, $$.
Southeast of Long Beach. State 103 south to junction with US 101, US 101 east .5 mile, Sandridge Road north .8 mile.

LOOMIS

DAISY (Okanogan National Forest)
3 units, trailers to 18', stream, elev. 4800', $.
Northwest of Loomis. CR 9425 2.1 miles north, CR 390 1.0 mile northwest, FSR 390 14.3 miles west.

IRON GATE (Okanogan National Forest)
1 tent unit, horse trails, corral, stock water, hitch rail & truck dock, elev. 6200'.
West of Loomis. CR 9425 2.1 miles north, CR 4066 1.0 miles north, FSR 39 15.3 miles west, Daisy Creek Road 5.0 miles northwest to campground.

THE STAGE STOP AT SULLY'S (Private)
18 campsites w/hookups for water/electricity/sewer, reservations - (509)223-3275, groceries, ice, restaurant/tavern, $$.
In Loomis. Located at city center on Main Street.

MARBLEMOUNT

ALPINE PARK (Private)
48 campsites, 33 w/hookups for water/electricity/sewer, 15 tent units, reservation information - (206)873-4142, showers, laundry, river, fishing, $$.
East of Marblemount. State 20 1.8 miles east.

BACON CREEK (Mt. Baker-Snoqualmie National Forest)
6 units, some trailers, fishing, hiking, elev. 4000', $.
North of Marblemount 5 miles via State 20.

COLONIAL CREEK (North Cascades National Park)
164 campsites, trailers to 22', information - (206)855-1331, wheelchair access, drinking water, flush toilets, picnic shelter, summer interpretive program, trailer waste disposal, at Diablo Lake, fishing, boat launch, hiking, $$.
East of Marblemount. State 20 16.0 miles east.

GOODELL CREEK (North Cascades National Park)
22 campsites, trailers to 22', drinking water, on Skagit River, fishing, hiking, $.
East of Marblemount. State 20 13.0 miles east.

NEWHALEM CREEK (North Cascades National Park)
129 campsites, trailers to 22', drinking water, flush toilets, wheelchair access, trailer waste disposal, on Newhalem Creek at Skagit River, fishing, hiking, $$.
East of Marblemount. State 20 14.0 miles east.

METALINE FALLS

CRAWFORD STATE PARK (State of Washington)
10 primitive tent sites, wheelchair access, large limestone cave - guided tours - open summer only, $.
Northwest of Metaline Falls. Take State 31 north approximately 9.0 miles and follow signs to Gardner Cave and Crawford State Park.

CRESCENT LAKE (Colville National Forest)
13 units, trailers to 32', fishing, hiking trails, elev. 2600', $.
North of Metaline Falls. State 31 11.0 miles north.

MILLPOND (Colville National Forest)
10 units, trailers to 22', well, stream, fishing, elev. 2400', $$.
East of Metaline Falls. State 31 1.5 miles east, CR 9345 3.5 miles east.

MT. LINTON RV PARK (Private)
26 campsites w/hookups for water/electricity/sewer, reservation information -(509)446-4553, showers, laundry, playfield, river, fishing, $$-$$$.
South of Metaline Falls. State 31 south to Metaline; located at city center.

SULLIVAN LAKE (Colville National Forest)
35 units, trailer to 32', 1 group site - reservation required (509)446-2681, piped water, boating, fishing, water skiing, elev. 2600', $$-$$$.
East of Metaline Falls. State 31 1.5 miles east, CR 9345 5.0 miles east.

MONTESANO

CHETWOOT (Olympic National Forest)
8 tent units, lake, boat launch, interpretive service, boating, swimming, fishing, water skiing, hiking trails, hike-in or boat-in only, elev. 800', $.
South of Montesano. CR 58 12.0 miles north, FSR 220 21.0 miles north, FSR 234 2.5 miles north, Trail 878 .5 miles east.

COHO (Olympic National Forest)
46 units, trailers to 32', piped water, lake, flush toilets, wheelchair access, paved nature trail, elev. 900', $$.
North of Montesano. CR 58 12.0 miles north, FSR 220 20.0 miles north, FSR 234 1.5 miles north.

LAKE SYLVIA STATE PARK (State of Washington)
35 tent units, group sites - reservations advised (206)249-3621, community kitchen/shelter, wheelchair access, boat rental, snack bar, groceries, trailer waste disposal, boat launch, fishing, swimming, $$-$$$.
North of Montesano. Campground is just off State 12, north of Montesano.

MAPLEWOOD MANOR RV PARK (Private)
104 campsites, 16 w/hookups for water/electricity/sewer, plus 88 w/hookups for water & electricity, reservation information - (206)482-2888, showers, laundry, trailer waste disposal, $$.
East of Montesano. US 12 10.0 miles east, Fairgrounds Rd. east to park, in Elma.

SCHAFER STATE PARK (State of Washington)
47 tent units, 6 trailer sites w/hookups for water & electricity, community kitchen/shelter, trailer waste disposal, beach access, fishing, on East Fork of Satsop River, $$.
Northeast of Montesano. State 12 east of Montesano just past Brady to Satsop River Road, follow this approximately 5.0 miles to campground.

TENAS (Olympic National Forest)
9 tent units, no picnic tables, interpretive services, hike-in or boat-in only, lake, boat launch, swimming, fishing, water skiing, hiking trails, elev. 800', $.
North of Montesano. CR 58 12.0 miles north, FSR 220 20.0 miles north, FSR 22022 2.0 miles north, Trail 878 .5 mile west.

WYNOOCHEE FALLS (Olympic National Forest)
18 tent units, well, river, fishing, elev. 1000', $.
North of Montesano. CR 141 18.5 miles north, FSR 220 26.7 miles north, FSR 2312 10.0 miles northeast.

MOSES LAKE

BIG SUN RESORT & RV PARK (Private)
50 campsites w/hookups for water/electricity/sewer, reservation information -(509)765-8294, wheelchair access, showers, laundry, ice, playground, on Moses Lake, swimming, fishing, boat launch, boat rental, $$.
In Moses Lake. Leave I-90 at exit #176 and take Broadway north .5 mile, campground is west at 2300 W. Marina Drive.

COMFORT INN RV PARK (Private)
30 campsites w/hookups for water/electricity/sewer, reservation information -(509)659-1007, wheelchair access, showers, laundry, groceries, swimming pool, therapy pool, nearby golf, $$$.
East of Moses Lake. I-90 east to exit #221; located along frontage road.

COTTAGE RV PARK & MOTEL (Private)
19 campsites w/hookups for water/electricity/sewer, reservation information -(509)659-0721, showers, trailer waste disposal, $$.
East of Moses Lake. I-90 east to exit #220, located in Ritzville at city center.

FISH HAVEN (Private)
83 campsites, 80 w/hookups for water/electricity/sewer, plus 3 w/hookups for water, reservations (509)346-2366, showers, groceries, close to O'Sullivan Dam Lake, swimming, fishing, senior discount, $$-$$$.
South of Moses Lake. Leave I-90 at exit #179, State 17 10.0 miles south, O'Sullivan Road 11.0 miles west.

MAR DON RESORT (Private)
350 campsites, 110 w/hookups for water/electricity/sewer, 55 w/hookups for water & electricity, 60 w/out hookups, plus beach tent area, information -(509)765-5061, flush toilets, showers, cafe/lounge, playground, large fish supply & grocery store, on Potholes Reservoir, 2 fishing docks, 2 boat launches, boat rental (no motors for rent), swimming beach, hiking, $$-$$$.
Southwest of Moses Lake. Located on Potholes Reservoir, 18.0 miles southwest of Moses Lake.

OASIS PARK (Private)
66 campsites, 28 w/hookups for water/electricity/sewer, plus 38 w/hookups for electricity, reservation information - (509)754-5102, wheelchair access, showers, laundry, groceries, swimming pool, mini-golf, nearby golf course, playfield, trailer waste disposal, pond, swimming, fishing, hiking, $$-$$$.
Northwest of Moses Lake. State 171 northwest 17.0 miles, State 282 northwest 5.0 miles, State 28 southwest 1.0 miles; in Ephrata.

ODESSA GOLF & RV PARK (Private)
12 campsites w/hookups for water & electricity, reservations - (509)982-0093, on Odessa Golf Course (9-hole), golfers stay for free, $$.
Northeast of Moses Lake. I-90 east 27.0 miles, State 21 north 19.0 miles; State 28 to west end of Odessa and campground.

POTHOLES STATE PARK (State of Washington)
66 tent units, 60 trailer sites w/hookups for water/electricity/sewer, trailer waste disposal, on Potholes Reservoir, boat launch, fishing, water skiing, $$.
Southwest of Moses Lake. State 17 10.0 miles southeast, Potholes Reservoir Road 13.0 miles west.

SOAP LAKES SMOKIAM CAMPGROUND (City)
52 campsites w/hookups for water/electricity/sewer, reservation information -(509)246-1366, showers, playground, lake, swimming, fishing, boat launch, $$.
Northwest of Moses Lake. State 171 northwest 17.0 miles, State 17 north 9.0 miles.

WILLOWS TRAILER VILLAGE (Private)
76 campsites, 35 w/hookups for water/electricity/sewer, 30 w/hookups for water & electricity, plus 11 tent units, reservation information - (509)765-7531, showers, laundry, groceries, fishing supplies, playfield, trailer waste disposal, $$-$$$.
South of Moses Lake. Leave I-90 at exit #179, State 17 south 2.0 miles, CR M southeast .3 mile.

NACHES

AMERICAN FORKS (Wenatchee National Forest)
15 units, trailers to 22', picnic area, well, river, fishing, elev. 2800', $.
Northwest of Naches. US 12 4.3 miles west, State 410 27.8 miles northwest, FSR 174 .2 mile southwest.

AMERICAN RIDGE LODGE (Wenatchee National Forest)
10 group sites, trailers to 18', reservations required (509)653-2205, shelter, no water, sledding, elev. 3000', $$$.
Northwest of Naches. US 12 4.3 miles north, State 410 27.8 miles northwest, FSR 174 .1 mile southwest, FSR 174B .5 mile southwest.

BOULDER CAVE (Mt. Baker-Snoqualmie National Forest)
22 tent units, community kitchen, stream, fishing, hiking, elev. 2400', $.
Northwest of Naches. US 12 4.3 miles west, State 410 23.0 miles northwest, campground is across river from Naches Highway.

BUMPING LAKE (Wenatchee National Forest)
12 units, trailers to 22', well, boat launch, boating, swimming, fishing, water skiing, elev. 3400', $.
Northwest of Naches. US 12 4.3 miles west, State 410 27.8 miles northwest, FSR 174 11.1 miles southwest, FSR 174D .3 mile west.

CEDAR SPRINGS (Wenatchee National Forest)
15 units, trailers to 22', well, fishing, elev. 2800', $.
Northwest of Naches. US 12 4.3 miles west, State 410 27.8 miles northwest, FSR 174 .5 mile southwest.

CLEAR LAKE NORTH (Wenatchee National Forest)
35 units, trailers to 22', group sites - reservations required (509)653-2205, lake - speed limits, boating, fishing, elev. 3000', $$-$$$.
Southwest of Naches. US 12 35.6 miles west, State 43 .9 mile south, FSR 1312 .5 mile south.

COTTON WOOD (Wenatchee National Forest)
16 units, trailers to 22', well, river, fishing, elev. 2300', $.
Northwest of Naches. US 12 4.3 miles west, State 410 17.7 miles northwest.

COUGAR FLAT (Wenatchee National Forest)
12 units, trailers to 18', well, river, fishing, elev. 3100', $.
Northwest of Naches. US 12 4.3 miles west, State 410 27.8 miles northwest, FSR 174 6.0 miles southwest.

CRANE PARK (Wenatchee National Forest)
6 units, no trailers, lake, boating, swimming, fishing, water skiing, elev. 3000', $.
Southwest of Naches. US 12 23.0 miles west, FSR 143 2.9 miles south, FSR 1382 1.0 miles west.

DEEP CREEK (Wenatchee National Forest)
6 units, trailers to 18', Trailhead into Cougar Lakes Area, elev. 4300', $.
West of Naches. US 12 4.3 miles west, State 410 27.8 miles northwest, FSR 174 13.3 miles southwest, FSR 162 7.0 miles southwest.

EAST POINT (Mt. Baker-Snoqualmie National Forest)
4 tent units, no trailers, lake, fishing, water skiing, hiking, elev. 3000', $.
Southwest of Naches. US 12 23.0 miles west, FSR 143 2.9 miles south,
FSR 1382 2.0 miles west.

GRANITE LAKE (Wenatchee National Forest)
8 units, trailers to 18', boating, swimming, fishing, elev. 5000', $.
West of Naches. US 12 4.3 miles west, State 410 27.8 miles northwest,
FSR 174 13.9 miles southwest, FSR 163 3.7 miles southwest.

GREY CREEK (Wenatchee National Forest)
5 units, trailers to 18', fishing, elev. 4000', $.
Southwest of Naches. US 12 23.0 miles west, FSR 143 4.5 miles south,
FSR 133 5.7 miles southwest.

HAUSE CREEK (Wenatchee National Forest)
42 units, trailers to 22', piped water, flush toilets, wheelchair access,
fishing, elev. 2500'', $$.
Southwest of Naches. US 12 21.9 miles west.

HELLS CROSSING (Wenatchee National Forest)
17 units, trailers to 18', picnic area, well, river, fishing, elev. 3200', $.
Northwest of Naches. US 12 4.3 miles west, State 410 33.7 miles north-
west.

HUCKLEBERRY (Mt. Baker-Snoqualmie National Forest)
8 tent units, river, fishing, berry picking, elev. 5300', $.
Northwest of Naches. US 12 4.3 miles west, State 410 24.0 miles north-
west, FSR 197 3.0 miles northwest, FSR 182 7.0 miles to campground.

INDIAN CREEK (Wenatchee National Forest)
39 units, trailers to 22', piped water, lake, groceries, ice, elev. 3000', $$.
Southwest of Naches. US 12 31.8 miles west.

INDIAN FLAT (Wenatchee National Forest)
11 units, trailers to 18', well, river, fishing, elev. 2600', $.
Northwest of Naches. US 12 4.3 miles west, State 410 26.6 miles northwest.

JUNGLE CREEK (Mt. Baker-Snoqualmie National Forest)
9 tent units, stream, fishing, hiking, elev. 2700', $.
Northwest of Naches. US 12 4.3 miles west, State 410 24.0 miles northwest, FSR 197 3.0 miles northwest to campground.

KANER FLAT (Wenatchee National Forest)
34 units, 6 group sites, trailers to 22', picnic area, well, river, fishing,
historic wagon train campsite along the Old Naches Trail, elev. 2600', $.
Northwest of Naches. US 12 4.3 miles west, State 410 24.9 miles northwest, FSR 197 2.5 miles northwest.

LITTLE NACHES (Wenatchee National Forest)
12 units, trailers to 18', river, fishing, elev. 2500', $.
Northwest of Naches. US 12 4.3 miles west, State 410 24.9 miles northwest, FSR 197 .1 mile northwest.

LODGE POLE (Wenatchee National Forest)
34 units, trailers to 22', picnic area, well, river, fishing, elev. 3500', $.
Northwest of Naches. US 12 4.3 miles west, State 410 40.6 miles northwest. Campground is located 8.3 miles from Chinook Pass & Mt. Rainier
National Park.

LONESOME COVE (Wenatchee National Forest)
5 tent units, lake, boating, swimming, fishing, water skiing, elev. 3000', $.
Southwest of Naches. US 12 23.0 miles west, FSR 143 2.9 miles south,
FSR 1382 2.0 miles southwest.

LONGMIRE MEADOW (Wenatchee National Forest)
13 units, trailers to 18', river, fishing, elev. 2800', $.
Northwest of Naches. US 12 4.3 miles west, State 410 24.3 miles northwest, FSR 197 4.1 miles northwest.

LOST LAKE (Wenatchee National Forest)
3 tent units, boating, swimming, fishing, elev. 3500', $.
West of Naches. US 12 23.0 miles west, FSR 143 .2 mile south, FSR 1402
4.6 miles southeast.

MORSE CREEK (Mt. Baker-Snoqualmie National Forest)
8 tent units, no trailers, fishing, elev. 3700', $.
Northwest of Naches. US 12 4.3 miles west, State 410 41.6 miles northwest, campground is just south of the highway 6.3 miles from Chinook
Pass & Mt. Rainier National Park.

RIVER BEND (Wenatchee National Forest)
6 units, trailers to 18', piped water, fishing, elev. 2500', $.
Southwest of Naches. US 12 21.8 miles west.

SAWMILL FLAT (Wenatchee National Forest)
27 units, trailers to 22', picnic area, well, river, wheelchair access, fishing,
elev. 2500', $.
Northwest of Naches. US 12 4.3 miles west, State 410 23.7 miles northwest.

SECTION 3 LAKE (Wenatchee National Forest)
3 tent units, elev. 6000', $.
Southwest of Naches. US 12 32.4 miles west, FSR 143 5.5 miles south,
FSR 1311 5.7 miles south, FSR 1314 4.0 miles southwest.

SILVER COVE (Wenatchee National Forest)
5 campsites, trailers okay, piped water, boating, fishing, swimming, water
skiing, elev. 3000', $.
Southwest of Naches. US 12 23.0 miles west, FSR 143 6.1 miles southwest
to campground.

SODA SPRINGS (Wenatchee National Forest)
26 units, trailers to 18', well, fishing, natural mineral springs, elev. 3100',
$$.
Northwest of Naches. US 12 4.3 miles west, State 410 27.8 miles north-
west, FSR 174 4.8 miles southwest.

SOUTH FORK BAY (Wenatchee National Forest)
5 units, trailers to 18', river, boating, fishing, water skiing, elev. 2900', $.
Southwest of Naches. US 12 23.0 miles west, FSR 143 4.0 miles south,
FSR 1326 .1 mile south.

SQUAW ROCK RESORT (Private)
64 campsites, 28 w/hookups for water/electricity/sewer, plus 36 w/hookups
for water & electricity, reservations - (509)658-2926, showers, laundry,
groceries, playground, swimming pool, trailer waste disposal, on Naches
River, fishing, hiking, $$$.
Northwest of Naches. US 12 west 4.0 miles, State 410 northwest 15.0
miles.

WILLOWS (Wenatchee National Forest)
16 units, trailers to 18', river, fishing, elev. 2400', $.
West of Naches. US 12 20.0 miles west.

WINDY POINT (Wenatchee National Forest)
15 units, trailers to 22', well, river, fishing, elev. 2000', $.
West of Naches. US 12 12.7 miles west.

NEWHALEM

DEVIL'S PARK (Okanogan National Forest)
Tenting areas in Pasayten Wilderness, horse trails, meager grazing, scarce water in late summer, creek, $.
East of Newhalem. State 20 approximately 15 miles east to Devil's Park Trailhead #738 located on north side of highway, take trail 3.5 miles to campground.

DIABLO LAKE RESORT CAMPGROUND (Private)
15 campsites w/hookups for water & electricity, restrooms, groceries & fishing supplies, restaurant/lounge, game room, on Diablo Lake, marina - boat rentals -outboards/sailboats/canoes, swimming, fishing, $$-$$$.
East of Newhalem. State 20 9.0 miles east.

McMILLAN PARK (Okanogan National Forest)
Tenting areas in Pasayten Wilderness, horse trails, meager grazing, scarce water in late summer, creek, $.
East of Newhalem. State 20 approximately 15 miles east to Devil's Park Trailhead #738 located on north side of highway, take trail 2.0 miles to campground.

NEWPORT

CIRCLE MOON (Private)
54 campsites, 34 w/hookups for water/electricity/sewer, plus 20 w/out hookups, tents okay, reservations - (509)447-3735, showers, playground, trailer waste disposal, $$.
West of Newport. US 2 southwest 13.0 miles, State 211 north 4.0 miles.

JERRY'S LANDING RV PARK (Private)
25 trailer sites, 16 w/hookups for water/electricity/sewer, plus 9 w/hookups for water & electricity, trailers to 35', reservation information - (509)292-2337, showers, groceries, trailer waste disposal, lake, swimming, fishing, boat launch, boat rental, $$.
Southwest of Newport. US 2 southwest approximately 19.0 miles, Oregon Road west 1.0 mile to Eloika Lake.

PEND OREILLE PARK (Pend Oreille County)
40 campsites, reservations - (509)292-8432, drinking water, flush toilets, showers, old growth timber, hiker/horse trails, $$.
Southwest of Newport. US 2 southwest 16.0 miles.

PIONEER PARK (Colville National Forest)
13 units, 1 group site, trailers to 22', piped water, on Box Canyon Reservoir, wheelchair access, boat launch, boating, fishing, water skiing, elev. 2100', $$.
North of Newport. US 2 .5 mile northeast, CR CH007 2.0 miles north.

WATERS EDGE CAMPGROUND (Private)
40 campsites, 19 w/hookups for water/electricity/sewer, 4 w/hookups for water & electricity, plus 17 tent units, reservation information - (509)292-2111, showers, laundry, ice, trailer waste disposal, lake, swimming, fishing, boat launch, boat rental, $$-$$$.
Southwest of Newport. US 2 southwest approximately 22.0 miles, Bridges Road .5 mile west.

NORTH BEND

CAMP JOY (Mt. Baker-Snoqualmie National Forest)
10 tent units, stream, fishing, hiking, elev. 1800', $.
Southeast of North Bend 15 miles via I-90 and Bandera Airfield Road.

DENNY CREEK (Mt. Baker-Snoqualmie National Forest)
34 units, 3 group sites, trailers to 22', well, fishing, elev. 2200', $$-$$$.
Southeast of North Bend. Take I-90 17.0 miles southeast, FSR 58 2.2 miles northeast.

MINE CREEK (Dept. of Natural Resources)
17 campsites, river, wheelchair access, $.
East of North Bend. Campground is located 8.0 miles east of North Bend on Middle Fork Snoqualmie River.

MOUNT PHELPS (Dept. of Natural Resources)
11 campsites, $.
Northeast of North Bend. Campground is located along North Fork of Snoqualmie River, 18.0 miles northeast of North Bend.

MOUNT SI (Dept. of Natural Resources)
6 campsites, picnic area, hike-in only, drinking water, hiking trails, $$.
Northeast of North Bend. Campground is located 2.0 miles northeast of town on CCC Road to Mount Si Trailhead, take trail to summit and campsites.

SNOQUALMIE RIVER CAMPGROUND (Private)
40 trailer sites w/hookups for electricity, reservation information - (206)222-5545, showers, playground, trailer waste disposal, on Snoqualmie River, swimming, fishing, $$.
Northwest of North Bend. I-90 northwest to exit #22, north 3.5 miles to Raging River Bridge, 44th Place southeast 1.0 mile.

TINKHAM (Mt. Baker-Snoqualmie National Forest)
40 units, 7 group sites, trailers to 22', well, river, wheelchair access, fishing, elev. 1800', $$.
Southeast of North Bend. Take I-90 10.0 miles southeast, FSR 55 1.5 miles southeast.

WAGNER BRIDGE (Dept. of Natural Resources)
10 campsites, $.
Northeast of North Bend. Campground is located along North Fork Snoqualmie River, 15.0 miles northeast of North Bend.

OKANOGAN

AMERICAN LEGION PARK (City of Okanogan)
49 campsites, information - (509)422-3600, drinking water, flush toilets, showers, picnic shelter, on Okanogan River, fishing, $.
In Okanogan. Located on State 215 at north edge of town.

CONCONULLY STATE PARK (State of Washington)
65 tent units, 10 trailer sites w/hookups for water, community kitchen, trailer waste disposal, boat launch, fishing, swimming, nature trail, $$.
Northwest of Okanogan. US 97 2.4 miles north, Conconully road 18.0 miles northwest to campground.

COUNTY FAIRGROUNDS (Okanogan County)
90 campsites, 50 w/hookups for water/electricity/sewer, plus 40 w/hookups for water & electricity, tents okay, reservations - (509)422-1621, showers, on Okanogan River, fishing, $$.
North of Okanogan. Located on east side of Okanogan River; 1.0 mile north of town.

EAST SIDE PARK CAMPGROUND (City)
76 campsites, 36 w/hookups for water/electricity/sewer, plus 40 tent units, reservation information - (509)826-1170, showers, tennis, swimming pool, playfield, trailer waste disposal, river, boat launch, $$.
Northeast of Okanogan. State 20 north 5.0 miles to Omak; located near Stampede Fairgrounds area.

OLYMPIA

AMERICAN HERITAGE KOA (Private)
105 campsites, 24 w/hookups for water/electricity/sewer, 52 w/hookups for water & electricity, plus 29 tent units, reservations - (206)943-8778, showers, laundry, groceries, swimming pool, playfield, playground, trailer waste disposal, $$$.
South of Olympia. Take exit #99 off I-5 and go east .3 mile, turn south to 9610 Kimmie Street SW.

BLACK LAKE RV PARK (Private)
65 campsites, 32 w/hookups for water/electricity/sewer, 18 w/hookups for water & electricity, plus 15 w/out hookups, reservations - (206)357-6775, showers, groceries, trailer waste disposal, on Black Lake, swimming, fishing, boat launch, boat rental, $$.
Southwest of Olympia. I-5 to exit #104, US 101 2.0 miles west, Black Lake Blvd. 2.0 miles south.

COACH POST MOTOR HOME & RV PARK (Private)
25 trailer sites, 20 w/hookups for water/electricity/sewer, plus 5 w/hookups for water & electricity, no tents, reservation information - (206)754-7580, showers, laundry, playfield, $$.
Southwest of Olympia. I-5 to exit #104, US 101 west 3.0 miles to Kaiser Road and campground.

COLUMBUS PARK (Private)
76 campsites, 48 w/hookups for water/electricity/sewer, plus 28 w/hookups for water & electricity, trailers to 35', reservations - (206)786-9460, wheelchair access, showers, laundry, picnic shelter, playground, playfield, trailer waste disposal, on Black Lake, stream, swimming, fishing, boat launch, paddle boat rental, $$.
Southwest of Olympia. I-5 to exit #104, US 101 west 2.0 miles to Black Lake Blvd., south 3.5 miles to campground.

DEEP LAKE RESORT (Private)
48 campsites, 13 w/hookups for water/electricity/sewer, 30 w/hookups for water & electricity, plus 5 tent units, trailers to 35', reservations - (206)352-7388, showers, laundry, groceries, playfield, playground, trailer waste disposal, lake, swimming, fishing, boat launch & rental, $$-$$$.
South of Olympia. I-5 to exit #95, Maytown Road east 2.5 miles, Tilley Road north .5 mile.

FALL CREEK (Dept. of Natural Resources)
8 campsites, drinking water, creek, wheelchair access, horse & hiking trails, horse facilities, $$.
Southwest of Olympia. Campground is located 5.0 miles west of Delphi entrance to Capitol Forest Multiple Use Area, on Fall Creek.

HOLLYWOOD (Dept. of Natural Resources)
10 campsites, drinking water, trails for horses/hikers/trailbikes, $$.
Southwest of Olympia. Campground is 6.0 miles northwest of Littlerock on Waddell Creek, in Capitol Forest Multiple Use Area.

MARGARET McKENNY (Dept. of Natural Resources)
18 campsites, drinking water, trails for horses/hikers/trailbikes, horse facilities, $$.
Southwest of Olympia. Campground is 3.0 miles northwest of Littlerock along Waddell Creek Road, in Capitol Forest Multiple Use Area.

MARTIN WAY RV PARK (Private)
14 trailer sites, 10 w/hookups for water/electricity/sewer, plus 4 w/hookups for water & electricity, no tents, reservation information - (206)491-6840, showers, laundry, playfield, $$.
Northeast of Olympia. I-5 to exit #111, State 510 east .8 mile, Martin Way south .1 mile to park.

MILLERSYLVANIA STATE PARK (State of Washington)
135 tent units, 52 trailer sites w/hookups for water & electricity, group sites - reservations advised (206)753-1519, community kitchen, wheelchair access, trailer waste disposal, boat launch, fishing, swimming, fitness trail, old-growth trees, $$-$$$.
South of Olympia. Take I-5 south of Olympia about 10.0 miles.

MIMA FALLS TRAILHEAD (Dept. of Natural Resources)
3 campsites, trails for hikers & horses, horse facilities, $.
Southwest of Olympia. Campground is 4.0 miles west of Littlerock at trailhead, in Capitol Forest Multiple Use Area.

MT. MOLLY (Dept. of Natural Resources)
10 campsites, drinking water, trails for horses/hikers/trailbikes, $$.
Southwest of Olympia. Campground is 6.0 miles northwest of Littlerock on Waddell Creek, in Capitol Forest Multiple Use Area.

NISQUALLY PLAZA RV PARK (Private)
55 trailer sites, 27 w/hookups for water/electricity/sewer, 21 w/hookups for water & electricity, plus 7 w/out hookups, no tents, reservation information -(206)491-3831, showers, laundry, groceries, swimming pool, playfield, playground, trailer waste disposal, river, fishing, boat launch, $$-$$$.
North of Olympia. I-5 to 7.0 miles north of town to exit #114.

NORTH CREEK (Dept. of Natural Resources)
5 campsites, drinking water, trails for hikers & horses, $$.
Southwest of Olympia. Campground is 6.0 miles northeast of Oakville on Cedar Creek Road, in Capitol Forest Multiple Use Area.

OLYMPIA KOA (Private)
105 campsites, 28 w/hookups for water/electricity/sewer, 45 w/hookups for water & electricity, plus 32 tent units, reservations - (206)352-2551, showers, laundry, groceries, picnic shelter, swimming pool, playground, trailer waste disposal, $$$.
South of Olympia. Take exit #99 off I-5 and go east .3 mile, turn north and travel 1.0 mile on Kimmie to 83rd Avenue, campground is .3 mile at 1441 83rd Avenue SW.

PORTER CREEK (Dept. of Natural Resources)
16 campsites, drinking water, trails for hikers/horses/trailbikes, horse facilities, $$.
Southwest of Olympia. Campground is 5.0 miles northeast of Porter, on Porter Creek Road, in Capitol Forest Multiple Use Area.

SALMON SHORE RESORT (Private)
50 campsites, 25 w/hookups for water/electricity/sewer, 15 w/hookups for water & electricity, plus 10 w/hookups for electricity, trailers to 35', reservation information - (206)357-8618, showers, laundry, groceries, picnic shelter, trailer waste disposal, lake, swimming, fishing, boat launch, boat rental, playfield, playground, $$.
Southwest of Olympia. I-5 to exit #104, US 101 west 2.0 miles to Black Lake Blvd., south 3.3 miles to resort.

SHERMAN VALLEY "Y" (Dept. of Natural Resources)
11 campsites, drinking water, trails for hikers & horses, $$.
Southwest of Olympia. Campground is 9.0 miles west of Littlerock along Cedar Creek, in Capitol Forest Multiple Use Area.

STAN'S RV PARK (Private)
41 campsites, 33 w/hookups for water & electricity, plus 8 w/out hookups, small tents okay, reservations - (206)943-3614, showers, playfield, trailer waste disposal, $$-$$$.
South of Olympia. Take exit #99 off I-5 to park; located at 2430 93rd Avenue SW.

ORIENT

SUMMIT LAKE (Colville National Forest)
5 units, no trailers, well, boat launch, boating, fishing, elev. 3600', $.
Northeast of Orient. CR 1510 3.8 miles east, CR 1500 5.0 miles north.

PACIFIC BEACH

BLUE PACIFIC MOTEL & TRAILER PARK (Private)
19 trailer sites, 13 w/hookups for water/electricity/sewer, plus 6 w/hookups for water & electricity, trailers to 30', no tents, reservation information -(206)289-2262, showers, playfield, playground, stream, $$$.
South of Pacific Beach. State 109 south 10.0 miles.

DRIFTWOOD ACRES OCEAN CAMPGROUND (Private)
45 campsites, 20 w/hookups for water/electricity/sewer, plus 25 w/hookups for water & electricity, reservation information - (206)289-3484, showers, trailer waste disposal, ocean access, river, swimming, fishing, $$$.
South of Pacific Beach. State 109 7.0 miles south, campground is located just north of Copalis Beach bridge.

HIDE-AWAY MOTEL & RV PARK (Private)
45 campsites, 2 w/hookups for water/electricity/sewer, 33 w/hookups for water & electricity, plus 10 w/out hookups, reservation information - (206)289-2182, showers, trailer waste disposal, $$$.
South of Pacific Beach. State 109 7.0 miles south, campground is located just north of Copalis Beach bridge.

LOOKOUT TRAILER COURT (Private)
20 trailer sites w/hookups for water/electricity/sewer, reservation information - (206)289-2220, showers, $$$.
South of Pacific Beach. State 109 10.5 miles, in Ocean City.

OCEAN CITY STATE PARK (State of Washington)
149 tent units, 29 trailer sites w/hookups for water/electricity/sewer, group sites - reservations advised (206)289-3553, community kitchen, wheelchair access, trailer waste disposal, fishing, beach access, $$-$$$.
South of Pacific Beach. State 109 south 12.0 miles to State 115; campground is located 2.0 miles north of Ocean Shores.

PACIFIC BEACH STATE PARK (State of Washington)
118 tent units, 20 trailer sites w/hookups for water & electricity, trailer waste disposal, fishing, beachcombing, clamming, $$.
At Pacific Beach. Campground is located off State 109 in Pacific Beach.

RIVERSIDE TRAILER COURT (Private)
68 trailer sites, 53 w/hookups for water/electricity/sewer, plus 15 w/hookups for water & electricity, reservation information - (206)289-2111, showers, rec room, trailer waste disposal, river, fishing, $$$.
South of Pacific Beach. State 109 7.0 miles south, campground is located just north of Copalis Beach bridge.

ROAD HOST USA RV PARKS (Private)
30 trailer sites w/hookups for water/electricity/sewer, adults only, reservation information - (206)289-3976, showers, rec room, $$.
South of Pacific Beach. State 109 8.5 miles south.

ROD'S BEACH RESORT & RV PARK (Private)
80 trailer sites w/hookups for water/electricity/sewer, no tents, reservation information - (206)289-2222, showers, groceries, trailer waste disposal, heated swimming pool, ocean access, fishing, rec room, playground, $$$.
South of Pacific Beach. State 109 7.5 miles south, park is located just south of Copalis Beach.

STURGEON TRAILER HARBOR (Private)
70 trailer sites, 54 w/hookups for water/electricity/sewer, plus 16 w/hookups for water & electricity, no tents, reservation information - (206)289-2101, showers, rec room, $$$.
South of Pacific Beach. State 109 10.5 miles south to Ocean City and park.

SURF & SAND RV PARK (Private)
44 campsites, 39 w/hookups for water/electricity/sewer, plus 5 w/hookups for water & electricity, reservation information - (206)289-2707, showers, trailer waste disposal, ocean access, fishing, $$$.
South of Pacific Beach. State 109 7.2 miles south, park is located in Copalis Beach on beach access road.

TIDELANDS ON THE BEACH RV PARK (Private)
55 campsites, 16 w/hookups for water/electricity/sewer, plus 39 w/hookups for water & electricity, reservation information - (206)289-8963, showers, rec room, playfield, playground, trailer waste disposal, ocean access, swimming, fishing, $$-$$$.
South of Pacific Beach. State 109 8.1 miles south.

PACKWOOD

ALPINE (Gifford Pinchot National Forest)
6 tent units, creek, hike-in only, elev. 5800', $.
Southeast of Packwood. US 12 2.0 miles southwest, FSR 21 11.0 miles south, FSR 2150 3.0 miles northwest to Chambers Lake Campground, Trail #96 4.3 miles to campground.

BYPASS (Gifford Pinchot National Forest)
5 tent units, creek, hike-in only, elev. 5500', $.
Southeast of Packwood. US 12 2.0 miles southwest, FSR 21 11.0 miles south, FSR 2150 3.0 miles northwest to Chambers Lake Campground, Trail #96 4.0 miles to campground.

CHAMBERS LAKE (Gifford Pinchot National Forest)
7 tent units, no trailers, fishing, hiking, elev. 4500', $.
Southeast of Packwood 40 miles. US 12 2.0 miles southwest, FSR 21 11.0 miles south, FSR 2150 3.0 miles northwest to campground.

HATCHERY R.V. CAMP (Gifford Pinchot National Forest)
25 units, trailers to 22', river, wheelchair access, fishing, elev. 1400', $$.
Northeast of Packwood. US 12 7.1 miles northeast, FSR 01272 .8 mile west to campground. Located 4 miles south of Mt. Rainier National Park.

LA WIS WIS (Gifford Pinchot National Forest)
100 units, trailers to 18', piped water, river, flush toilets, fishing, hiking, elev. 1400', $$.
Northeast of Packwood. US 12 2.1 miles northeast, FSR 1272 .6 mile west. Located 4 miles south of Mt. Rainier National Park.

LOST LAKE (Gifford Pinchot National Forest)
2 camp areas, 8 tent units, lake, hike-in only, elev. 5200', $.
Southeast of Packwood. Leave US 12 in Packwood on Packwood Lake Road, follow 4.0 miles to end, take Trail #78 4.0 miles to Packwood Lake, continue on Trail #78 3.6 miles to Lost Lake.

OHANAPECOSH (Mt. Rainier National Park)
232 campsites, trailers to 30', trailer waste disposal, on Ohanapecosh River, fishing, hiking, elev. 2000', $$.
Northeast of Packwood. US 12 northeast 8.0 miles, State 123 north; campground is located 1.5 miles south of Mt. Rainier National Park's Stevens Canyon Entrance.

PACKWOOD LAKE (Gifford Pinchot National Forest)
18 tent units, piped water, boating, fishing, water skiing, hike-in only, elev. 2900', $.
Southeast of Packwood. Leave US 12 in Packwood on Packwood Lake Road, follow 4.0 miles to end, take Trail #78 4.0 miles to Packwood Lake.

PACKWOOD RV PARK (Private)
66 campsites w/hookups for water/electricity/sewer, reservation information -(206)494-5145, showers, playfield, trailer waste disposal, $$-$$$.
In Packwood. Located at city center.

WALUPT LAKE (Gifford Pinchot National Forest)
44 units, trailers to 22', lake - speed limits, wheelchair access, boating, fishing, trail to Goat Rocks Wilderness, elev. 3900', $$.
Southeast of Packwood. US 12 2.7 miles southwest, FSR 2100 16.4 miles southeast, FSR 2160 4.5 miles east.

POMEROY

CENTRAL FERRY STATE PARK (State of Washington)
60 trailer sites w/hookups for water/electricity/sewer, picnic shelter, wheelchair access, trailer waste disposal, on Snake River, boat launch, boating, fishing, water skiing, $$.
Northwest of Pomeroy. US 12 13.0 miles northwest, State 127 9.0 miles north.

CHIEF TIMOTHY STATE PARK (State of Washington)
33 tent units, 33 trailer sites w/hookups for water/electricity/sewer, picnic shelter, wheelchair access, trailer waste disposal, boat launch, docks for boat campers, fishing, water sports, interpretive center on Lewis & Clark Expedition, groceries, $$.
East of Pomeroy. US 12 22.0 miles east.

LYONS FERRY STATE PARK (State of Washington)
50 tent units, some trailers - no hookups, picnic shelter, wheelchair access, trailer waste disposal, at confluence of Snake & Palouse Rivers, boat launch, fishing, swimming, $$.
Northwest of Pomeroy. US 12 13.0 miles northwest, State 261 25.0 miles northwest to campground.

PALOUSE FALLS STATE PARK (State of Washington)
10 primitive campsites, picnic shelter, 190' waterfall, $.
Northwest of Pomeroy. US 12 13.0 miles northwest, State 261 30.0 miles northwest, park entry road 2.6 miles west.

PANJAB TRAILHEAD (Umatilla National Forest)
7 tent units, fishing, hiking, horse trails, elev. 3400', $.
Southwest of Pomroy. CR 101 17.6 miles southwest, FSR 47 12.1 miles southwest, FSR 4713 2.3 miles south.

PORT ANGELES

BAYVIEW & RV PARK (Private)
21 trailer sites w/hookups for water/electricity/sewer, reservation informa-
tion - (206)963-2542, showers, laundry, ocean access, fishing, $$$.
Northwest of Port Angeles. US 101 5.0 miles west, State 112 47.0 miles
west/northwest to Sekiu, Airport Road north .01 mile.

CAROL'S CRESCENT BEACH (Private)
60 trailer sites w/hookups for water/electricity/sewer, reservation informa-
tion - (206)928-3344, showers, laundry, playfield, ocean access, swimming,
fishing, $$$.
West of Port Angeles. US 101 5.0 miles west, State 112 6.5 miles west to
Joyce, Crescent Beach Road 3.0 miles north.

CITY CENTER TRAILER PARK (Private)
30 trailer sites w/hookups for water/electricity/sewer, trailers to 35', reser-
vation information - (206)457-7092, showers, laundry, propane, creek, $$.
In Port Angeles. Located at 127 South Lincoln.

COHO RESORT (Private)
150 campsites, 44 w/hookups for water/electricity/sewer, 50 w/hookups for
water & electricity, plus 56 tent units, reservation information -
(206)963-2333, showers, laundry, ice, trailer waste disposal, ocean access,
fishing, boat launch, boat rental, $$.
Northwest of Port Angeles. US 101 5.0 miles west, State 112 47.0 miles
west/northwest to Sekiu, located on east end of town.

CONESTOGA QUARTERS RV PARK (Private)
38 campsites, 34 w/hookups for water/electricity/sewer, plus 4 w/hookups
for water & electricity, reservation information - (206)452-4637, wheelchair
access, showers, ice, playground, trailer waste disposal, hiking, $$$.
East of Port Angeles. US 101 7.0 miles east.

CURLEY'S RESORT (Private)
12 trailer sites w/hookups for water/electricity/sewer, trailers to 22', no
tents, reservation information - (206)963-2281, showers, laundry, ocean ac-
cess, fishing, $$.
Northwest of Port Angeles. US 101 5.0 miles west, State 112 47.0 miles
west/northwest to Sekiu.

D & B RV PARK (Private)
25 campsites, 18 trailer sites w/hookups for water/electricity/sewer, plus 7
w/hookups for water & electricity, reservation information - (206)457-6821,
showers, charter fishing, $$.
East of Port Angeles. US 101 7.0 miles east.

DUNGENESS RECREATION AREA (Clallam County)
65 campsites, information - (206)683-5847, wheelchair access, showers,
playground, trailer waste disposal, ocean access, pond, swimming, fishing,
boat launch, hiking, $$.
East of Port Angeles. US 101 east 10.0 miles Kitchen Road 4.0 miles north.

ELMER'S TRAILER PARK (Private)
12 trailer sites w/hookups for water/electricity/sewer, reservations -
(206)457-4392, showers, laundry, $$$.
East of Port Angeles. US 101 east 1.5 miles.

FAIRHOLM CAMPGROUND (Olympic National Park)
87 campsites, trailers to 21', groceries, trailer waste disposal, on Crescent Lake, swimming, fishing, boat launch, boat rental, hiking, $$.
West of Port Angeles. US 101 west/southwest 26.0 miles.

HEART O' THE HILLS (Olympic National Park)
105 campsites, trailers to 21', wheelchair access, hiking, $$.
South of Port Angeles. US 101 to Race Street, south 6.0 miles to campground.

LOG CABIN RESORT (Private)
40 campsites w/hookups for water/electricity/sewer, reservations - (206)928-3325, wheelchair access, showers, laundry, groceries, restaurant/lounge, trailer waste disposal, on Crescent Lake - no fishing license required on lake, swimming, fishing, boat launch, boat rental, hiking, $$$.
West of Port Angeles. US 101 west/southwest 16.0 miles to milepost #232, East Beach Road north 3.0 miles.

LYRE RIVER (Dept. of Natural Resources)
10 campsites, drinking water, $.
West of Port Angeles. Campground is 22 miles west of Port Angeles, off State 112, on Lyre River.

LYRE RIVER PARK (Private)
75 campsites, 55 w/hookups for water/electricity/sewer, plus 20 w/hookups for water & electricity, reservations - (206)928-3436, wheelchair access, showers, laundry, groceries, rec room, trailer waste disposal, ocean access, on Lyre River, swimming, fishing, small boat launch, hiking, $$$.
West of Port Angeles. US 101 5.0 miles west, State 112 15.0 miles west, West Lyre River Road north .5 mile.

NEAH BAY RESORT (Private)
50 campsites w/hookups for water/electricity/sewer, reservation information -(206)645-2288, showers, groceries, ocean access, fishing, boat launch, boat rental, $$$.
Northwest of Port Angeles. US 101 5.0 miles west, State 112 58.0 miles west/northwest.

OLSON'S RESORT (Private)
90 campsites, 30 w/hookups for water/electricity/sewer, plus 60 w/out hookups, reservation information - (206)963-2311, showers, groceries, ocean access, fishing, boat launch, boat rental, $-$$.
Northwest of Port Angeles. US 101 5.0 miles west, State 112 47.0 miles west/northwest to Sekiu.

PORT ANGELES KOA (Private)
31 campsites, 18 w/hookups for water/electricity/sewer, plus 13 w/hookups for water & electricity, reservations - (206)457-5916, showers, laundry, groceries, swimming pool, playground, trailer waste disposal, $$$.
East of Port Angeles. US 101 5.0 miles east.

SALT CREEK RECREATION AREA (Clallam County)
80 campsites, drinking water, flush toilets, playground, trailer waste disposal, ocean access, stream, swimming, fishing, hiking, $-$$.
Northwest of Port Angeles. US 101 5.0 miles west, State 112 9.0 miles west, Camp Hayden Road 3.5 miles north.

SAM'S TRAILER & RV PARK (Private)
26 campsites, 20 w/hookups for water/electricity/sewer, plus 6 w/out hookups, reservation information - (206)963-2402, showers, laundry, ocean access, fishing, $$.
Northwest of Port Angeles. US 101 west 5.0 miles, State 112 west 44.0 miles to Clallam Bay, located on east end of Clallam Bay.

SILVER KING RESORT (Private)
175 campsites, 140 w/hookups for water & electricity, plus 35 w/out hookups, reservation information - (206)928-3858, showers, laundry, groceries, trailer waste disposal, ocean access, fishing, boat launch, $$-$$$.
Northwest of Port Angeles. US 101 west 5.0 miles, State 112 west 30.0 miles to Jim Creek Recreation Area.

SOLEDUCK (Olympic National Park)
80 campsites, trailers to 21', groceries, trailer waste disposal, on Soleduck River, swimming, fishing, hiking, $$.
West of Port Angeles. US 101 28.0 miles west/southwest, Soleduck River Road 12.0 miles southeast.

THUNDERBIRD RESORT (Private)
40 campsites w/hookups for water/electricity/sewer, reservation information -(206)645-2450, showers, laundry, ice, trailer waste disposal, ocean access, fishing, boat launch, $$$.
Northwest of Port Angeles. US 101 west 5.0 miles, State 112 61.0 miles west/northwest, in Neah Bay.

TRETTEVIKS TRAILER PARK (Private)
22 campsites, 10 w/hookups for water/electricity/sewer, plus 12 w/hookups for water & electricity, reservation information - (206)963-2688, laundry, ocean access, sandy beach, swimming, fishing, $$.
Northwest of Port Angeles. US 101 5.0 miles west, State 112 55.0 miles west/northwest.

TYEE MOTEL & RV PARK (Private)
30 trailer sites w/hookups for water/electricity/sewer, reservation information - (206)645-2223, showers, laundry, trailer waste disposal, ocean access, fishing, $$$.
Northwest of Port Angeles. US 101 west 5.0 miles, State 112 61.0 miles west/northwest, in Neah Bay.

VAN RIPER'S RESORT & RV PARK (Private)
42 trailer sites w/hookups for water & electricity, reservation information -(206)963-2334, showers, ice, trailer waste disposal, ocean access, fishing, boat launch, boat rental, $$.
Northwest of Port Angeles. US 101 5.0 miles west, State 112 47.0 miles west/northwest to Sekiu.

WELCOME INN TRAILER & RV PARK (Private)
75 trailer sites w/hookups for water/electricity/sewer, reservation information - (206)457-1553, showers, laundry, trailer waste disposal, playfield, $$-$$$.
In Port Angeles. US 101 2.0 miles west.

WESTWIND RESORT (Private)
26 campsites, 6 w/hookups for water/electricity/sewer, 15 w/hookups for water & electricity, plus 5 w/hookups for water, reservation information - (206)645-2751, showers, laundry, ice, ocean access, fishing, $$.
Northwest of Port Angeles. US 101 west 5.0 miles, State 112 61.0 miles west/northwest, in Neah Bay.

PORT TOWNSEND

FORT FLAGLER STATE PARK (State of Washington)
116 tent units, group sites - reservations advised (206)385-1259, picnic shelter, wheelchair access, groceries, trailer waste disposal, boat launch, fishing, scuba diving area, clamming, crabbing, 1898 historical fort, Youth Hostel, $$-$$$.
Southeast of Port Townsend. Leave Port Townsend on State 20, after about 5.0 miles take the road marked Hadlock and Fort Flagler State Park.

FORT WORDEN STATE PARK (State of Washington)
50 units, trailers okay, hookups for water/electricity/sewer, community kitchen, wheelchair access, snack bar, groceries, trailer waste disposal, boat launch, scuba diving area, fishing, full conference facilities & housing in historic buildings, Youth Hostel, $$.
In Port Townsend. Located at Port Townsend's northern edge.

OLD FORT TOWNSEND STATE PARK (State of Washington)
40 tent units, 3 primitive sites, some trailers, community kitchen, beach access, playfield, fishing, clamming beach, historic 1859 fort w/group facilities - reservations required (206)385-4730, $$-$$$.
South of Port Townsend. Campground is 3.0 miles east of Port Townsend, east of Highway 20.

POINT HUDSON RV PARK (Private)
18 trailer sites w/hookups for water/electricity/sewer, no tents, information -(206)385-2828, showers, laundry, groceries, ocean access, fishing, boat launch, $$$.
In Port Townsend. Located at the docks; follow Water Street to end.

SMITTY'S ISLAND RETREAT (Private)
40 campsites w/hookups for water/electricity/sewer, reservation information -(206)385-2165, ocean access, fishing, $$.
Southeast of Port Townsend. Leave Port Townsend on State 20, after about 5.0 miles take the road marked Hadlock/Fort Flagler State Park; located 1.0 mile south of park.

PUYALLUP

HENLEY'S SILVER LAKE RESORT (Public)
45 campsites, 12 w/hookups for water/electricity/sewer, 17 w/hookups for water & electricity, plus 16 tent units, reservation information - (206)832-3580, trailer waste disposal, lake, fishing, boat launch, boat rental, hiking, $$.
South of Puyallup. State 161 26.0 miles south, State 7 northwest 4.0 miles.

MAJESTIC MOBILE MANOR & RV PARK (Private)
123 trailer sites w/hookups for water/electricity/sewer, reservation information - (206)845-3144, showers, laundry, swimming pool, groceries, rec room, trailer waste disposal, stream, fishing, $$-$$$.
West of Puyallup. State 167 (River Road) 3.0 miles west.

NORTHWEST TREK WILDLIFE PARK (Private)
35 campsites, trailers to 35', reservation information - (206)832-6116, wildlife park, wheelchair access, restrooms, lounge, $$.
South of Puyallup. State 161 south 16.0 miles.

RAINBOW RESORT (Private)
42 trailer sites w/hookups for water/electricity/sewer, reservation information - (206)879-5115, showers, laundry, groceries, rec room, playground, trailer waste disposal, lake, swimming, fishing, boat launch, boat rental, $$-$$$.
South of Puyallup. State 161 south 15.0 miles, Tanwax Drive .5 mile east.

TANWAX RESORT (Private)
25 campsites, 16 w/hookups for water/electricity/sewer, plus 9 tent units, trailers to 32', reservation information - (206)879-5533, showers, trailer waste disposal, lake, fishing, boat rental, $$.
South of Puyallup. State 161 south 15.0 miles, Tanwax Drive .5 mile east.

T-J'S RV PARK (Private)
20 trailer sites w/hookups for water/electricity/sewer, adults only, no tents, reservation information - (206)847-7153, $$.
South of Puyallup. State 161 south 3.0 miles.

QUEETS

KALALOCH (Olympic National Park)
179 campsites, groceries, trailer waste disposal, ocean access, swimming, fishing, hiking, $$.
North of Queets. US 101 6.0 miles north.

QUILCENE

BIG QUILCENE (Olympic National Forest)
3 tent units, no trailers, picnic area, piped water,fishing, hiking, elev. 1400', $.
Southwest of Quilcene 7 miles via Townsend Creek Road #2812.

FALLS VIEW CAMPGROUND (Olympic National Forest)
30 units, trailers to 32', picnic area, piped water, flush toilets, hiking trails, elev. 500', $$.
Southwest of Quilcene. US 101 3.5 miles southwest. Campground is located 5 miles from Quilcine Bay.

RAINBOW (Olympic National Forest)
9 tent units, piped water, trails to Big Quilcene River, elev. 800', $.
Southwest of Quilcene. US 101 4.5 miles southwest.

QUINAULT

FALLS CREEK (Olympic National Forest)
22 units, trailers to 18', picnic area, piped water, flush toilets, boat launch, boating, swimming, fishing, elev. 200', $$.
Northeast of Quinault. CR 5 .2 mile northeast.

OLALLIE (Olympic National Forest)
14 tent units, piped water, community kitchen, flush toilets, boat launch, lake, fishing, swimming, elev. 200', $$.
Southwest of Quinault. CR 5 1.5 miles southwest.

RAIN FOREST RESORT & RV PARK (Private)
31 campsites w/hookups for water/electricity/sewer, information - (206)288-2535, showers, laundry, groceries, on Lake Quinault, swimming, fishing, boat launch, boat rental, $$$.
East of Quinault. Leave US 101 on South Shore Road, resort is 3.5 miles east.

WILLABY (Olympic National Forest)
19 units, trailers to 22', picnic area, piped water, stream, flush toilets, boat launch, boating, swimming, fishing, hiking trails, elev. 200', $$.
Southwest of Quinault. CR 5 .5 mile southwest.

RANDLE

ADAMS FORK (Gifford Pinchot National Forest)
27 units, trailers to 22', well, swimming, fishing, on Cispus River, elev. 2600', $.
Southeast of Randle. County Road 3.1 miles south, FSR 23 15.7 miles southeast, FSR 21 4.7 miles southeast, FSR 56 .2 mile east to campground.

BLUE LAKE (Gifford Pinchot National Forest)
3 tent units, hike-in, fishing, elev. 4900', $.
Southeast of Randle. County Road 3.1 miles south, FSR 23 11.2 miles southeast, Trail 3.0 miles.

BLUE LAKE CREEK (Gifford Pinchot National Forest)
11 units, trailers to 32', well, fishing, hiking, on Cispus River, elev. 1900', $.
Southeast of Randle. County Road 3.1 miles south, FSR 23 13.2 miles southeast.

IRON CREEK (Gifford Pinchot National Forest)
54 units, trailers to 32', piped water, fishing, hiking, on Lower Cispus River, elev. 1200', $$.
Southeast of Randle. County Road 3.1 miles south, FSR 23 8.7 miles, FSR 1134 1.0 miles, FSR 76 6.0 miles west, FSR 26 .5 mile west.

MAPLE GROVE RESORT (Private)
70 campsites, 35 w/hookups for water & electricity, 28 w/hookups for water, plus 7 w/out hookups, reservation information - (206)497-2741, wheelchair access, showers, laundry, groceries, snack bar, picnic shelter, playfield, playground, trailer waste disposal, river, fishing, hiking, nearby golf, $$-$$$.
In Randle. Leave US 12 on Cispus Road, resort is .3 mile south.

MAPLE LEAF (Gifford Pinchot National Forest)
18 units, some trailers, well, picnic area, elev. 1000', $.
East of Randle 6 miles via US 12.

MIDWAY (Gifford Pinchot National Forest)
2 units, creek, horse trails & ramp, hiking, access to Pacific Crest Trail, elev. 4500'.
Southeast of Randle. Take County Road 3.1 miles south, FSR 23 28.9 miles southeast, FSR 2329 11.2 miles southeast.

NORTH FORK (Gifford Pinchot National Forest)
33 units, trailers to 32', piped water, fishing, hiking, on North Fork Cispus River, bicycling, elev. 1500', $$.
Southeast of Randle. County Road 3.1 miles south, FSR 23 8.7 miles southeast.

NORTH FORK GROUP (Gifford-Pinchot National Forest)
3 group sites, trailers to 32', reservations required (206)497-7565, piped water, river, fishing, hiking, bicycling, elev. 1500', $$$.
Southeast of Randle. County Road 3.1 miles south, FSR 23 8.7 miles southeast.

RYAN LAKE (Gifford Pinchot National Forest)
3 tent units, fishing, hiking, elev. 3200', $.
Southeast of Randle. Take County Road 3.1 miles south, FSR 23 8.7 miles southeast, FSR 1134 1.0 mile , FSR 76 6.0 miles west, FSR 26 approximately 12 miles southwest to campground.

TAKHLAKH (Gifford Pinchot National Forest)
34 units, trailers to 22', piped water, lake - speed limits, boat launch, fishing, boating, swimming, hiking trails, lava flow 1 mile east, elev. 4500', $.
Southeast of Randle. County Road 3.1 miles south, FSR 23 28.9 miles southeast, FSR 2329 1.6 miles north.

TOWER ROCK (Gifford Pinchot National Forest)
22 units, trailers to 22', piped water, on Cispus River, fishing, elev. 1100', $$.
Southeast of Randle. County Road 3.1 miles south, FSR 23 5.4 miles southeast, FSR 28 1.4 miles south, FSR 76 1.8 miles west.

WOBBLY LAKE (Gifford Pinchot National Forest)
3 tent units, fishing, hike-in only, elev. 3400'.
Southeast of Randle 36 miles. County Road 3.1 miles south, FSR 23 9.7 miles southeast, FSR 22 8.0 miles, Wobbly Lake Trail 2 miles.

RAYMOND

BAYSHORE RV PARK (Private)
56 campsites, 41 w/hookups for water/electricity/sewer, plus 15 w/hookups for water & electricity, reservation information - (206)267-2625, showers, laundry, rec room, trailer waste disposal, ocean access, swimming, fishing, $$.
Northwest of Raymond. State 105 west 19.0 miles, park is located in Tokeland at 2941 Kindred.

BRUCEPORT PARK (City)

15 campsites, 2 w/hookups for water, plus 13 tent units, reservation information - (206)875-6315, picnic shelter, playground, $.
Southwest of Raymond. US 101 south 11.0 miles.

GYPSY TRAIL RV & MOTOR HOME PARK (Private)

18 trailer sites w/hookups for water/electricity/sewer, no tents, reservation information - (206)875-5165, showers, laundry, trailer waste disposal, $$.
Southwest of Raymond. US 101 south 5.0 miles to South Bend; park is located on Central, .1 mile off US 101.

HAPPY TRAILS KOA (Private)

43 campsites, 6 w/hookups for water/electricity/sewer, 26 w/hookups for water & electricity, plus 11 w/hookups for water, reservations - (206)875-6344, showers, laundry, groceries, rec room, playground, sandy beach, trailer waste disposal, $$$.
Southwest of Raymond. US 101 15.5 miles southwest, Bay Center Road west 3.0 miles.

TIMBERLAND RV PARK (Private)

24 campsites w/hookups for water/electricity/sewer, reservation information -(206)942-3325, showers, ocean access, nearby fishing & golf, $$.
North of Raymond. US 101 north to junction with State 105, west .2 mile to Crescent Street; park is 2 blocks south.

REPUBLIC

BLACK BEACH RESORT (Private)

116 campsites, 110 w/hookups for water/electricity/sewer, plus 6 w/hookups for water & electricity, reservations - (509)775-3989, laundry, groceries, playground, trailer waste disposal, Lake Curlew, swimming, fishing, boat launch, $$-$$$.
North of Republic. West Curlew Lake Road north 8.0 miles, Black Beach Road east 1.0 mile.

CURLEW LAKE STATE PARK (State of Washington)

64 tent units, 18 trailer sites w/hookups for water/electricity/sewer, wheelchair access, trailer waste disposal, boat launch, fishing, trails, gold mining district, winter sports, $$.
Northeast of Republic. State 21 10.0 miles northeast.

CURLEW POINT RV PARK (Private)

32 campsites, 26 w/hookups for water/electricity/sewer, plus 6 tent units, reservations - (509)775-3643, showers, laundry, groceries, trailer waste disposal, on Curlew Lake, swimming, fishing, boat launch, boat rental, $$-$$$.
North of Republic. State 21 north 10.0 miles.

FERRY LAKE (Colville National Forest)

9 units, trailers to 22', well, boat launch, boating, fishing, elev. 3300', $$.
Southwest of Republic. State 21 7.0 miles south, FSR 53 6.0 miles southwest, FSR 5330 1.0 mile north, FSR 100 .5 mile north.

LONG LAKE (Colville National Forest)
12 units, trailers to 22', well, lake - no motors, boating, fly fishing, elev. 3200', $$.
Southwest of Republic. State 21 7.0 miles south, FSR 53 8.0 miles southwest, FSR 400 1.5 miles south to campground.

PINE POINT RESORT (Private)
32 campsites w/hookups for water/electricity/sewer, reservations - (509)775-3643, showers, laundry, groceries, trailer waste disposal, on Curlew Lake, swimming, fishing, boat launch, boat rental, playground, $$.
North of Republic. State 21 north 10.0 miles.

SWAN LAKE (Colville National Forest)
29 units, trailers to 32', community kitchen, well, boat launch, boating, swimming, fishing, hiking trails, elev. 3600', $$.
Southwest of Republic. State 21 7.0 miles south, FSR 5300 8.0 miles southwest.

TEN MILE (Colville National Forest)
9 units, trailers to 18', picnic area, piped water, stream, fishing, elev. 2200', $$.
South of Republic. State 21 10.0 miles south.

TIFFANYS RESORT (Private)
22 campsites, 14 w/hookups for water/electricity/sewer, 2 w/hookups for water & electricity, plus 6 w/out hookups, reservations - (509)775-3152, showers, laundry, groceries, playground, on Curlew Lake, swimming, fishing, boat launch, boat rental, $$$.
North of Republic. West Curlew Lake Road north 10.0 miles.

RICHLAND

BEACH RV PARK (Private)
36 trailer sites w/hookups for water/electricity/sewer, reservation information - (509)588-5959, showers, laundry, ice, river, fishing, $$-$$$.
Northwest of Richland. I-82 west 11.0 miles to Benton City exit, located in Benton City on Abby Avenue.

CHARBONNEAU PARK (Corps)
55 campsites, 15 w/hookups for water/electricity/sewer, 24 w/hookups for electricity, 16 tent units, reservation information - (509)547-7781, showers, wheelchair access, rec room, playground, trailer waste disposal, lake, swimming, fishing, boat launch, $$.
Northeast of Richland. I-82 5.0 miles east to State 14, 4.0 miles northeast to Pasco, State 12 3.0 miles south, State 124 8.0 miles east, Sun Harbor Drive 2.0 miles north.

COLUMBIA MOBILE VILLAGE (Private)
20 trailer sites w/hookups for water/electricity/sewer, reservation information - (509)783-3314, playfield, playground, $$.
Southeast of Richland. State 12 5.0 miles to Kennewick, State 14 to Clearwater Avenue, 1.3 miles west.

COLUMBIA PARK (Benton County)

100 campsites, 18 w/hookups for water & electricity, plus 82 w/out hookups, reservations - (509)783-3711, showers, trailer waste disposal, nearby boat launch on Columbia River, bike/hike trails, $$.
Southeast of Richland. US 12 southeast to Columbia Center exit and follow signs.

DESERT GOLD TRAILER PARK & MOTEL (Private)

69 trailer sites w/hookups for water/electricity/sewer, reservation - (509)627-1000, showers, laundry, groceries, swimming pool, therapy pool, $$$.
Southeast of Richland. US 12 southeast to Columbia Drive SE and look for signs.

FISHHOOK PARK (Corps)

41 campsites, reservation information - (509)547-7781, wheelchair access, showers, playground, trailer waste disposal, lake, swimming, fishing, boat launch, elev. 4500', $$.
Northeast of Richland. I-82 5.0 miles east to State 14, 4.0 miles northeast to Pasco, State 12 3.0 miles south, State 124 15.0 miles east, Page Road 4.0 miles north.

GREEN TREE RV PARK (Private)

70 trailer sites w/hookups for water/electricity/sewer, reservation information - (503)547-6220, showers, laundry, ice, $$$.
Northeast of Richland. I-82 east to exit #13, park is just north on 4th Avenue.

HOOD PARK (Corps)

69 trailer sites w/hookups for electricity, reservation information - (509)547-7781, wheelchair access, showers, playground, trailer waste disposal, lake, swimming, fishing, boat launch, elev. 3500', $$.
Northeast of Richland. I-82 5.0 miles east to State 14, 4.0 miles northeast to Pasco, State 12 3.0 miles south, located at junction with State 124.

PLYMOUTH PARK (Corp)

32 campsites, 17 w/hookups for water/electricity/sewer, plus 15 tent units, reservation information - (509)525-5632, wheelchair access, showers, trailer waste disposal, lake, river, swimming, fishing, boat launch, $$.
Southwest of Richland. I-82 29.0 miles south to Plymouth, park is located 1.0 mile west of Umatilla Bridge.

SAN JUAN ISLANDS

CYPRESS ISLAND/PELICAN BEACH (Dept. of Natural Resources)

6 campsites, boat-in only, buoys, hiking trails, $.
In San Juan Islands. On Cypress Island, 4.0 miles north of Cypress Head, on northeast side.

LOPEZ ISLAND/SPENCER SPIT STATE PARK (State of Washington)

28 tent units, some trailers - no hookups, group sites - reservations advised (206)468-2251, picnic shelter, trailer waste disposal, fishing, beachcombing, clamming, $$-$$$.
On Lopez Island. This island is accessible via the Anacortes ferry and is located on the northeast side of the island.

LUMMI ISLAND (Dept. of Natural Resources)
4 campsites, boat-in only, $.
In San Juan Islands. Located on southeast tip of Lummi Island, 1.0 miles
south of Reil Harbor.

ORCAS ISLAND/MORAN STATE PARK (State of Washington)
136 units, some trailers - no hookups, picnic shelter, wheelchair access,
trailer waste disposal, boat rental, boat launch, fishing, located on top of
Mt. Constitution, $$.
In San Juan Islands. On northeast side of Orcas Island. This island is ac-
cessible via Washington State Ferry.

ORCAS ISLAND/OBSTRUCTION PASS (Dept. of Natural Resources)
9 campsites, boat-in or hike-in only, buoys, hiking trails, $.
In San Juan Islands. Campground is located 5.0 miles southwest of
Rosario, on Orcas Island.

ORCAS ISLAND/POINT DOUGHTY (Dept. of Natural Resources)
4 campsites, boat-in only, buoys, $.
In San Juan Islands. Campground is on north end of Orcas Island; 3.0
miles northwest of Eastsound.

ORCAS ISLAND/TOWN & COUNTRY (Private)
24 trailer sites w/hookups for water/electricity/sewer, reservation informa-
tion - (206)378-4717, showers, laundry, playground, trailer waste disposal,
ocean access, lake, fishing, $$-$$$.
On Orcas Island. Located northeast of Friday Harbor.

ORCAS ISLAND/WEST BEACH RESORT (Private)
62 campgrounds, 21 w/hookups for water/electricity/sewer, 15 w/hookups
for water & electricity, plus 26 tent units, reservation information -
(206)376-2240, showers, laundry, groceries, ocean access, swimming,
fishing, boat launch, boat rental, $$-$$$.
On Orcas Island. Located west of Eastsound 3.5 miles.

STRAWBERRY/LOON ISLAND (Dept. of Natural Resources)
6 campsites, boat-in only, $.
In San Juan Islands. Located .5 mile west of Cypress Island.

STUART ISLAND STATE PARK (State of Washington)
19 primitive sites, boat-in only, buoys & floats, nearby fishing, $.
Northwest of San Juan Island. Stuart Island is northwest of San Juan
Island.

SUCIA ISLAND STATE PARK (State of Washington)
51 primitive sites, boat-in only, buoys & floats, picnic shelter, scuba diving
area, crabbing, clamming, geological formations, $.
North of Orcas Island. Sucia Island is approximately 2.5 miles north of
Orcas Island.

TURN ISLAND STATE PARK (State of Washington)
10 primitive sites, boat-in only, bouys, fishing, no drinking water, trails, $.
East of San Juan Island. Turn Island is close to San Juan Island's Friday
Harbor.

SEATTLE

AQUA BARN RANCH (Private)
195 campsites, 105 w/hookups for water/electricity/sewer, 65 w/hookups for water & electricity, plus 25 tent units, reservation information - (206)255-4618, wheelchair access, showers, laundry, ice, swimming pool, therapy pool, playground, trailer waste disposal, river, fishing, $$$.
Southeast of Seattle. I-5 south to I-405 eastbound, exit 4A to State 169, east 3.5 miles.

BLAKE ISLAND STATE PARK (State of Washington)
41 tent units, boat-in only - floats & buoys, group sites - reservations advised (206)947-0905, picnic shelter, wheelchair access, scuba diving area, fishing, nature trail, hiking, $-$$$.
West of Seattle. On Blake Island in Puget Sound, 3.0 miles west of Seattle.

RIVER BEND RV PARK (Private)
42 trailer sites w/hookups for water/electricity/sewer, adults only, no tents, reservation information - (206)255-2613, showers, laundry, rec room, trailer waste disposal, $$$.
Southeast of Seattle. I-5 south to I-405 eastbound, exit 4A to State 169, east 4.5 miles

SEATTLE NORTH RV PARK (Private)
152 campsites, 100 w/hookups for water/electricity/sewer, 31 w/hookups for water & electricity, plus 21 w/hookups for water, reservation information -(206)481-1972, showers, laundry, groceries, swimming pool, therapy pool, rec room, playground, trailer waste disposal, $$$.
Northeast of Seattle. I-5 to exit #182, I-405 to Bothell exit #26, park is 1 block south.

SEATTLE SOUTH KOA (Private)
152 campsites, 133 w/hookups for water/electricity/sewer, plus 19 w/hookups for water & electricity, reservations - (206)872-8652, wheelchair access, showers, laundry, groceries, heated swimming pool, lounge, playground, rec room, nearby golf, $$$.
Southeast of Seattle. I-5 south to exit #152, east on Orillia Road.

THE HAYLOFT (Private)
53 trailer sites w/hookups for water/electricity/sewer, adults only, trailers to 35', reservation information - (206)743-2289, trailer waste disposal, rec room, $$$.
North of Seattle. I-5 north to Lynnwood exit #183, 164th Street west 1.3 miles, 36th Street/35th Avenue north .8 mile.

TRAILER INNS RV PARK (Private)
100 trailer sites w/hookups for water/electricity/sewer, no tents, reservation information - (206)747-9181, showers, laundry, ice, swimming pool, therapy pool, sauna, rec room, playground, $$$.
East of Seattle. I-90 east to Bellevue exit #11A, follow signs.

TWIN CEDARS RV PARK (Private)
70 trailer sites w/hookups for water/electricity/sewer, reservation information - (206)742-5540, showers, laundry, ice, trailer waste disposal, stream, lounge, wheelchair access, $$$.
North of Seattle. I-5 north to Lynnwood exit #183, 164th Street 1.3 miles west, State 99 south to 17826.

WILLOW VISTA MOBILE/RV PARK (Private)
25 campsites w/hookups for water/electricity/sewer, reservation information -(202)872-8264, showers, laundry, swimming pool, trailer waste disposal, $$-$$$.
Southeast of Seattle. I-5 south to I-405, east to State 167, south to 84th Avenue; located to the north at 21740 84th Avenue.

SEQUIM

DIAMOND POINT RV PARK & CAMPGROUND (Private)
41 campsites, 31 w/hookups for water/electricity/sewer, plus 10 tent units, reservation information - (206)683-2284, showers, laundry, ice, trailer waste disposal, ocean access, fishing, boat launch, $$-$$$.
East of Sequim. US 101 east 10.0 miles, Diamond Point Road north 3.3 miles.

RAINBOW'S END RV PARK (Private)
52 campsites, 12 w/hookups for water/electricity/sewer, 17 w/hookups for water & electricity, plus 23 w/out hookups, reservation information - (206)683-3863, wheelchair access, showers, laundry, trailer waste disposal, trout pond, stream, fishing, $$$.
West of Sequim. US 101 west 1.5 miles.

SEQUIM BAY MARINA (Private)
43 campsites w/hookups for water/electricity/sewer, reservations - (206)683-4050, showers, laundry, trailer waste disposal, fishing, $$$.
Northwest of Sequim. Take West Sequim Bay Road 2.5 miles northwest.

SEQUIM BAY STATE PARK (State of Washington)
60 tent units, 26 trailer sites w/hookups for water/electricity/sewer, wheelchair access, community kitchen/shelter, trailer waste disposal, boat launch, fishing, scuba diving area, moorage camping, $-$$.
East of Sequim. Take US 101 4.0 miles east to campground.

SEQUIM WEST RV PARK & MOTEL (Private)
29 trailer sites w/hookups for water/electricity/sewer, no tents, reservations -(206)683-4144, showers, laundry, ice, $$$.
In Sequim. Located at 740 West Washington (Highway 101).

SLAB (Olympic National Forest)
6 tent units, stream, fishing, hiking, elev. 2600', $.
Southwest of Sequim 17 miles. US 101 east to Canyon Creek Road #2926, follow this to campground.

SOUTH SEQUIM BAY RV PARK (Private)
30 campsites, 24 w/hookups for water/electricity/sewer, plus 6 w/hookups for electricity, reservations - (206)683-7194, showers, playfield, trailer waste disposal, ocean access, pond, $$-$$$.
East of Sequim. US 101 east 5.0 miles, Old Blyn Highway northeast .3 mile.

SUNSHINE MOBILE HOME/RV PARK (Private)
57 campsites, 49 w/hookups for water/electricity/sewer, plus 8 w/out hookups, reservation information - (206)683-4769, showers, laundry, ice, stream, nearby golf & fishing, $$-$$$.
West of Sequim. US 101 west 4.0 miles.

SHELTON

BROWN CREEK (Olympic National Forest)
20 units, trailers to 22', well, swimming, fishing, hiking trails, elev. 600', $.
Northwest of Shelton. US 101 7.5 miles north, CR 242 5.3 miles northwest,
FSR 226 8.7 miles north, FSR 2285 .5 mile east.

JARRELL'S COVE MARINA (Private)
10 campsites, trailers to 27', reservations - (206)426-8823, showers, laundry, groceries, marina w/gasoline & diesel, playground, ocean access,
swimming, fishing, hiking, $$.
Northeast of Shelton. State 3 north 8.0 miles, Spencer Lake Road east 4.0
miles, N. Island Drive 3.0 miles north, Haskell Hill Road west 1.0 mile.

SQUAXIN ISLAND STATE PARK (State of Washington)
20 tent sites, primitive, picnic shelter, boat-in only - bouys & floats, large
lawn area, beautiful scenery, $.
East of Shelton. Squaxin Island is between Harstene Island and Shelton.

SKYKOMISH

BECKLER RIVER (Mt. Baker-Snoqualmie National Forest)
27 units, trailers to 22', picnic area, well, fishing, on site caretaker, elev.
900', $$.
Northeast of Skykomish. US 2 1.0 mile east, FSR 65 2.0 mile north.

FOSS RIVER (Mt. Baker-Snoqualmie National Forest)
5 units, some trailers, fishing, hiking, elev. 1400', $.
Southeast of Skykomish. US 2 2.0 miles east, FSR 2622 4.5 miles south.
Campground is located 2 miles north of Alpine Lakes Wilderness
Boundary.

MILLER RIVER (Mt. Baker-Snoqualmie National Forest)
24 units, group sites - reservation required (206)677-2414, trailers to 22',
well, swimming, fishing, elev. 1000', $$$.
Southwest of Skykomish. US 2 2.5 miles west, FSR 64 1.0 mile southeast,
FSR 6410 1.0 miles south. Campground is 6 miles north of Alpine Lakes
Wilderness Boundary.

MONEY CREEK (Mt. Baker-Snoqualmie National Forest)
25 units, trailers to 22', group sites, picnic area, well, swimming, fishing, on
site caretaker, elev. 900', $$-$$$.
West of Skykomish. US 2 2.5 miles west, FSR 6400 .1 mile southeast..

TYE CANYON (Mt. Baker-Snoqualmie National Forest)
2 tent units, no trailers, stream, fishing, hiking, elev. 2200', $.
East of Skykomish 10 miles via US 2.

WEST FORK MILLER RIVER (Mt. Baker-Snoqualmie National Forest)
4 tent units, no trailers, fishing, elev. 1700', $.
South of Skykomish 8 miles via Miller River Road #2516, staying right
when road forks.

SPOKANE

BARBARS RESORT (Private)
25 campsites, 20 w/hookups for water & electricity, plus 5 w/hookups for electricity, trailers to 35', reservation information - (509)299-3830, showers, groceries, playground, trailer waste disposal, lake, swimming, fishing, boat launch, boat rental, $$.
Southwest of Spokane. I-90 southwest to exit #264, Salnaive Road 2.0 miles north.

BERNIE'S LAST RESORT (Private)
40 campsites, 8 w/hookups for water/electricity/sewer, 12 w/hookups for water & electricity, plus 20 tent units, reservation information - (509)299-7273, showers, laundry, rec room, trailer waste disposal, lake, swimming, fishing, boat launch, boat rental, $$-$$$.
Southwest of Spokane. I-90 to 7.0 miles southwest to exit #270, south .02 mile to Medical Lake turnoff, take this 3.2 miles northwest to Medical Lake, Four Lakes Road will lead you to the resort.

DRAGOON CREEK (Dept. of Natural Resources)
25 campsites, drinking water, wheelchair access, $$.
North of Spokane. US 395 north approximately 9.0 miles to Dragoon Creek and campground.

FISHTRAP LAKE RESORT (Private)
20 trailer sites w/hookups for water & electricity, reservation information -(509)235-2284, groceries, trailer waste disposal, lake, swimming, fishing, boat launch, boat rental, $$.
Southwest of Spokane. I-90 southwest to exit #254, Fishtrap Road southeast 3.5 miles to resort.

HOMESTEAD (Dept. of Natural Resources)
16 campsites, picnic shelter, drinking water, wheelchair access, $$.
Northeast of Spokane. Campground is located 2.0 miles northeast of Newman Lake, near Idaho border.

KOA OF SPOKANE (Private)
190 campsites, 91 w/hookups for water/electricity/sewer, 59 w/hookups for water & electricity, plus 40 tent units, reservations - (509)924-4722, showers, laundry, groceries, swimming pool, game room, playground, trailer waste disposal, $$$.
East of Spokane. I-90 east to exit #293, Barker Road north 1.3 miles.

LAST ROUNDUP MOTEL/RV PARK & CAMPGROUND (Private)
23 campsites, 13 w/hookups for water/electricity/sewer, plus 10 tent units, reservation information - (509)257-2583, showers, laundry, ice, playfield, $$.
Southwest of Spokane. I-90 southwest to Sprague exit #245, campground is east .5 mile.

LEWIS BROTHERS RESORT (Private)
25 campsites, 12 w/hookups for water/electricity/sewer, plus 13 w/hookups for water & electricity, reservation information - (509)235-2341, showers, laundry, groceries, playground, trailer waste disposal, lake, swimming, fishing, boat launch, boat rental, $$.
Southwest of Spokane. I-90 southwest 7.0 miles to Cheney exit #270, State 904 south 6.0 miles to Cheney, Badger Lake Road 9.5 miles south.

LIBERTY LAKE PARK (Spokane County)
21 trailer sites w/hookups for water & electricity, trailers to 35', no pets, reservation information - (509)456-4730, wheelchair access, playground, trailer waste disposal, lake, swimming, fishing, hiking, $-$$.
East of Spokane. I-90 east to exit #296, Liberty Lake Road south approximately 4.0 miles to park.

LONG LAKE (Dept. of Natural Resources)
16 campsites, drinking water, lake, boat launch, Indian paintings, $$.
Northwest of Spokane. State 291 to Long Lake, campground is 3.0 miles east of Long Lake Dam over Lapray Bridge Road #1108.

MOUNT SPOKANE STATE PARK (State of Washington)
12 tent units, some trailers - no hookups, picnic shelter, wheelchair access, hiking, horse trails, winter sports, $$.
Northeast of Spokane. US 2 10.0 miles northeast, State 206 19.0 miles northeast.

OVERLAND STATION (Private)
32 trailer sites w/hookups for water/electricity/sewer, reservation information - (509)747-1703, showers, laundry, groceries, playground, $$-$$$.
In Spokane. I-90 to exit #272 and campground.

PARKLAND MOTEL & RV PARK (Private)
15 trailer sites w/hookups for water/electricity/sewer, no tents, reservation information - (509)535-1626, ice, playground, $$$.
In Spokane. I-90 east to exit #283-B, .8 mile to Havana Street, north .03 mile, Sprague Avenue east to 4412 and park.

PEACEFUL PINES RV PARK (Private)
30 campsites, 10 w/hookups for water/electricity/sewer, 6 w/hookups for water & electricity, plus 14 w/out hookups, reservation information - (509)235-4966, showers, trailer waste disposal, $$.
Southwest of Spokane. I-90 southwest 7.0 miles to Cheney exit #270, State 904 south/southwest 7.0 miles, located 1.0 mile west of Cheney.

PICNIC PINES ON SILVER LAKE (Private)
42 campsites, 30 w/hookups for water/electricity/sewer, plus 12 tent units, reservation information - (509)299-3223, ice, rec room, playground, on Silver Lake, swimming, fishing, boat launch, boat rental, $$.
Southwest of Spokane. I-90 southwest 7.0 miles to exit #270, south .02 mile to Medical Lake turnoff, take this 3.5 miles northwest to Medical Lake and Silver Lake Road, this will lead you to the campground.

RICHARD'S RESORT (Private)
50 trailer sites w/hookups for water & electricity, reservation information -(509)235-2331, groceries, playground, on Badger Lake, swimming, fishing, boat launch, boat rental, $$-$$$.
Southwest of Spokane. I-90 southwest 7.0 miles to Cheney exit #270, State 904 south 6.0 miles to Cheney, Badger Lake Road south 15.0 miles to resort.

RIVERSIDE STATE PARK (State of Washington)
101 tent units, some trailers - no hookups, group sites - reservations advised (509)456-3964, community kitchen/shelter, Spokane House Interpretive Center, boat launch, fishing, horse trails & rental, ORV area, $$-$$$.
Northwest of Spokane. Located 6.0 miles northwest of Spokane.

SANDY BEACH RESORT (Private)

26 trailer sites, 12 w/hookups for water/electricity/sewer, plus 14 w/hookups for water & electricity, no tents, reservation information - (509)255-6222, showers, laundry, groceries, rec room, playground, lake, swimming, fishing, boat launch, boat rental, $$$.

East of Spokane. I-90 east to exit #296, south 1.0 mile to Sprague Avenue, east .8 mile to resort.

SHADOWS RV PARK & CAMPGROUND (Private)

60 campsites, 14 w/hookups for water/electricity/sewer, plus 46 w/hookups for water & electricity, trailers to 35', reservations - (509)467-6951, showers, laundry, ice, trailer waste disposal, $$$.

North of Spokane. US 395 north of city center 5.0 miles to junction with US 2, Division Street exit to campground.

SMOKEY TRAIL RV CAMPSITE (Private)

70 campsites, 20 w/hookups for water/electricity/sewer, 10 w/hookups for water & electricity, 10 w/hookups for electricity, plus 30 tent units, reservation information - (509)747-9415, showers, laundry, groceries, playground, trailer waste disposal, hiking, nearby golf, $$-$$$.

Southwest of Spokane. I-90 southwest to exit #272, Hallet Road east 1.0 mile, Mallon Road .5 mile south.

SPRAGUE LAKE RESORT (Private)

60 campsites, 30 w/hookups for water/electricity/sewer, plus 30 tent units, reservation information - (509)257-2864, showers, laundry, ice, playground, trailer waste disposal, lake, swimming, fishing, boat launch, boat rental, $$.

Southwest of Spokane. I-90 southwest to Sprague exit #245, go through Sprague city center and head west 2.0 miles to lake and resort.

TRAILER INNS RV PARK (Private)

158 trailer sites w/hookups for water/electricity/sewer, no tents, pets okay, reservation information - (509)535-1811, showers, laundry, ice, swimming pool, therapy pool, sauna, lounge, game room, playground, $$$.

In Spokane. I-90 east to exit #285, follow signs to park at 6021 East Fourth Avenue.

UNITED CAMPGROUND OF SPOKANE (Private)

72 trailer sites w/hookups for water/electricity/sewer, 78 w/hookups for water & electricity, reservation information - (509)928-3300, showers, laundry, groceries, heated swimming pool, game room, lounge, playfield, playground, trailer waste disposal, $$$.

East of Spokane. I-90 east to exit #293 and campground.

WILLIAMS LAKE RESORT (Private)

65 campsites, 7 w/hookups for water/electricity/sewer, 28 w/hookups for water & electricity, plus 30 w/hookups for electricity, reservation information -(509)235-2391, groceries, playground, trailer waste disposal, lake, swimming, fishing, boat launch, boat rental, $$-$$$.

Southwest of Spokane. I-90 southwest 7.0 miles to Cheney exit #270, State 904 south 6.0 miles to Cheney, Cheney Plaza Road 11.5 miles south, Willams Lake Road 3.5 miles west.

TACOMA

DASH POINT STATE PARK (State of Washington)
108 tent units, 28 trailer sites w/hookups for water & electricity, group sites - reservations advised - (206)593-2206, picnic shelter, trailer waste disposal, fishing, $$-$$$.
Northeast of Tacoma. State 509 5.0 miles northeast to campground.

FIR ACRES MOTOR HOME/RV PARK (Private)
14 trailer sites w/hookups for water/electricity/sewer, reservation information - (206)588-7894, showers, laundry, $$$.
South of Tacoma. I-5 south to exit #125, east .1 mile on Bridgeport Way SW.

GIG HARBOR/TACOMA KOA (Private)
137 campsites, 52 w/hookups for water/electricity/sewer, 41 w/hookups for water & electricity, plus 44 tent units, reservation information - (206)858-8138, showers, laundry, groceries, heated swimming pool, rec room, playground, trailer waste disposal, $$$.
Northwest of Tacoma. I-5 to Gig Harbor exit #132, State 16 6.0 miles, beyond Narrows Bridge, Burnham Drive 1.0 miles north.

KARWAN VILLAGE MOBILE HOME/RV PARK (Private)
10 trailer sites, 8 w/hookups for water/electricity/sewer, plus 2 w/out hookups, no tents, no pets, adults only, reservations - (206)588-2501, showers, laundry, $$$.
South of Tacoma. I-5 south to exit #129; northbound take exit #128. Park is west on 84th St.

KOPACHUCK STATE PARK (State of Washington)
41 tent units, some trailers - no hookups, group sites - reservations advised (206)265-3606, picnic shelter, wheelchair access, trailer waste disposal, on Henderson Bay in Puget Sound, boat fishing, nearby boat launch, clamming, $$-$$$.
Northwest of Tacoma. State 16 11.0 miles northwest, take road west then follow south to Kopachuck State Park.

SALTWATER STATE PARK (State of Washington)
52 tent sites, some trailers - no hookups, group sites - reservations advised (206)764-4128, community kitchen/shelter, wheelchair access, trailer waste disposal, on Puget Sound, scuba diving area, hiking, $$-$$$.
Northeast of Tacoma. I-5 16.0 miles north, State 516 2.0 miles west, State 509 2.0 miles south.

TANWAX (Dept. of Natural Resources)
10 campsites, picnic area w/shelter, drinking water, wheelchair access, horse facilities, $$.
South of Tacoma. Campground is 24.0 miles south of Tacoma via State 7, on Tanwax Creek.

TONASKET

AENEAS SPRING (Okanogan National Forest)
3 units, trailers to 32', elev. 3600', $.
Southeast of Tonasket. State 30 12.6 miles east, CR 164 9.2 miles southeast, FSR 30 4.5 miles southeast.

BEAVER LAKE (Okanogan National Forest)
11 units, trailers to 22', well, boat launch, boating, swimming, fishing, hiking trails, elev. 3000', $.
Northeast of Tonasket. State 20 20.1 miles east, FSR 32 11.0 miles northeast, FSR 3245 3.3 miles northwest.

BONAPARTE LAKE (Okanogan National Forest)
25 units, trailers to 32', picnic area, piped water, flush toilets, groceries, gasoline, ice, boat launch, boat rental, cafe-snack bar, boating, swimming, fishing, water skiing, hiking trails, elev. 3600', $$-$$$.
Northeast of Tonasket. State 20 20.1 miles east, FSR 32 6.0 miles north. Located .3 mile from Bonaparte Lake Resort.

BONAPARTE LAKE RESORT (Private)
32 campsites, 18 w/hookups for water/electricity/sewer, plus 14 tent sites, reservation information - (509)486-2828, showers, laundry, cafe, groceries, ice, playground, trailer waste disposal, lake, swimming, fishing, boat launch, boat rental, elev. 3500', $$.
East of Tonasket. State 20 20.0 miles east, Bonaparte Road 6.0 miles north.

MACK'S LAKESHORE BORDER RV PARK (Private)
41 campsites, 11 w/hookups for water/electricity/sewer, plus 30 w/hookups for water & electricity, reservation information - (509)476-3114, showers, laundry, trailer waste disposal, lake, swimming, fishing, boat launch, $$-$$$.
North of Tonasket. US 97 north 25.0 miles; at border.

OSOYOOS LAKE STATE PARK (State of Washington)
80 tent units, some trailers - no hookups, picnic shelter, snackbar, trailer waste disposal, boat launch, fishing, swimming, water skiing, winter nesting area for Canada Geese, $$.
North of Tonasket. State 97 18.5 north, north of Oroville.

RAINBOW RESORT (Private)
40 campsites, 26 w/hookups for water/electricity/sewer, plus 14 w/hookups for water & electricity, reservations - (509)223-3700, showers, ice, on Spectacle Lake, swimming, fishing, boat launch, boat rental, $$$.
Northwest of Tonasket. US 97 north approximately 7.0 miles to Loomis Road; west 6.0 miles to resort.

SPECTACLE FALLS RESORT (Private)
30 campsites w/hookups for water/electricity/sewer, reservations - (509)223-4141, ice, trailer waste disposal, on Spectacle Lake, swimming, fishing, boat launch, boat rental, $$.
Northwest of Tonasket. US 97 north approximately 7.0 miles to Loomis Road; west 8.0 miles to resort.

SPECTACLE LAKE RESORT (Private)
40 campsites, 34 w/hookups for water/electricity/sewer, plus 6 tent units, reservations - (509)223-3433, laundry, ice, swimming pool, playfield, playground, trailer waste disposal, on Spectacle Lake, swimming, fishing, boat launch, boat rental, $$$.
Northwest of Tonasket. US 97 north approximately 7.0 miles to Loomis Road; west 5.0 miles to resort.

UPPER BEAVER LAKE (Okanogan National Forest)
5 tent units, well, hiking, elev. 3000', $.
Northeast of Tonasket. State 20 20.1 miles east, FSR 3245 3.3 miles
northeast.

WEST FORK SAN POIL (Okanogan National Forest)
8 units, trailers to 32', stream, fishing, elev. 2300', $.
Southeast of Tonasket. State 30 12.6 miles east, CR 9455 25.6 miles
southeast, FSR 359 3.2 miles southeast.

TROUT LAKE

BIRD CREEK (Dept. of Natural Resources)
7 campsites, picnic area, $.
Northeast of Trout Lake. Take road east to Glenwood, campground is 6.0
miles northwest of Glenwood along the Bird Creek County Road, on Bird
Creek.

CULTUS CREEK (Gifford Pinchot National Forest)
57 units, trailers to 18', piped water, stream, wheelchair access, trailhead
to Indian Heaven Backcountry, elev. 4000', $.
Northwest of Trout Lake. State 141 5.5 miles southwest, FSR 2400 12.6
miles northwest.

ISLAND CAMP (Dept. of Natural Resources)
6 campsites, winter sports, $.
Northeast of Trout Lake. Take road east to Glenwood, campground is 8.0
miles northwest of Glenwood along the Bird Creek County Road, on Bird
Creek.

PETERSON GROUP CAMP (Gifford Pinchot National Forest)
1 group unit, trailers to 22', reservations required (509)395-2501, piped
water, stream, wheelchair access, hiking, elev. 2800', $$$.
Southwest of Trout Lake. State 141 5.5 miles southwest, FSR 2400 2.5
miles west.

PETERSON PRAIRIE (Gifford Pinchot National Forest)
19 units, trailers to 18', piped water, stream, wheelchair access, elev.
2800', $$.
Southwest of Trout Lake. State 141 5.5 miles southwest, FSR 2400 2.5
miles west.

TILLICUM (Gifford Pinchot National Forest)
49 units, trailers to 18', piped water, stream, hiking, berry picking, elev.
4300', $.
Northwest of Trout Lake. State 141 5.5 miles southwest, FSR 2400 19.1
miles northwest.

TIMBERLINE MT. ADAMS (Gifford Pinchot National Forest)
3 tent units, no trailers, hiking, mountain climbing, elev. 6300', $.
North of Trout Lake. CR 17 1.9 miles north, FSR 80 3.5 miles north, FSR
8040 9.0 miles north.

TWISP

BLACK PINE LAKE (Okanogan National Forest)
21 units, trailers to 22', picnic area, piped water, lake - no motors, wheelchair access, boat launch, boating, fishing, hiking trails, elev. 4200', $$.
Southwest of Twisp. CR 9114 11.0 miles west, FSR 43 8.0 miles south.

CRATER CREEK (Okanogan National Forest)
2 tent units, fishing, hiking trails, elev. 2800', $.
Southwest of Twisp. State 20 2.0 miles east, State 153 12.2 miles south, CR 1029 .1 mile west, FSR 4340 5.8 miles northwest.

HIDDEN (Okanogan National Forest)
3 units, trailers to 18', no water, elev. 3500', $.
East of Twisp. State 20 12.5 miles east, FSR 42 2.0 miles north, FSR 42H .4 mile north.

J R (Okanogan National Forest)
6 units, trailers to 18', piped water, stream, wheelchair access, bicycling, elev. 3900', $.
East of Twisp. State 20 12.1 miles east.

LOUP LOUP (Okanogan National Forest)
20 units, trailers to 22', piped water, stream, bicycling, elev. 4200', $.
East of Twisp. State 20 13.0 miles east, FSR 42 .6 mile north.

LYDA (Okanogan National Forest)
3 units, no trailers, stream, elev. 4300', $.
East of Twisp. State 20 13.0 miles east, FSR 3523 3.4 miles north.

PARADISE VALLEY RV RESORT (Private)
96 campsites, 28 w/hookups for water/electricity/sewer, 18 w/hookups for water & electricity, plus 50 w/out hookups, reservations - (509)997-4572, wheelchair access, showers, laundry, groceries, picnic shelter, playground, trailer waste disposal, river, swimming, fishing, paddle boat rental, playfield, hiking, 5-hole putting green, $$.
West of Twisp. Twisp River Road west 1.5 miles, Poorman Creek Road southwest 1.0 miles.

POPLAR FLAT (Okanogan National Forest)
15 units, trailers to 22', picnic area, piped water, river, wheelchair access, fishing, hiking trails, elev. 2900', $.
West of Twisp. CR 9114 10.8 miles west, FSR 44 9.4 miles northwest.

RIVER BEND RV PARK (Private)
60 campsites, 36 w/hookups for water/electricity/sewer, plus 24 w/hookups for water & electricity, reservation information - (509)997-3500, showers, laundry, groceries, picnic shelter, playfield, playground, trailer waste disposal, river, fishing, $$-$$$.
Southeast of Twisp. State 20 6.0 miles southeast.

WAR CREEK (Okanogan National Forest)
11 units, trailers to 22', well, fishing, hiking trails, elev. 2400', $.
West of Twisp. CR 9114 10.8 miles west, FSR 44 3.3 miles west.

USK

BLUESLIDE RESORT (Private)
60 campsites, 31 w/hookups for water/electricity/sewer, 20 w/hookups for electricity, plus 9 w/out hookups, reservations - (509)445-1327, wheelchair access, showers, laundry, groceries, playground, trailer waste disposal, on Pend Oreille River, swimming, fishing, boat launch, boat rental, hiking, $$.
North of Usk. State 20 21.0 miles north.

BROWNS LAKE (Colville National Forest)
17 units, trailers to 22', piped water, lake - no motors, boat launch, boating, fishing, elev. 3400', $$.
Northeast of Usk. FSR 50 6.5 miles northeast, FSR 5030 3.0 miles north.

SKOOKUM CREEK (Dept. of Natural Resources)
14 campsites, drinking water, $$.
East of Usk. Campground is 4.0 miles east of Usk on Skookum Creek.

SOUTH SKOOKUM LAKE (Colville National Forest)
15 units, trailers to 22', picnic area, well, lake - speed limits, boat launch, boating, fishing, hiking, elev. 3600', $$.
Northeast of Usk. FSR 50 7.5 miles northeast.

VANCOUVER

BATTLE GROUND LAKE STATE PARK (State of Washington)
35 tent units, 15 primitive horse camps, group sites - reservations advised (206)687-4621, community kitchen, wheelchair access, snack bar, trailer waste disposal, boat launch, scuba diving area, fishing, swimming, horse trails, $-$$$.
Northeast of Vancouver. At Vancouver, take the Battle Ground exit off I-5 heading east, follow this road 21.0 miles to Battle Ground Lake State Park.

BEACON ROCK STATE PARK (State of Washington)
35 tent units, group sites - reservations advised (206)427-8265, community kitchen/picnic shelter, wheelchair access, trailer waste facility, on Columbia River, boat launch, fishing, trail to top of Beacon Rock, $$-$$$.
East of Vancouver. State 14 35.0 miles east to Beacon Rock and campground.

BEAVER BAY CAMP (Pacific Power)
63 campsites, group sites - reservations required (503)243-4778, showers, trailer waste disposal, on Lewis River, boat launch, fishing, swimming, water skiing, $-$$.
Northeast of Vancouver. I-5 north to exit #21, State 503 east 30.0 miles.

BIG FIR CAMPGROUND (Private)
80 campsites, 6 w/hookups for water/electricity/sewer, 23 w/hookups for water & electricity, plus 51 tent units, reservation information - (206)887-8970, showers, groceries, trailer waste disposal, stream, fishing, $$$.
Northeast of Vancouver. I-5 to exit #14, east 4.0 miles to campground.

COLD CREEK (Dept. of Natural Resources)
7 campsites, picnic area w/shelter, drinking water, hiking trails, horse facilities, $$.
Northeast of Vancouver. Campground is 11.0 miles southeast of Yacolt on Cedar Creek.

COUGAR CAMP (Pacific Power)
45 campsites, group sites - reservations required - (503)243-4778, tenting area - reservations advised, showers, on Lewis River, boat launch, fishing, swimming, water skiing, $-$$.
Northeast of Vancouver. I-5 north to exit #21, State 503 east 26.0 miles.

DOUGLAS CREEK (Dept. of Natural Resources)
7 campsites, picnic area, drinking water, hiking trails, $.
East of Vancouver. State 14 east 16.0 miles to Camas/Washougal, campground is located 19.0 miles northeast in Washougal River Valley, in Yacolt Multiple Use Area.

JONES CREEK (Dept. of Natural Resources)
7 campsites, drinking water, trailbike trails, $.
East of Vancouver. State 14 east 16.0 miles to Camas/Washougal, campground is located 9.0 miles northeast on Jones Creek, in Yacolt Multiple Use Area.

LEWIS RIVER RV PARK (Private)
85 campsites, 25 w/hookups for water/electricity/sewer, 45 w/hookups for water & electricity, plus 15 tent units, trailers to 60', reservation - (206)225-9556, wheelchair access, showers, laundry, groceries, swimming pool, trailer waste disposal, river, fishing, boat rental, golf, $$$.
Northeast of Vancouver. I-5 north to 20.0 miles to exit #21, State 503 east 5.0 mile.

99 MOBILE LODGE & RV PARK (Private)
60 trailer sites w/hookups for water/electricity/sewer, no tents, reservation information - (206)573-0351, showers, laundry, trailer waste disposal, $$.
North of Vancouver. I-5 north to 134th Street exit; located on Hwy. 99 to 129th Street.

PARADISE POINT STATE PARK (State of Washington)
70 tent units, 9 primitive sites, trailer waste disposal, beach access, East Fork Lewis River access, boat launch, fishing, hiking trail, $.
North of Vancouver. I-5 15.0 miles north to campground.

ROCK CREEK CAMP (Dept. of Natural Resources)
9 campsites, drinking water, trails for hikers & horses, horse facilities, $$.
Northeast of Vancouver. Campground is located 9.0 miles southeast of Yacolt along Dole Valley County Road, on Rock Creek.

SWIFT CAMP (Pacific Power)
93 campsites, picnic area, drinking water, trailer waste disposal, on Lewis River, boat launch, fishing, swimming, water skiing, $.
Northeast of Vancouver. I-5 north to exit #21, State 503 east 26.0 miles.

VOLCANO VIEW CAMPGROUND (Private)
78 campsites, 23 w/hookups for water/electricity/sewer, 25 w/hookups for water & electricity, plus 30 tent units, reservation information - (206)231-4329, showers, groceries, rec room, playfield, trailer waste disposal, $$-$$$.
Northeast of Vancouver. I-5 north to State 503 exit #21, State 503 24.0 miles to Amboy, south 1.0 mile.

WOODLAND/BRATTON CANYON (Dept. of Natural Resources)
10 campsites, picnic area w/shelter, wheelchair access, drinking water, $$.
Northeast of Vancouver. I-5 north 20.0 miles north to Woodland, campground is 3.0 miles east of Woodland on CR 38.

WAUCONDA

BETH LAKE (Okanogan National Forest)
8 units, 2 group sites, trailers to 32', picnic area, piped water, flush toilets, lake - speed limits, boat launch, boating, swimming, fishing, hiking trails, elev. 2900', $$.
North of Wauconda. State 20 2.0 miles west, CR 4953 5.0 miles north, FSR 32 6.0 miles north, FSR 3245 3.3 miles northwest.

LOST LAKE (Okanogan National Forest)
21 units, 3 group sites, trailers to 32', piped water, picnic area, flush toilets, boat launch, interpretive services, boating, swimming, fishing, hiking trails, elev. 3800', $$.
North of Wauconda. State 20 2.0 miles west, FSR 33 10.5 miles northeast, FSR 50 6.5 miles northwest.

SWEAT CREEK (Okanogan National Forest)
9 units, trailers to 32', picnic area, well, elev. 3500', $.
Southeast of Wauconda. State 20 8.5 miles southeast.

WENATCHEE

BEEHIVE SPRINGS (Wenatchee National Forest)
4 tent units, no trailers, picnic area, piped water, elev. 4100', $.
Southwest of Wenatchee. Leave US 2 on Squilchick Road #2107, follow this 10 miles to campground.

LINCOLN ROCK STATE PARK (State of Washington)
27 tent units, some trailers - no hookups, picnic shelter, trailer waste disposal, boat launch, fishing, boating, water skiing, $$.
North of Wenatchee. State 28 and US 2 6.0 miles north. Campground is adjacent to Rocky Reach Hydro Electric Dam.

SQUILCHUCK STATE PARK (State of Washington)
Group camping only - reservations required (509)844-3044, $$$.
Southwest of Wenatchee. Leave Wenatchee heading southwest on Squilchuck Road, campground is 9.0 miles southwest of Wenatchee.

WENATCHEE RIVER COUNTY PARK (Chelan County)
105 campsites, 40 w/hookups for water/electricity/sewer, 24 w/hookups for water & electricity, plus 41 tent sites, information - (509)662-2525, showers, playground, trailer waste disposal, on Wenatchee River, fishing, $$-$$$.
Northwest of Wenatchee. State 28 4.0 miles north, US 2/97 west 5.0 miles.

WESTPORT

COHO RV PARK (Private)
80 campsites w/hoookups for water/electricity/sewer, reservations - (206)268-0111, showers, laundry, ice, ocean access, fishing, fish charter, $$$.
In Westport. Located in dock area.

G & M TRAILER PARK & BOAT MOORAGE (Private)
30 campsites, 22 w/hookups for water/electricity/sewer, plus 8 w/hookups for water & electricity, reservations - (206)268-0265, showers, ice, ocean access, fishing, $$.
In Westport. Located in dock area on north side of boat basin.

GRAYLAND BEACH STATE PARK (State of Washington)
60 trailer sites, hookups for water/electricity/sewer, wheelchair access, fishing, interpretive self-guided trail, beachcombing, kite flying, $$.
South of Westport. State 105 south 4.0 miles to Grayland and campground.

HOLAND CENTER RV PARK (Private)
80 trailer sites w/hookups for water/electricity/sewer, reservation information - (206)268-9582, showers, $$.
In Westport. Located 2 blocks off docks on State 105.

ISLANDER RV PARK (Private)
65 trailer sites w/hookups for water/electricity/sewer, no tents, reservation -(206)268-9166, wheelchair access, showers, laundry, ice, swimming pool, coffee shop, lounge, ocean access, fishing, fish charter, fish cleaning area, $$-$$$.
In Westport. Located on Revetment Drive at northwest end of boat basin.

KENANNA RV PARK (Private)
90 campsites w/hookups for water/electricity/sewer, reservation information -(206)267-3515, showers, rec room, playfield, playground, trailer waste disposal, ocean access, sandy beach, fishing, $$$.
South of Westport. State 105 south to Grayland, campground is 2.0 miles south of Grayland.

OCEAN GATE RESORT (Private)
40 campsites, 24 w/hookups for water/electricity/sewer, plus 16 tent units, reservation information - (206)267-1956, showers, laundry, picnic shelter, playground, trailer waste disposal, ocean access, fishing, $$-$$$.
South of Westport. State 105 south to Grayland, located in Grayland.

PACIFIC MOTEL & TRAILER PARK (Private)
80 campsites w/hookups for water/electricity/sewer, some tent units, reservations - (206)268-9325, showers, heated swimming pool, $$-$$$.
South of Westport. State 105 just south of town.

TOTEM RV PARK (Private)
75 campsites, 44 w/hookups for water/electricity/sewer, 24 w/hookups for water & electricity, plus 7 w/out hookups, tents okay, reservations - (206)268-0025, showers, laundry, groceries, drive-in restaurant, picnic shelter, trailer waste disposal, ocean access, fishing, $$-$$$.
In Westport. Located in dock area.

TWIN HARBORS STATE PARK (State of Washington)
272 units, 49 w/hookups for water/electricity/sewer, group sites - reservations advised (206)268-6502, wheelchair access, trailer waste disposal, fishing, beachcombing, nature trail, $$-$$$.
South of Westport. State 105 south 3.0 miles to campground.

TWIN SPRUCE RV PARK (Private)
49 campsites, 41 w/hookups for water/electricity/sewer, plus 8 w/hookups for water & electricity, reservation information - (206)267-1275, showers, laundry, ice, rec room, near beach, $$-$$$.
South of Westport. State 105 south to Grayland, Schmid Road east .1 mile.

WESTERN SHORES MOTEL & TRAILER PARK (Private)
25 campsites w/hookups for water/electricity/sewer, reservation information -(206)267-6115, ice, playground, $$.
South of Westport. State 105 south to Grayland, located in Grayland.

WESTPORT CITY PARK (City)
40 campsites, restrooms, tennis, playground, $$.
In Westport. Located in city center; on Washington Avenue, one block west of Montesano.

WILBUR

BELLS TRAILER PARK (Private)
20 trailer sites w/hookups for water/electricity/sewer, reservations - (509)647-5888, showers, laundry, ice, picnic area, $$$.
In Wilbur. Located at eastern edge of town; 1 block off US 2.

BLUE LAKE RESORT (Private)
75 campsites, 23 w/hookups for water/electricity/sewer, 33 w/hookups for water & electricity, plus 19 tent units, reservation information - (509)632-5364, showers, groceries, playfield, playground, lake, swimming, fishing, boat launch, boat rental, $$.
Southwest of Wilbur. US 2 southwest 32.0 miles, State 17 south 10.0 miles.

COULEE CITY PARK (City)
60 campsites, 34 w/hookups for water/electricity/sewer, plus 26 tent units, trailers to 24', reservation information - (509)632-5331, showers, playground, trailer waste disposal, lake, swimming, fishing, boat launch, $-$$.
Southwest of Wilbur. US 2 southwest 30.0 miles, located in Coulee City at northern edge of town.

COULEE LODGE RESORT (Private)
45 campsites, 22 w/hookups for water/electricity/sewer, 11 w/hookups for water & electricity, plus 12 tent units, reservation information - (509)632-5565, wheelchair access, showers, laundry, groceries, trailer waste disposal, lake, swimming, fishing, boat launch, boat rental, $$.
Southwest of Wilbur. US 2 southwest 32.0 miles, State 17 south 8.0 miles.

COULEE PLAYLAND RESORT & RV PARK (Private)
46 campsites w/hookups for water/electricity/sewer, reservation information -(509)633-2671, showers, laundry, groceries, playground, trailer waste disposal, lake, swimming, fishing, boat launch, boat rental, $$-$$$.
Northwest of Wilbur. State 174 19.0 miles northwest, State 155 1.0 mile west.

CURLY'S CAMPGROUND (Private)
22 campsites, 16 w/hookups for water/electricity/sewer, plus 6 tent units, reservation information - (509)633-0750, showers, $$.
Northwest of Wilbur. State 174 20.0 miles northwest, located 1.0 mile northwest of Grand Coulee.

HAWK CREEK (Coulee Dam Recreation Area)
18 campsites, reservation information - (509)633-0881, lake, fishing, boat launch, $$.
East of Wilbur. US 2 east to Creston, Fort Spokane Highway 17.0 miles north.

KELLER FERRY (Coulee Dam Recreation Area)
Campsites, trailers okay - no hookups, group campsites, drinking water, picnic area, cafe/snack bar, groceries, trailer & boat waste disposal, boat ramp & dock, boat fuel, swimming/lifeguard, $$-$$$.
North of Wilbur. State 21 approximately 14 miles to Keller Ferry landing and campground.

LAKEVIEW TERRACE RV PARK (Private)
15 trailer sites w/hookups for water/electricity/sewer, reservation information - (509)633-2169, showers, laundry, playfield, playground, $$.
Northwest of Wilbur. State 174 16.0 miles northwest, located 3.0 mile southeast of Grand Coulee.

LEE MOTEL & RV PARK (Private)
28 trailer sites w/hookups for water/electricity/sewer, reservation information - (509)633-1992, showers, laundry, $$$.
Northwest of Wilbur. State 174 18.0 miles northwest, located 1.0 mile southeast of Grand Coulee.

SMITTY'S RV PARK (Private)
42 trailer sites w/hookups for water/electricity/sewer, reservation information - (509)632-5772, showers, laundry, lake, swimming, fishing, $$$.
Southwest of Wilbur. US 2 southwest 27.5 miles, located north of highway.

SPRING CANYON (Coulee Dam Recreation Area)
Campsites, trailers okay - no hookups, group campsites, drinking water, picnic area, handicap access, cafe/snack bar, groceries, trailer & boat waste disposal, boat dock & ramp, boat fuel, swimming/lifeguard, summer amphitheater programs, $$-$$$.
Northwest of Wilbur. State 174 approximately 14.0 miles northwest to campground road, follow this 1.1 miles north to campground.

STEAMBOAT ROCK STATE PARK (State of Washington)
100 trailer sites w/hookups for water/electricity/sewer, wheelchair access, on Banks Lake, snackbar, boat launch, fishing, water skiing, scuba diving area, nearby horse trails, winter sports, $$.
Northwest of Wilbur. State 174 19.0 miles northwest, State 155 7.2 miles southwest, campground road will take you northwest.

SUN LAKES PARK RESORT (Private)
110 trailer sites w/hookups for water/electricity/sewer, no tents, reservation information - (509)632-5291, showers, laundry, groceries, trailer waste disposal, swimming pool, playfield, playground, lake, swimming, fishing, boat launch, boat rental, mini-golf, golf, hiking, $$$.
Southwest of Wilbur. US 2 southwest 32.0 miles, State 17 south 7.0 miles.

SUN LAKES STATE PARK (State of Washington)
175 tent units, 18 trailer sites w/hookups for water/electricity/sewer, group sites - reservations advised (509)632-5583, cabins, wheelchair access, snackbar, groceries, trailer waste disposal, boat & horse rental, boat launch, fishing, swimming, horse trails, $$-$$$.
Southwest of Wilbur. US 2 32.0 miles southwest, State 17 5.0 miles southwest.

SUN VILLAGE RESORT (Private)
115 campsites, 95 w/hookups for water/electricity/sewer, plus 20 w/hookups for water & electricity, reservation information - (509)632-5664, showers, laundry, groceries, playfield, playground, trailer waste disposal, lake, swimming, fishing, boat launch, boat rental, $$$.
Southwest of Wilbur. US 2 southwest 32.0 miles, State 17 south 8.0 miles.

THE RIVER RUE RV PARK (Private)
27 trailer sites w/hookups for water/electricity/sewer, reservations - (509)647-2647, wheelchair access, showers, groceries, deli/snack bar, playfield, playground, trailer waste disposal, near Lake Roosevelt & fishing, $$.
North of Wilbur. State 21 14.0 miles north.

WILBUR MOTEL & RV PARK (Private)
30 trailer sites, 20 w/hookups for water/electricity/sewer, plus 10 w/hookups for water & electricity, reservation information - (509)647-5608, showers, nearby golf, $$.
In Wilbur. Located at west end of town.

WINTHROP

ANDREWS CREEK (Okanogan National Forest)
1 tent unit, horse corral, fishing, hiking, elev. 3000', $.
North of Winthrop. CR 1213 6.6 miles north, FSR 392 15.3 miles north.

BALLARD (Okanogan National Forest)
7 units, trailers to 22', well, river, fishing, elev. 2600', $.
Northwest of Winthrop. State 20 13.2 miles northwest, CR 1163 6.9 miles northwest, FSR 5400 2.1 miles northwest.

BLACK LAKE (Okanogan National Forest)
3 tent units in Pasayten Wilderness, horse trails, meager grazing, lake, hike-in only, $.
North of Winthrop. CR 1213 6.6 miles north, FSR 392 14.5 miles north, Trail #500 out of Lake Creek Campground 5.0 miles to campsites.

BUCK LAKE (Okanogan National Forest)
4 units, trailers to 18', piped water, boating, fishing, elev. 3200', $.
North of Winthrop. CR 1213 6.6 miles north, FSR 51 2.8 miles north, FSR 5130 .6 mile northwest, FSR 100 2.3 miles northwest.

CHANCELLOR (Okanogan National Forest)
6 tent units, shelter, fishing, hiking, river, elev. 4800', $$.
Northwest of Winthrop. State 20 13.2 miles northwest, CR 1163 6.9 miles northwest, FSR 5400 to campground which is located at end of road.

CUTTHROAT (Okanogan National Forest)
3 tent units, piped water, fishing, hiking, elev. 4000', $.
Northwest of Winthrop. State 20 26 miles northwest; campground is 4 miles north of Washington Pass.

DERRY'S RESORT ON PEARRYGIN LAKE (Private)
154 campsites, 55 w/hookups for water/electricity/sewer, 9 w/hookups for water & electricity, plus 90 tent units, reservations - (509)996-2322, showers, laundry, groceries, playfield, playground, trailer waste disposal, on Pearrygin Lake, swimming, fishing, boat launch, $$-$$$.
Northeast of Winthrop. Riverside north .5 mile, Bluff Street east 2.0 miles, Pearrygin Lake Road east 1.0 mile to campground.

EARLY WINTERS (Okanogan National Forest)
20 units, trailers to 18', piped water, river, wheelchair access, fishing, elev. 2400', $$.
Northwest of Winthrop. State 20 16.0 miles northwest.

FALLS CREEK (Okanogan National Forest)
9 units, trailers to 18', well, waterfall, fishing, elev. 2300', $.
North of Winthrop. CR 1213 6.6 miles north, FSR 5160 5.3 miles north.

5Y RESORT (Private)
90 campsites, 28 w/hookups for water/electricity/sewer, plus 62 w/out hookups, reservation information - (509)996-2448, showers, laundry, playfield, on Pearrygin Lake, swimming, fishing, boat launch, $$$.
Northeast of Winthrop. Riverside north .5 mile, Bluff Street east 2.0 miles, Pearrygin Lake Road .5 mile to resort.

FLAT (Okanogan National Forest)
12 units, trailers to 18', well, stream, wheelchair access, fishing, elev. 2600', $.
North of Winthrop. CR 1213 6.6 miles north, FSR 51 2.8 miles north, FSR 5130 2.0 miles northwest.

GATE CREEK (Okanogan National Forest)
3 tent units, 1 trailer to 22', well, fishing, elev. 2800', $.
Northwest of Winthrop. State 20 13.2 miles northwest, CR 1163 4.5 miles northwest.

KLIPCHUCK (Okanogan National Forest)
46 units, trailers to 32', piped water, stream, flush toilets, wheelchair access, fishing, hiking trails, elev. 3000', $$.
Northwest of Winthrop. State 20 17.2 miles northwest, FSR 300 1.2 miles northwest.

LAKE CREEK (Okanogan National Forest)
3 tent units, fishing, elev. 2800', $.
North of Winthrop. CR 1213 6.6 miles north, FSR 392 14.5 miles north.

LONE FIR (Okanogan National Forest)
27 units, trailers to 22', piped water, river, wheelchair access, fishing, hiking trails, provides access to Silver Star Glacier, elev. 3800', $$.
Northwest of Winthrop. State 20 26.8 miles northwest.

MEMORIAL (Okanogan National Forest)
2 units, trailers to 18', well, river, fishing, elev. 2000', $.
North of Winthrop. CR 1213 6.6 miles north, FSR 392 1.0 mile north.

METHOW RIVER/WINTHROP KOA (Private)
100 campsites, 16 w/hookups for water/electricity/sewer, 56 w/hookups for water & electricity, plus 23 tent units, reservations - (206)996-2258, showers, laundry, groceries, trailer waste disposal, heated swimming pool, river, fishing, playground, $$$.
Southeast of Winthrop. State 20 1.0 mile south.

PEARRYGIN LAKE STATE PARK (State of Washington)
26 tent units, 30 trailer sites w/hookups for water/electricity/sewer, 27 trailer sites w/water hookups, wheelchair access, trailer waste disposal, boat launch, fishing, winter sports, $$.
North of Winthrop. Leave State 20 at Winthrop, campground is 5.0 miles north.

PINE-NEAR TRAILER PARK (Private)
28 campsites w/hookups for water/electricity/sewer, plus tenting area, reservations - (509)996-2391, showers, laundry, trailer waste disposal, $$-$$$.
At Winthrop. Riverside north .5 mile, Bluff Street east .1 mile, park is on Castle, right across from Shaffer Museum.

RATTLESNAKE (Okanogan National Forest)
3 tent units, well, stream, fishing, hiking, elev. 2700', $.
Northwest of Winthrop. State 20 13.2 miles northwest, CR 1163 6.9 miles northwest, FSR 5400 2.5 miles northwest, FSR 3700 1.5 miles west.

RIVER BEND (Okanogan National Forest)
5 units, trailers to 22', well, river, fishing, elev. 2700', $.
Northwest of Winthrop. State 20 13.2 miles northwest, CR 1163 6.9 miles northwest, FSR 5400 2.5 miles northwest, FSR 60 .5 mile west.

SHEEP MOUNTAIN (Okanogan National Forest)
Tenting areas in Pasayten Wilderness, horse trails, meager grazing, creeks & lakes on route, $.
North of Winthrop. CR 1213 6.6 miles north, FSR 392 15.3 miles north, take trail at Andrews Creek Campground northwest approximately 50 miles to camping area.

SPANISH CAMP (Okanogan National Forest)
Tenting areas in Pasayten Wilderness, horse trails, grazing area, lake, hike-in only, $.
North of Winthrop. CR 1213 6.6 miles north, FSR 392 15.3 miles north, take trail at Andrews Creek Campground northwest approximately 20 miles to camping area.

THIRTYMILE (Okanogan National Forest)
9 tent units, well, horse corral, stream, fishing, hiking, elev. 3600', $$.
North of Winthrop. CR 1213 6.6 miles north, FSR 392 23.4 miles north.

YACOLT

SUNSET (Gifford Pinchot National Forest)
10 units, trailers to 22', picnic area, well, stream, wheelchair access -includes trail, fishing, elev. 1000', $.
East of Yacolt. CR 16 3.0 miles southeast, CR 12 8.0 miles east.

YAKIMA

CIRCLE H RV RANCH (Private)
36 campsites w/hookups for water/electricity/sewer, reservation information -(509)457-3683, wheelchair access, showers, laundry, swimming pool, spa, therapy pool, lounge, playground, $$$.
In Yakima. I-82 to exit #34, 18th Street north .3 mile.

GRANGER RV PARK (Private)
45 campsites w/hookups for water/electricity/sewer, reservation information -(509)854-1300, showers, laundry, ice, trailer waste disposal, $$$.
Southeast of Yakima. I-82 southeast 23.0 miles to Granger, State 223 .3 mile south.

NORTH FORK (Dept. of Natural Resources)
2 campsites, $.
West of Yakima. Campground is 32.0 miles west of Yakima on North Fork of Ahtanum Creek, in Ahtum Multiple Use Area.

TRAILER INNS RV PARK (Private)
101 trailer sites w/hookups for water/electricity/sewer, no tents, pets okay, reservation information - (509)452-9561, showers, laundry, trailer waste disposal, swimming pool, therapy pool, sauna, lounge, playground, $$$.
In Yakima. I-82 to exit #31; located at 1610 N. First Street.

YAKIMA KOA (Private)
117 campsites, 37 w/hookups for water/electricity/sewer, 37 w/hookups for water & electricity, 6 w/hookups for electricity, plus 37 tent units, reservations -(509)248-5882, showers, laundry, groceries, playground, trailer waste disposal, river, fishing, boat rental, $$$.
In Yakima. I-82 to exit #34, State 24 east 1.0 mile, Keyes Road north .3 mile.

YAKIMA SPORTSMAN STATE PARK (State of Washington)
28 tent units, 36 trailer sites w/hookups for water/electricity/sewer, community kitchen/shelter, trailer waste disposal, children's fishing pond, river fishing for adults, $$.
East of Yakima. Campground is located 1.0 mile east of Yakima.

WARNING: The following books will cause you to spend less money while enjoying more quality family time!

Ki² offers two unique guidebooks that together will lead you to nearly 2,000 free recreational attractions in Washington and Oregon. **OREGON FREE** and **WASHINGTON FREE** show you where to find the ghost towns, covered bridges, historic sites, museums, parks and public lands, bicycle paths, hot springs, hiking trails, scenic areas, natural wonders, caves, rockhounding spots, waterfalls, art collections, wildlife refuges, and more, all for free!

Each book covers the entire state, from corner to corner, letting you know exactly where to find those fun, free, family attractions. The books are set up in an easy to use manner and include brief descriptions of each attraction plus directions and schedules where necessary.

FREE CAMPGROUNDS OF WASHINGTON & OREGON details only the cost free campgrounds, about 600 in all. Great for campers who want to get closer to nature. Each campground has a complete listing of facilities available and easy to follow directions.

THE NORTHWEST GOLFER is a guide to the public golf courses in Washington and Oregon. It details 252 public and semi-private courses and includes full reservation information. A quick tee bar immediately tells you how many holes are available, the total yardage and par. Next you learn how to get to the course, what they charge, whether or not they rent carts or clubs and their operating schedule. You'll also find out what the terrain is like, if you'll find lots of hazards and what facilities the course has to offer, plus a little more.

WASHINGTON IN YOUR POCKET — A Guide to Recreational Attractions in Washington's Northwest Corner details the wealth of family attractions found in the most heavily populated part of the state. Whatcom, Skagit, Island, Snohomish, King, Clallam and Jefferson Counties have been included. Includes nearly 200 easily accessible attractions. Zoos, archeological sites, museums, trails, the San Juan Islands, Olympic National Park, scenic and natural wonders, historic sites, tours, and wildlife areas are all covered.

All Ki² books carry a moneyback guarantee when returned in saleable condition, within 10 days of purchase.

ORDER INFORMATION

✂ --

Please send:

___ A CAMPER'S GUIDE TO OR & WA @ $9.95 ea.. _____
___ FREE-CAMPGROUNDS OF WA & OR $6.95 ea. _____
___ THE NORTHWEST GOLFER @ $9.95 ea....... _____
___ OREGON FREE @ $9.95 ea................. _____
___ WASHINGTON FREE @ $9.95 ea............. _____
___ WASHINGTON IN YOUR POCKET @ $4.95 ea.. _____
     Free fourth class shipping on all prepaid orders.

TOTAL enclosed $

Name _____

Address _____

City/State/Zip Code _____

Send this order coupon to Ki² Enterprises, P.O. Box 13322,
Portland, Oregon 97213.

                                               C'G

✂ --

Please send:

___ A CAMPER'S GUIDE TO OR & WA @ $9.95 ea.. _____
___ FREE CAMPGROUNDS OF WA & OR $6.95 ea. _____
___ THE NORTHWEST GOLFER @ $9.95 ea....... _____
___ OREGON FREE @ $9.95 ea................. _____
___ WASHINGTON FREE @ $9.95 ea............. _____
___ WASHINGTON IN YOUR POCKET @ $4.95 ea.. _____
     Free fourth class shipping on all prepaid orders.

TOTAL enclosed $

Name _____

Address _____

City/State/Zip Code _____

Send this order coupon to Ki² Enterprises, P.O. Box 13322,
Portland, Oregon 97213.

                                               C'G

INDEX

Tidewater – 100.
Tillamook – 100, 101.
Tollgate – 101, 102.
Troy – 102.
Tygh Valley – 102.
Ukiah – 102, 103.
Union – 103.
Unity – 103.
Vale – 103, 104.
Vernonia – 104.
Waldport – 104, 105, 106.
Wamic – 106.
Warm Springs – 106.
Warrenton – 35.
Welches – 106, 107.
Westfir – 107.
Weston – 107.
White City – 107, 108.
Yachats – 109.
Zigzag – 106.

Scuba diving – 116, 117, 120, 125, 133, 134, 141, 144, 170, 177, 178, 179, 184, 188, 193.

Showers – 33, 34, 35, 36, 37, 38, 39, 40, 41, 42, 43, 44, 45, 46, 47, 48, 49, 50, 51, 52, 53, 54, 57, 58, 59, 60, 61, 62, 63, 65, 66, 67, 68, 69, 71, 72, 73, 74, 75, 76, 78, 79, 80, 81, 82, 83, 85, 86, 87, 88, 89, 90, 91, 92, 93, 94, 95, 96, 97, 98, 99, 100, 101, 102, 104, 105, 106, 107, 108, 109, 115, 116, 117, 118, 119, 120, 121, 122, 123, 124, 125, 126, 127, 128, 129, 130, 131, 132, 133, 134, 135, 136, 137, 138, 139, 143, 144, 145, 146, 147, 148, 149, 150, 151, 152, 153, 154, 155, 158, 159, 160, 161, 162, 163, 164, 165, 166, 167, 168, 169, 170, 171, 172, 173, 174, 175, 176, 177, 178, 179, 180, 181, 182, 183, 184, 185, 187, 188, 189, 190, 191, 192, 193, 194, 195, 196, 197.

Swimming – 33, 34, 35, 36, 37, 38, 39, 40, 43, 44, 45, 46, 47, 48, 49, 50, 51, 52, 53, 54, 55, 56, 57, 58, 59, 60, 61, 62, 63, 64, 65, 66, 67, 68, 69, 70, 71, 72, 73, 74, 75, 76, 77, 78, 79, 80, 81, 82, 83, 84, 85, 86, 87, 88, 89, 90, 91, 92, 93, 94, 95, 96, 97, 98, 99, 100, 010, 102, 103, 104, 106, 107, 108, 109, 115, 117, 118, 119, 120, 121, 122, 123, 124, 125, 126, 127, 128, 129, 130, 132, 133, 134, 136, 137, 138, 139, 140, 141, 142, 143, 144, 146, 147, 148, 149, 150, 151, 152, 153, 154, 155, 156, 157, 158, 159, 160, 161, 162, 163, 164, 165, 166, 167, 168, 169, 171, 172, 173, 174, 175, 176, 177, 178, 179, 180, 181, 182, 183, 184, 185, 187, 188, 189, 191, 192, 193, 194, 195, 196, 197.

Swimming Pool – 34, 35, 36, 37, 43, 44, 49, 51, 52, 60, 63, 65, 67, 68, 73, 80, 81, 89, 92, 93, 98, 99, 106, 107, 108, 118, 120, 121, 125, 127, 128, 129, 132, 133, 136, 144, 146, 149, 150, 151, 154, 155, 158, 161, 163, 164, 168, 171, 176, 178, 179, 181, 183, 184, 185, 189, 191, 193, 196, 197.

Trailers okay – 33, 34, 35, 36, 37, 38, 39, 40, 41, 42, 43, 44, 45, 46, 47, 48, 49, 50, 51, 52, 53, 54, 55, 56, 57, 58, 59, 60, 61, 62, 63, 64, 65, 66, 67, 68, 69, 70, 71, 72, 73, 74, 75, 76, 77, 78, 79, 80, 81, 82, 83, 84, 85, 86, 87, 88, 89, 90, 91, 92, 93, 94, 95, 96, 97, 98, 99, 100, 101, 102, 103, 104, 105, 106, 107, 108, 109, 115, 116, 117, 118, 119, 120, 121, 122, 123, 124, 125, 126, 127, 128, 129, 130, 131, 132, 133, 134, 135, 136, 137, 138, 139, 140, 141, 142, 143, 144, 145, 146, 147, 148, 149, 150, 151, 152, 153, 154, 155, 156, 157, 158, 159, 160, 161, 162, 163, 164, 165, 166, 167, 168, 169, 170, 171, 172, 173, 174, 175, 176, 177, 178, 179, 180, 181, 182, 183, 184, 185, 186, 187, 188, 189, 190, 191, 192, 193, 194, 195, 196 197.

Trailer waste disposal – 33, 34, 35, 36, 37, 39, 40, 41, 42, 43, 44, 45, 46, 47, 48, 49, 50, 51, 52, 53, 54, 55, 56, 57, 58, 59, 60, 61, 62, 63, 65, 66, 67, 68, 69, 70, 71, 72, 73, 74, 75, 76, 77, 78, 79, 80, 81, 82, 83, 84, 85, 86, 87, 88, 89, 90,

91, 92, 93, 94, 95, 96, 97, 98, 99,
100, 101, 102, 103, 104, 105,
106, 107, 108, 109, 115, 116,
117, 118, 119, 120, 121, 122,
123, 124, 125, 126, 127, 128,
129, 130, 131, 132, 133, 134,
135, 136, 137, 138, 139, 140,
141, 143, 144, 145, 146, 147,
148, 149, 150, 151, 152, 153,
154, 155, 158, 159, 160, 161,
162, 163, 164, 165, 166, 167,
168, 169, 170, 171, 172, 173,
174, 175, 176, 177, 178, 179,
180, 181, 182, 183, 184, 185,
187, 188, 189, 190, 191, 192,
193, 194, 195, 196, 197.

Washington cities – 115-197.

Allyn – 117.
Amboy – 115, 190.
Anacortes – 115, 176.
Ashford – 115.
Asotin – 115.
Battle Ground – 188.
Belfair – 115, 116, 117.
Bellevue – 178.
Benton City – 175.
Blaine – 117, 118, 119.
Bothell – 178.
Brady – 154.
Bridgeport – 125.
Brinnon – 119.
Burlington – 119, 120, 121.
Carson – 121, 122.
Castle Rock – 122, 123.
Cathlamet – 147.
Chehalis – 124.
Chelan – 124, 125.
Cheney – 181, 182, 183.
Chewelah – 125, 126.
Chinook – 144, 145.
Clallam Bay – 169.
Cle Elum – 126, 127, 128.
Colfax – 128.
Colville – 129.
Conconully – 129, 130, 131.
Concrete – 131, 132.
Cook – 133.
Copalis Beach – 164, 165.
Cougar – 133.
Coulee City – 192.
Coupeville – 133, 134.
Creston – 193.
Curlew – 134.
Darrington – 135.

Dayton – 135.
Doty – 124.
Easton – 127.
Eastsound – 177.
Elbe – 136.
Eldon – 136.
Ellensburg – 136
Elma – 154.
Entiat – 136, 137.
Enumclaw – 137, 138.
Ephrata – 155.
Everett – 138.
Ferndale – 118.
Forks – 138, 139, 140.
Fort Spokane – 140.
Friday Harbor – 177.
Gifford – 144.
Gig Harbor – 184.
Glacier – 140.
Glenwood – 186.
Gold Bar – 146.
Goldendale – 141.
Grand Coulee – 193.
Granite Falls – 141, 142, 143.
Grayland – 191, 192.
Hadlock – 170.
Hoodsport – 143, 144.
Humptulips – 144.
Hunters – 144.
Ilwaco – 144, 145.
Index – 146.
Ione – 147.
Joyce – 167.
Kalama – 147, 148.
Kelso – 147, 148.
Kennewick – 175.
Kettle Falls – 148, 149.
Klipsan Beach – 152.
La Conner – 121.
La Push – 139.
Leavenworth – 149, 150.
Littlerock – 162, 163.
Long Beach – 151, 152.
Longbranch – 116, 117.
Loomis – 152.
Lynden – 118, 119.
Lynnwood – 178.
Marblemount – 152, 153.
Marys Corner – 124.
Metaline Falls – 153.
Montesano – 153, 154.
Moses Lake – 154, 155.
Naches – 156, 157, 158, 159.
Neah Bay – 169, 170.